digits™

Student Companion

Accelerated Grade 7
Volume 2

PEARSON

Boston, Massachusetts • Chandler, Arizona • Glenview, Illinois • Upper Saddle River, New Jersey

Acknowledgments for illustrations and composition: Rory Hensley, David Jackson, Jim Mariano, Rich McMahon, Lorie Park, Ted Smykal, Ralph Voltz, and Laserwords

ISBN-13: 978-0-13-330641-5
ISBN-10: 0-13-330641-0
1 2 3 4 5 6 7 8 9 10 V001 17 16 15 14

digits™ System Requirements

► Supported System Configurations

	Operating System (32-bit only)	Web Browser* (32-bit only)	Java® Version**
PC	Windows® XP (SP3) Windows Vista (SP1) Windows 7	Internet Explorer® 7 Internet Explorer 8 Internet Explorer 9 Mozilla Firefox® 11 Google Chrome™	1.4.2 1.5 [5.0 Update 11 or higher] 1.6 [6.0 through Update 18]
Mac	Macintosh® OS 10.6.x, 10.7.x	Safari® 5.0 Safari 5.1 Google Chrome™	1.5 [5.0 Update 16 or higher]

* Pop-up blockers must be disabled in the browser.
** Java (JRE) plug-in must be installed and JavaScript® must be enabled in the browser.

► Additional Requirements

Software	Version
Adobe® Flash®	Version 10.4 or higher
Adobe Reader® (required for PC*)	Version 8 or higher
Word processing software	Microsoft® Word®, Open Office, or similar application to open ".doc" files

* Macintosh® OS 10.6 has a built-in PDF reader, Preview.

Screen Resolution
PC
Minimum: 1024 x 768*
Maximum: 1280 x 1024
Mac
Minimum: 1024 x 768*
Maximum: 1280 x 960
*recommended for interactive whiteboards

Internet Connection
Broadband (cable/DSL) or greater is recommended.

AOL® and AT&T™ Yahoo!® Users
You cannot use the AOL or AT&T Yahoo! browsers. However, you can use AOL or AT&T as your Internet Service Provider to access the Internet, and then open a supported browser.

The trademarks referred to above are the property of their respective owners, none of whom have authorized, approved, or otherwise sponsored this product.

► For *digits*™ Support

go to **http://support.pearsonschool.com/index.cfm/digits**

My Name: _____

My Teacher's Name: _____

My School: _____

Dana Sara Javier Jay

Francis (Skip) Fennell
digits Author

Approaches to mathematics content and curriculum, educational policy, and support for intervention

Eric Milou
digits Author

Approaches to mathematical content and the use of technology in middle grades classrooms

Art Johnson
digits Author

Approaches to mathematical content and support for English language learners

William F. Tate
digits Author

Approaches to intervention, and use of efficacy and research

Helene Sherman
digits Author

Teacher education and support for struggling students

Grant Wiggins
digits Consulting Author

Understanding by Design

Stuart J. Murphy
digits Author

Visual learning and student engagement

Randall I. Charles
digits Advisor

Janie Schielack
digits Author

Approaches to mathematical content, building problem solvers, and support for intervention

Jim Cummins
digits Advisor

Supporting English Language Learners

Jacquie Moen
digits Advisor

Digital Technology

Go online for all your cool digits™ stuff!

Be sure to save your login information by writing it here.

My Username: _____

My Password: _____

First, go to **MyMathUniverse.com**. From there you can explore the **Channel List**, which includes fun and interactive games and videos, or select your program and log in.

Play some cool math **games!**

Complete your **homework** online**!**

Discover math **tricks** and **tips!**

Check out fun **videos!**

ACTIVe-book

No more pencils! No more books! Why? Because the Student Companion you have in front of you can also be found online in ACTIVe-book format. You can access your ACTIVe-book on a tablet or on a computer, so any questions you can answer in your Student Companion you can also master online.

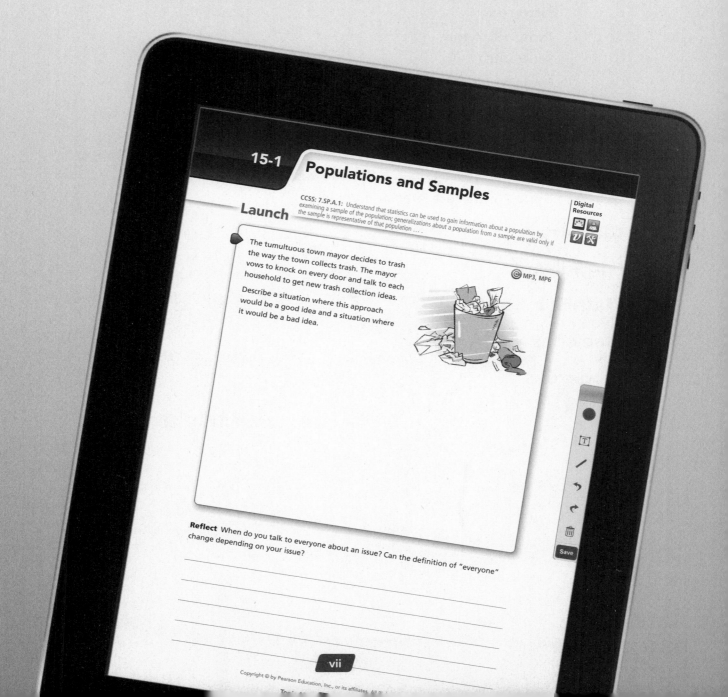

15-1

Populations and Samples

Launch

CCSS: 7.SP.A.1: Understand that statistics can be used to gain information about a population by examining a sample of the population; generalizations about a population from a sample are valid only if the sample is representative of that population ... .

Digital Resources

The tumultuous town mayor decides to trash the way the town collects trash. The mayor vows to knock on every door and talk to each household to get new trash collection ideas.

Describe a situation where this approach would be a good idea and a situation where it would be a bad idea.

© MP3, MP6

Reflect When do you talk to everyone about an issue? Can the definition of "everyone" change depending on your issue?

Welcome to digits™

Using the Student Companion

digits is designed to help you master mathematics skills and concepts in a way that's relevant to you. As the title **digits** suggests, this program takes a digital approach. The Student Companion supports your work on **digits** by providing a place to demonstrate your understanding of lesson skills and concepts in writing.

Your companion supports your work on **digits** in so many ways!

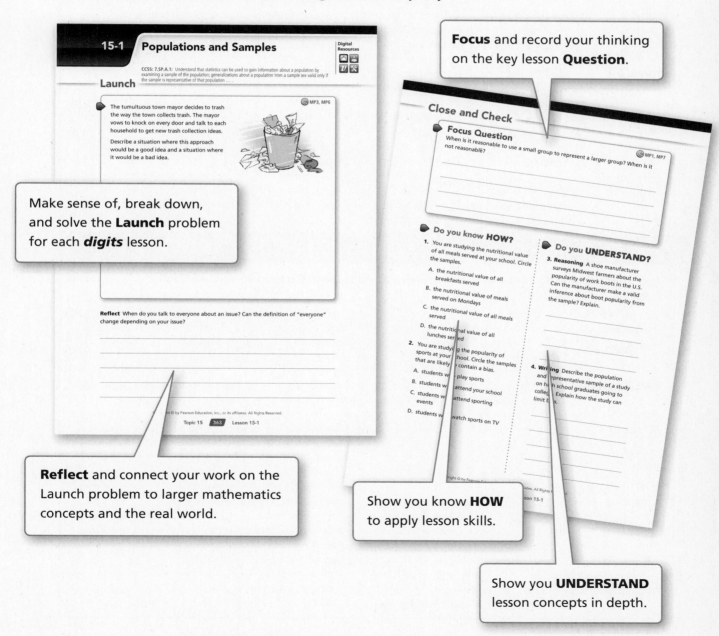

Focus and record your thinking on the key lesson **Question**.

Make sense of, break down, and solve the **Launch** problem for each **digits** lesson.

Reflect and connect your work on the Launch problem to larger mathematics concepts and the real world.

Show you know **HOW** to apply lesson skills.

Show you **UNDERSTAND** lesson concepts in depth.

Number	Standard for Mathematical Content

7.RP Ratios and Proportional Relationships

Analyze proportional relationships and use them to solve real-world and mathematical problems.

7.RP.A.1	Compute unit rates associated with ratios of fractions, including ratios of lengths, areas and other quantities measured in like or different units.
7.RP.A.2	Recognize and represent proportional relationships between quantities.
7.RP.A.2a	Decide whether two quantities are in a proportional relationship, e.g., by testing for equivalent ratios in a table or graphing on a coordinate plane and observing whether the graph is a straight line through the origin.
7.RP.A.2b	Identify the constant of proportionality (unit rate) in tables, graphs, equations, diagrams, and verbal descriptions of proportional relationships.
7.RP.A.2c	Represent proportional relationships by equations.
7.RP.A.2d	Explain what a point (x, y) on the graph of a proportional relationship means in terms of the situation, with special attention to the points $(0, 0)$ and $(1, r)$ where r is the unit rate.
7.RP.A.3	Use proportional relationships to solve multistep ratio and percent problems. Examples: simple interest, tax, markups and markdowns, gratuities and commissions, fees, percent increase and decrease, percent error.

7.NS The Number System

Apply and extend previous understandings of operations with fractions to add, subtract, multiply, and divide rational numbers.

7.NS.A.1	Apply and extend previous understandings of addition and subtraction to add and subtract rational numbers; represent addition and subtraction on a horizontal or vertical number line diagram.
7.NS.A.1a	Describe situations in which opposite quantities combine to make 0. For example, a hydrogen atom has 0 charge because its two constituents are oppositely charged.
7.NS.A.1b	Understand $p + q$ as the number located a distance $|q|$ from p, in the positive or negative direction depending on whether q is positive or negative. Show that a number and its opposite have a sum of 0 (are additive inverses). Interpret sums of rational numbers by describing real-world contexts.
7.NS.A.1c	Understand subtraction of rational numbers as adding the additive inverse, $p - q = p + (-q)$. Show that the distance between two rational numbers on the number line is the absolute value of their difference, and apply this principle in real-world contexts.
7.NS.A.1d	Apply properties of operations as strategies to add and subtract rational numbers.
7.NS.A.2	Apply and extend previous understandings of multiplication and division and of fractions to multiply and divide rational numbers.

Number	Standard for Mathematical Content

7.NS The Number System (*continued*)

Apply and extend previous understandings of operations with fractions to add, subtract, multiply, and divide rational numbers.

Number	Standard for Mathematical Content
7.NS.A.2a	Understand that multiplication is extended from fractions to rational numbers by requiring that operations continue to satisfy the properties of operations, particularly the distributive property, leading to products such as $(-1)(-1) = 1$ and the rules for multiplying signed numbers. Interpret products of rational numbers by describing real-world contexts.
7.NS.A.2b	Understand that integers can be divided, provided that the divisor is not zero, and every quotient of integers (with non-zero divisor) is a rational number. If p and q are integers, then $\left(\frac{p}{q}\right) = \frac{(-p)}{q} = \frac{p}{(-q)}$. Interpret quotients of rational numbers by describing real- world contexts.
7.NS.A.2c	Apply properties of operations as strategies to multiply and divide rational numbers.
7.NS.A.2d	Convert a rational number to a decimal using long division; know that the decimal form of a rational number terminates in 0s or eventually repeats.
7.NS.A.3	Solve real-world and mathematical problems involving the four operations with rational numbers.

7.EE Expressions and Equations

Use properties of operations to generate equivalent expressions.

Number	Standard for Mathematical Content
7.EE.A.1	Apply properties of operations as strategies to add, subtract, factor, and expand linear expressions with rational coefficients.
7.EE.A.2	Understand that rewriting an expression in different forms in a problem context can shed light on the problem and how the quantities in it are related. For example, $a + 0.05a = 1.05a$ means that "increase by 5%" is the same as "multiply by 1.05."

Solve real-life and mathematical problems using numerical and algebraic expressions and equations.

Number	Standard for Mathematical Content
7.EE.B.3	Solve multi-step real-life and mathematical problems posed with positive and negative rational numbers in any form (whole numbers, fractions, and decimals), using tools strategically. Apply properties of operations to calculate with numbers in any form; convert between forms as appropriate; and assess the reasonableness of answers using mental computation and estimation strategies.
7.EE.B.4	Use variables to represent quantities in a real-world or mathematical problem, and construct simple equations and inequalities to solve problems by reasoning about the quantities.
7.EE.B.4a	Solve word problems leading to equations of the form $px + q = r$ and $p(x + q) = r$, where p, q, and r are specific rational numbers. Solve equations of these forms fluently. Compare an algebraic solution to an arithmetic solution, identifying the sequence of the operations used in each approach.
7.EE.B.4b	Solve word problems leading to inequalities of the form $px + q > r$ or $px + q < r$, where p, q, and r are specific rational numbers. Graph the solution set of the inequality and interpret it in the context of the problem.

Grade 7 Common Core State Standards *continued*

Number	Standard for Mathematical Content
7.G Geometry	
Draw construct, and describe geometrical figures and describe the relationships between them.	
7.G.A.1	Solve problems involving scale drawings of geometric figures, including computing actual lengths and areas from a scale drawing and reproducing a scale drawing at a different scale.
7.G.A.2	Draw (freehand, with ruler and protractor, and with technology) geometric shapes with given conditions. Focus on constructing triangles from three measures of angles or sides, noticing when the conditions determine a unique triangle, more than one triangle, or no triangle.
7.G.A.3	Describe the two-dimensional figures that result from slicing three- dimensional figures, as in plane sections of right rectangular prisms and right rectangular pyramids.
Solve real-life and mathematical problems involving angle measure, area, surface area, and volume.	
7.G.B.4	Know the formulas for the area and circumference of a circle and use them to solve problems; give an informal derivation of the relationship between the circumference and area of a circle.
7.G.B.5	Use facts about supplementary, complementary, vertical, and adjacent angles in a multi-step problem to write and solve simple equations for an unknown angle in a figure.
7.G.B.6	Solve real-world and mathematical problems involving area, volume and surface area of two- and three-dimensional objects composed of triangles, quadrilaterals, polygons, cubes, and right prisms.
7.SP Statistics and Probability	
Use random sampling to draw inferences about a population.	
7.SP.A.1	Understand that statistics can be used to gain information about a population by examining a sample of the population; generalizations about a population from a sample are valid only if the sample is representative of that population. Understand that random sampling tends to produce representative samples and support valid inferences.
7.SP.A.2	Use data from a random sample to draw inferences about a population with an unknown characteristic of interest. Generate multiple samples (or simulated samples) of the same size to gauge the variation in estimates or predictions.
Draw informal comparative inferences about two populations.	
7.SP.B.3	Informally assess the degree of visual overlap of two numerical data distributions with similar variabilities, measuring the difference between the centers by expressing it as a multiple of a measure of variability.
7.SP.B.4	Use measures of center and measures of variability for numerical data from random samples to draw informal comparative inferences about two populations.
Investigate chance processes and develop, use, and evaluate probability models.	
7.SP.C.5	Understand that the probability of a chance event is a number between 0 and 1 that expresses the likelihood of the event occurring. Larger numbers indicate greater likelihood. A probability near 0 indicates an unlikely event, a probability around $\frac{1}{2}$ indicates an event that is neither unlikely nor likely, and a probability near 1 indicates a likely event.

Number	Standard for Mathematical Content

7.SP Statistics and Probability (continued)

Investigate chance processes and develop, use, and evaluate probability models.

Number	Standard for Mathematical Content
7.SP.C.6	Approximate the probability of a chance event by collecting data on the chance process that produces it and observing its long-run relative frequency, and predict the approximate relative frequency given the probability.
7.SP.C.7	Develop a probability model and use it to find probabilities of events. Compare probabilities from a model to observed frequencies; if the agreement is not good, explain possible sources of the discrepancy.
7.SP.C.7a	Develop a uniform probability model by assigning equal probability to all outcomes, and use the model to determine probabilities of events.
7.SP.C.7b	Develop a probability model (which may not be uniform) by observing frequencies in data generated from a chance process.
7.SP.C.8	Find probabilities of compound events using organized lists, tables, tree diagrams, and simulation.
7.SP.C.8a	Understand that, just as with simple events, the probability of a compound event is the fraction of outcomes in the sample space for which the compound event occurs.
7.SP.C.8b	Represent sample spaces for compound events using methods such as organized lists, tables and tree diagrams. For an event described in everyday language (e.g., "rolling double sixes"), identify the outcomes in the sample space which compose the event.
7.SP.C.8c	Design and use a simulation to generate frequencies for compound events. For example, use random digits as a simulation tool to approximate the answer to the question: If 40% of donors have type A blood, what is the probability that it will take at least 4 donors to find one with type A blood?

Number	Standard for Mathematical Practice
MP1	Make sense of problems and persevere in solving them.
MP2	Reason abstractly and quantitatively.
MP3	Construct viable arguments and critique the reasoning of others.
MP4	Model with mathematics.
MP5	Use appropriate tools strategically.
MP6	Attend to precision.
MP7	Look for and make use of structure.
MP8	Look for and express regularity in repeated reasoning.

Number	Standard for Mathematical Content

8.NS The Number System

Know that there are numbers that are not rational, and approximate them by rational numbers.

8.NS.A.1	Know that numbers that are not rational are called irrational. Understand informally that every number has a decimal expansion; for rational numbers show that the decimal expansion repeats eventually, and convert a decimal expansion which repeats eventually into a rational number.
8.NS.A.2	Use rational approximations of irrational numbers to compare the size of irrational numbers, locate them approximately on a number line diagram, and estimate the value of expressions (e.g., π^2). For example, by truncating the decimal expansion of $\sqrt{2}$, show that $\sqrt{2}$ is between 1 and 2, then between 1.4 and 1.5, and explain how to continue on to get better approximations.

8.EE Expressions and Equations

Work with radicals and integer exponents.

8.EE.A.1	Know and apply the properties of integer exponents to generate equivalent numerical expressions. For example, $3^2 \times 3^{(-5)} = 3^{(-3)} = \frac{1}{(3^3)} = \frac{1}{27}$.
8.EE.A.2	Use square root and cube root symbols to represent solutions to equations of the form $x^2 = p$ and $x^3 = p$, where p is a positive rational number. Evaluate square roots of small perfect squares and cube roots of small perfect cubes. Know that $\sqrt{2}$ is irrational.
8.EE.A.3	Use numbers expressed in the form of a single digit times an integer power of 10 to estimate very large or very small quantities, and to express how many times as much one is than the other. For example, estimate the population of the United States as 3×10^8 and the population of the world as 7×10^9, and determine that the world population is more than 20 times larger.
8.EE.A.4	Perform operations with numbers expressed in scientific notation, including problems where both decimal and scientific notation are used. Use scientific notation and choose units of appropriate size for measurements of very large or very small quantities (e.g., use millimeters per year for seafloor spreading). Interpret scientific notation that has been generated by technology.

Understand the connections between proportional relationships, lines, and linear equations.

8.EE.B.5	Graph proportional relationships, interpreting the unit rate as the slope of the graph. Compare two different proportional relationships represented in different ways. For example, compare a distance-time graph to a distance-time equation to determine which of two moving objects has greater speed.
8.EE.B.6	Use similar triangles to explain why the slope m is the same between any two distinct points on a non-vertical line in the coordinate plane; derive the equation $y = mx$ for a line through the origin and the equation $y = mx + b$ for a line intercepting the vertical axis at b.

Number	Standard for Mathematical Content

8.EE Expressions and Equations (continued)

Analyze and solve linear equations and pairs of simultaneous linear equations.

8.EE.C.7	Solve linear equations in one variable.
8.EE.C.7a	Give examples of linear equations in one variable with one solution, infinitely many solutions, or no solutions. Show which of these possibilities is the case by successively transforming the given equation into simpler forms, until an equivalent equation of the form $x = a$, $a = a$, or $a = b$ results (where a and b are different numbers).
8.EE.C.7b	Solve linear equations with rational number coefficients, including equations whose solutions require expanding expressions using the distributive property and collecting like terms.

8.G Geometry

Understand congruence and similarity using physical models, transparencies, or geometry software.

8.G.A.1	Verify experimentally the properties of rotations, reflections, and translations:
8.G.A.1a	Verify experimentally the properties of rotations, reflections, and translations: Lines are taken to lines, and line segments to line segments of the same length.
8.G.A.1b	Verify experimentally the properties of rotations, reflections, and translations: Angles are taken to angles of the same measure.
8.G.A.1c	Verify experimentally the properties of rotations, reflections, and translations: Parallel lines are taken to parallel lines.
8.G.A.2	Understand that a two-dimensional figure is congruent to another if the second can be obtained from the first by a sequence of rotations, reflections, and translations; given two congruent figures, describe a sequence that exhibits the congruence between them.
8.G.A.3	Describe the effect of dilations, translations, rotations, and reflections on two-dimensional figures using coordinates.
8.G.A.4	Understand that a two-dimensional figure is similar to another if the second can be obtained from the first by a sequence of rotations, reflections, translations, and dilations; given two similar two- dimensional figures, describe a sequence that exhibits the similarity between them.
8.G.A.5	Use informal arguments to establish facts about the angle sum and exterior angle of triangles, about the angles created when parallel lines are cut by a transversal, and the angle-angle criterion for similarity of triangles.

Solve real-world and mathematical problems involving volume of cylinders, cones, and spheres.

8.G.C.9	Know the formulas for the volumes of cones, cylinders, and spheres and use them to solve real-world and mathematical problems.

Grade 8 Common Core State Standards *continued*

Number	Standard for Mathematical Practice
MP1	Make sense of problems and persevere in solving them.
MP2	Reason abstractly and quantitatively.
MP3	Construct viable arguments and critique the reasoning of others.
MP4	Model with mathematics.
MP5	Use appropriate tools strategically.
MP6	Attend to precision.
MP7	Look for and make use of structure.
MP8	Look for and express regularity in repeated reasoning.

Vocabulary

Language of Math for Topic 15

Lesson	Vocabulary New	Vocabulary Review
15-1 Populations and Samples	bias biased sample inference invalid inference population representative sample sample of a population subject valid inference	proportional
15-2 Estimating a Population		population proportional representative sample
15-3 Convenience Sampling	convenience sampling	representative sample
15-4 Systematic Sampling	systematic sampling	representative sample
15-5 Simple Random Sampling	simple random sampling	population
15-6 Comparing Sampling Methods		convenience sampling representative sample simple random sampling systematic sampling
15-7 Problem Solving		convenience sample systematic sample valid inference
Topic 15 Topic Review	bias convenience sample inference population representative sample simple random sampling systematic sampling	proportional

Vocabulary

Language of Math for Topic 16

Lesson	Vocabulary	
	New	**Review**
16-1 Statistical Measures	interquartile range mean median quartile range	box plot measure of center measure of variability
16-2 Multiple Populations and Inferences	comparative inference	inference population random sample
16-3 Using Measures of Center		comparative inference mean measure of center median
16-4 Using Measures of Variability		comparative inference interquartile range measure of variability range
16-5 Exploring Overlap in Data Sets	mean absolute deviation	absolute deviation deviation mean measure of variability
16-6 Problem Solving		measure of center measure of variability
Topic 16 Topic Review	comparative inference interquartile range mean mean absolute deviation median quartile range	inference measure of center measure of variability population random sample

Vocabulary

Language of Math for Topic 17

Lesson	Vocabulary	
	New	**Review**
17-1 Likelihood and Probability	probability of an event	decimal fraction percent
17-2 Sample Space	action event outcome sample space	probability of an event
17-3 Relative Frequency and Experimental Probability	experimental probability relative frequency trial	event probability of an event
17-4 Theoretical Probability	simulation theoretical probability	action outcome probability of an event sample space
17-5 Probability Models	probability model uniform probability model	action event outcome probability of an event relative frequency sample space theoretical probability
17-6 Problem Solving		uniform probability model
Topic 17 Topic Review	action event experimental probability outcome probability model probability of an event relative frequency sample space simulation theoretical probability trial uniform probability model	decimal fraction percent

Vocabulary

Language of Math for Topic 18

Lesson	Vocabulary	
	New	**Review**
18-1 Compound Events	compound event dependent events independent events	action
18-2 Sample Spaces		action outcome sample space
18-3 Counting Outcomes	counting principle	action event outcome sample space
18-4 Finding Theoretical Probabilities		theoretical probability
18-5 Simulation With Random Numbers		simulation
18-6 Finding Probabilities by Simulation		experimental probability simulation
18-7 Problem Solving		probability
Topic 18 Topic Review	compound event counting principle dependent events independent events	action event experimental probability outcome sample space simulation theoretical probability

Vocabulary

Language of Math for Topic 19

Lesson	Vocabulary	
	New	**Review**
19-1 Measuring Angles	acute angle angle obtuse angle right angle straight angle vertex of an angle	classify
19-2 Adjacent Angles	adjacent angles	angle vertex of an angle
19-3 Complementary Angles	complementary angles	adjacent angles right angle
19-4 Supplementary Angles	supplementary angles	adjacent angle straight angle
19-5 Vertical Angles	vertical angles	intersecting lines name
19-6 Problem Solving		acute angle obtuse angle
Topic 19 Topic Review	acute angle adjacent angles angle complementary angles obtuse angle right angle straight angle supplementary angles vertex of an angle vertical angles	classify intersecting lines

Vocabulary

Language of Math for Topic 20

Lesson	Vocabulary	
	New	**Review**
20-1 Center, Radius, and Diameter	center of a circle circle diameter radius	segment
20-2 Circumference of a Circle	circumference of a circle pi	diameter radius
20-3 Area of a Circle	area of a circle	pi
20-4 Circumference and Area of a Circle		area of a circle circumference of a circle
20-5 Problem Solving		circle
Topic 20 Topic Review	area of a circle circle circumference of a circle diameter pi radius	segment

Vocabulary

Language of Math for Topic 21

Lesson	Vocabulary	
	New	**Review**
21-1 Geometry Drawing Tools		parallelogram quadrilateral
21-2 Drawing 2-D Figures with Given Conditions 1	included angle included side	triangle
21-3 Drawing 2-D Figures with Given Conditions 2		included side net
21-4 2-D Slices of Right Rectangular Prisms	cross section	plane three-dimensional figure
21-5 2-D Slices of Right Rectangular Pyramids		cross section pyramid
21-6 Problem Solving		cross section
Topic 21 Topic Review	cross section included angle included side	net parallelogram plane pyramid three-dimensional figure triangle

Vocabulary

Language of Math for Topic 22

Lesson	Vocabulary	
	New	**Review**
22-1 Surface Areas of Right Prisms	lateral area of a prism surface area of a cube surface area of a prism	lateral face prism regular polygon
22-2 Volumes of Right Prisms	volume of a cube volume of a prism	base area edge of a three-dimensional figure height of a prism
22-3 Surface Areas of Right Pyramids	lateral area of a pyramid slant height of a pyramid surface area of a pyramid	lateral face pyramid
22-4 Volumes of Right Pyramids	volume of a pyramid	base area height of a pyramid
22-5 Problem Solving		prism
Topic 22 Topic Review	lateral area surface area volume	base area height of a prism height of a pyramid lateral face prism pyramid

Vocabulary

Language of Math for Topic 23

Lesson	Vocabulary	
	New	Review
23-1 Translations	image rigid motion transformation translation	vertex of a polygon
23-2 Reflections	line of reflection reflection	rigid motion transformation
23-3 Rotations	angle of rotation center of rotation rotation	rigid motion transformation
23-4 Congruent Figures	congruent figures	rigid motion
23-5 Problem Solving		rigid motion
Topic 23 Topic Review	congruent figures image reflection rigid motion rotation transformation translation	vertex of a polygon

Vocabulary

Language of Math for Topic 24

Lesson	Vocabulary	
	New	Review
24-1 Dilations	dilation enlargement reduction scale factor	transformation
24-2 Similar Figures	similar figures	dilation rigid motion
24-3 Relating Similar Triangles and Slope		similar figures slope
24-4 Problem Solving		dilation scale drawing rigid motion
Topic 24 Topic Review	dilation scale factor similar figures	rigid motion slope transformation

Vocabulary

Language of Math for Topic 25

Lesson	Vocabulary	
	New	**Review**
25-1 Angles, Lines, and Transversals	alternate interior angles corresponding angles transversal	congruent parallel lines
25-2 Reasoning and Parallel Lines	deductive reasoning	alternate interior angles corresponding angles parallel lines transversal
25-3 Interior Angles of Triangles		angle
25-4 Exterior Angles of Triangles	exterior angle of a triangle remote interior angles	straight angle
25-5 Angle-Angle Triangle Similarity		similar
25-6 Problem Solving		similar
Topic 25 Topic Review	alternate interior angles corresponding angles deductive reasoning exterior angle of a triangle remote interior angles transversal	angle congruent parallel lines straight angle

Vocabulary

Language of Math for Topic 26

Lesson	Vocabulary	
	New	**Review**
26-1 Surface Areas of Cylinders	base cylinder height lateral area lateral surface right cylinder surface area	net surface area
26-2 Volumes of Cylinders	volume	base cylinder height
26-3 Surface Areas of Cones	base cone height lateral area lateral surface right cone slant height surface area vertex	base area
26-4 Volumes of Cones	volume	base area cone height
26-5 Surface Areas of Spheres	radius sphere surface area	lateral area of a cylinder
26-6 Volumes of Spheres	volume of a sphere	volume of a cylinder
26-7 Problem Solving		cone cylinder
Topic 26 Topic Review	cone cylinder lateral area sphere surface area volume	net surface area

Digital Resources

CCSS: 7.SP.A.1: Understand that statistics can be used to gain information about a population by examining a sample of the population; generalizations about a population from a sample are valid only if the sample is representative of that population . . . .

Launch

© MP3, MP6

The tumultuous town mayor decides to trash the way the town collects trash. The mayor vows to knock on every door and talk to each household to get new trash collection ideas.

Describe a situation where this approach would be a good idea and a situation where it would be a bad idea.

Reflect When do you talk to everyone about an issue? Can the definition of "everyone" change depending on your issue?

_____

_____

_____

_____

_____

Got It?

PART 1 Got It (1 of 2)

You are studying the T-shirts being sold at a clothing store. Which are *samples*?

I. every other T-shirt in the store
II. all of the T-shirts in the store
III. all of the medium-sized T-shirts
IV. one T-shirt in the store
V. all of the striped T-shirts in the store

PART 1 Got It (2 of 2)

Suppose you have a sample of 15 people. Can you tell what population you are studying? Explain.

PART 2 Got It

You are studying the people in the United States. You want to know who goes sledding each year. Which samples are likely to contain a bias? Justify your reasoning.

I. Everyone in Colorado, Utah, and Vermont
II. 200 people from each state
III. Everyone in Florida, Louisiana, and Texas
IV. Everyone who owns a sled

Discuss with a classmate

What do you know about the term bias?
Choose one of the numbered statements that you identified as having a bias. Explain to your classmate why you think there is a bias in that sample.

Got It?

PART 3 Got It (1 of 2)

A magazine company studies a representative sample of people who read their magazine. In the sample, there are 12 women and 8 men. Which inference(s) about their readership is (are) valid?

I. 60% of the magazine's readers are women.
II. 8 out of 12 of the magazine's readers are men.
III. More men read the magazine than women.

PART 3 Got It (2 of 2)

Suppose you are studying the people in the United States who read newspapers. Would the sample "1 person from each state" be a representative sample made up of 50 subjects?

Close and Check

Focus Question

MP1, MP7

When is it reasonable to use a small group to represent a larger group? When is it not reasonable?

_____

_____

_____

_____

Do you know HOW?

1. You are studying the nutritional value of all meals served at your school. Circle the samples.

   A. the nutritional value of all breakfasts served

   B. the nutritional value of meals served on Mondays

   C. the nutritional value of all meals served

   D. the nutritional value of all lunches served

2. You are studying the popularity of sports at your school. Circle the samples that are likely to contain a bias.

   A. students who play sports

   B. students who attend your school

   C. students who attend sporting events

   D. students who watch sports on TV

Do you UNDERSTAND?

3. **Reasoning** A shoe manufacturer surveys Midwest farmers about the popularity of work boots in the U.S. Can the manufacturer make a valid inference about boot popularity from the sample? Explain.

   _____

   _____

   _____

   _____

4. **Writing** Describe the population and representative sample of a study on high school graduates going to college. Explain how the study can limit bias.

   _____

   _____

   _____

   _____

   _____

Estimating a Population

CCSS: 7.SP.A.2: Use data from a random sample to draw inferences about a population with an unknown characteristic of interest. Generate multiple samples (or simulated samples) of the same size to gauge the variation in estimates or predictions. .... Also, **7.SP.A.1.**

Launch

© MP2, MP4

A newspaper reporter arrives late to a game and sees a few remaining fans. The reporter knows nothing about the teams or the game but concludes that the home team lost. Describe how the reporter may have come to this conclusion.

Reflect Could the reporter be wrong? How?

_____

_____

_____

_____

_____

Got It?

PART 1 Got It (1 of 2)

In a representative sample of 24 seventh graders, there are three students with April birthdays. Suppose there are 448 students in the seventh grade. Estimate how many students in the seventh grade you can infer have April birthdays.

PART 1 Got It (2 of 2)

How do you know that there is a constant of proportionality between a representative sample and the population?

Got It?

PART 2 Got It (1 of 2)

You want to find the number of fiction books in your local library. There are 5,000 books in the library. You have three samples. The actual number of fiction books in the library is 1,500. Which sample(s) best represent the population?

Sample A: fiction, children's, biography, fiction, non-fiction, poetry, play
Sample B: 12 "fiction," 15 "non-fiction," and 12 "biography"
Sample C: 40 "fiction," 29 "non-fiction," 7 "poetry," 19 "drama," and 39 "children's"

PART 2 Got It (2 of 2)

How is the estimate of a population affected by the size of the sample?

Got It?

PART 3 Got It (1 of 2)

An apple orchard has 874 apple trees. Three gardeners each checked 75 apple trees in different areas of the orchard and noted the number of trees that are ready for picking. Each gardener used his or her results to estimate the total number of trees in the orchard that are ready for picking.

Gardener A: 11 apple trees ready for picking
Gardener B: 18 apple trees ready for picking
Gardener C: 13 apple trees ready for picking

a. What was each gardener's estimate?
b. Suppose the actual number of trees ready for picking is 161. How can you use the information in the samples to get the best estimate?

PART 3 Got It (2 of 2)

The three samples in the Example were the same size. What could explain the differences in the inspector's estimates?

Close and Check

Focus Question

When can you use a small group to estimate things about a larger group?

_____

_____

_____

_____

_____

Do you know HOW?

1. In a representative sample of 100 vehicles in a parking lot, there are 15 vans. There are 480 vehicles in the parking lot. Estimate how many of them are vans.

   ☐ vans

2. You want to find the number of red rubber bands there are in a bag of 540. The actual number of red rubber bands is 120. Which sample best represents the population?

   A. 1 red, 2 green, 1 blue rubber band

   B. 18 red, 28 green, 10 blue, 11 orange, and 23 purple rubber bands

   C. 61 red, 92 green, 29 blue, 28 orange, and 60 purple rubber bands

3. The widget factory samples 75 widgets and finds 3 defective ones. If the factory produces 500 widgets a day, how many defective widgets can they expect to produce?

   ☐ defective widgets

Do you UNDERSTAND?

4. **Reasoning** You record the number of students in your class who have green eyes. Is this enough information to estimate the total number of green-eyed students in the school? Explain.

   _____

   _____

   _____

5. **Error Analysis** Three friends each visit 10 of the 60 area homes to find how many have pets. One friend finds 3 homes; the others find 7 and 5. They conclude that 15 of 60 homes have pets. Explain their error.

   _____

   _____

   _____

   _____

   _____

This page intentionally left blank.

Convenience Sampling

CCSS: 7.SP.A.1: Understand that statistics can be used to gain information about a population by examining a sample of the population; generalizations about a population from a sample are valid only if the sample is representative of that population ... .

Launch

© MP1, MP3

The tumultuous town mayor wants to re-route the town bus routes. So, he goes to the two nearest bus stops and asks riders for their opinions.

Describe the good and not-so-good parts of this approach.

Reflect Describe a situation where just asking friends for their opinions would be a good idea.

_____

_____

_____

_____

_____

Got It?

PART 1 Got It

Suppose you are doing research on the students in your grade. Which of the description(s) is *not* an instance of convenience sampling?

I. You choose the first 20 students that you see.
II. You choose all of the students in your school band.
III. You choose all of the students in your classroom.
IV. You choose 10 students from each classroom.

PART 2 Got It

Suppose you are a news reporter, investigating the town's opinion of the new shopping center. What are three ways to choose a convenience sample of town residents to interview? Are the samples that you chose representative samples?

Explain.

Got It?

PART 3 Got It (1 of 2)

Use the convenience sample to estimate how many of the 1,165 cars on Highway 60 are red. Is your estimate accurate?

Convenience sample:
Out of the 40 cars that you can see, there are 16 red ones.

PART 3 Got It (2 of 2)

Suppose a business owner wants to determine what the site's visitors think of his Web site. He uses his e-newsletter list as his convenience sample. Does the sample have bias?

Explain.

Close and Check

> ## Focus Question
> ⒸMP2, MP6
>
> How do you sample in a way that is convenient? What are the advantages and disadvantages of convenience sampling?
>
> _____
>
> _____
>
> _____
>
> _____

Do you know HOW?

1. Suppose you are doing research on the most popular snack foods. Circle the examples of convenience sampling.

   A. You ask your friends.

   B. You ask each person shopping at a convenience store.

   C. You give a survey to each household in your neighborhood.

   D. You ask all the students who ride your bus.

2. You want to find out how many people support the school tax. Circle the representative sample.

   A. You ask every adult in your extended family.

   B. You ask the first 25 adults you see at the mall.

   C. You ask the parents of your friends.

Do you UNDERSTAND?

3. **Writing** A new industrial plant moves into a city of 300,000 people. You want to know if the citizens support the industrial development. Describe a convenience sample and tell whether it would be a representative sample.

   _____

   _____

   _____

   _____

4. **Reasoning** A reporter finds that 9 out of the 10 people he interviews at a concert like the band. Use his data to estimate how many of the 40,000 people in the town like the band. Is it an accurate estimate? Explain.

   _____

   _____

   _____

   _____

   _____

Systematic Sampling

Digital Resources

CCSS: 7.SP.A.1: Understand that statistics can be used to gain information about a population by examining a sample of the population; generalizations about a population from a sample are valid only if the sample is representative of that population ... .

Launch

© MP3, MP4

Your school holds a school-wide kickball tournament. Your gym teacher lines your class up and starts picking every third person to make up your class team.

Describe a possible benefit and a possible drawback of this sampling approach.

Reflect How could the gym teacher make the sampling method better? Provide one idea.

_____

_____

_____

_____

Got It?

A movie theater wants to survey their customers to make sure they are maintaining a customer-friendly environment. Which sampling description is an instance of systematic sampling?

I. You ask every movie-goer that walks into the theater.

II. Choose one customer that comes into the theater.

III. Starting with the first movie-goer, choose every 5th movie-goer that comes into the theater.

IV. Select the first 20 customers that walk into the theater.

Discuss with a classmate

Choose one of the numbered answer choices. If it is an answer choice you selected as correct, explain why it is an example, or instance, of systematic sampling. If you did not select it as a correct answer choice, explain why it is NOT an example of systematic sampling.

How are convenience and systematic sampling similar? How are they different?

Got It?

PART 2 Got It (1 of 2)

Suppose you want to determine how many students in your grade have had a dream about flying. Suppose there are 340 students in your grade. Describe how you would choose a systematic sample of 20 students. Is the sample a representative sample? Explain.

PART 2 Got It (2 of 2)

When might a systematic sample *not* be a representative sample?

Got It?

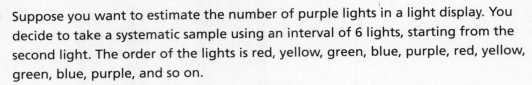

Suppose you want to estimate the number of purple lights in a light display. You decide to take a systematic sample using an interval of 6 lights, starting from the second light. The order of the lights is red, yellow, green, blue, purple, red, yellow, green, blue, purple, and so on.

Suppose there are a total of 300 light bulbs in the display. Using your systematic sample, how many purple light bulbs do you estimate are in the display? How accurate is your estimate? Explain.

Close and Check

Focus Question

⊙ MP3, MP5

How do you sample systematically? What are the advantages and disadvantages of systematic sampling?

_____

_____

_____

_____

Do you know HOW?

1. A moving company wants to survey their customers to find out what they like the most about the company's service. Circle the descriptions of systematic sampling.

   A. The company surveys every customer.

   B. The company chooses every 8th name from its alphabetized customer list to survey.

   C. The company sends a survey to every household.

   D. Each driver surveys every 5th customer.

2. Sixty people are in line for a show. Starting with the 3rd person, you ask every 5th person if they bought their ticket in advance. Nine people say yes. Based on the sample, how many people bought tickets in advance?

   [   ] people

Do you UNDERSTAND?

3. **Compare and Contrast** Describe a situation in which convenience sampling would be sufficient and a situation in which systematic sampling would be more appropriate.

   _____

   _____

   _____

   _____

   _____

4. **Writing** Fruit bars come in 5 flavors. Describe how to gather a systematic sample to find the least popular flavor in your grade.

   _____

   _____

   _____

   _____

   _____

This page intentionally left blank.

Simple Random Sampling

CCSS: 7.SP.A.1: Understand that statistics can be used to gain information about a population ... ; generalizations ... from a sample are valid only if the sample is representative ... . **7.SP.A.2:** Use data from a random sample to draw inferences about a population ... .

Launch

© MP3, MP5

The tumultuous town mayor decides he can't talk to every household to get ideas for a new trash plan. So, he puts all the town's phone numbers into a large hat and chooses at random some numbers to call.

Describe one possible benefit and one possible drawback of choosing a sample this way.

Reflect What makes the process of choosing phone numbers random in the problem?

_____

_____

_____

_____

_____

Got It?

You are doing research on the number of pink flowers in a large field of red flowers. Which is an instance of simple random sampling?

I.   You choose every 10th flower in the field starting with the third flower.
II. You choose 3 flowers from the field.
III. You choose the 50 flowers closest to you.
IV. You choose 50 flowers from different locations in the field.

How are systematic sampling and simple random sampling similar?
How are they different?

Got It?

PART 2 Got It

The table shows the names of the 50 brightest stars in the night sky. Describe how you would collect a sample of 9 stars using simple random sampling. Then choose a simple random sample.

Arcturus	Alnilam	Capella	Koo She	Regor
Achernar	Alnitak	Castor	Menkalinan	Regulus
Acrux	Alphard	Deneb	Miaplacidus	Rigel
Adhara	Altair	Dubhe	Mimosa	Rigil Kentaurus
Aldebaran	Antares	Elnath	Mirfak	Sargas
Algieba	Atria	Fomalhaut	Mirzam	Shaula
Alhena	Avior	Gacrux	Peacock	Sirius
Alioth	Bellatrix	Hadar	Polaris	Spica
Alkaid	Betelgeuse	Hamal	Pollux	Vega
Alnair	Canopus	Kaus Australis	Procyon	Wezen

Got It?

PART 3 Got It

You are studying the brightness of the stars in the night sky. The table shows the brightness of the nine stars in your simple random sample of the 50 brightest stars in the night sky. Based on this sample, how many stars can you infer are between 0.50 and 1.00 magnitude in brightness? Explain.

Number	Star	Brightness (magnitude)
1	Arcturus	−0.05
7	Alhena	1.93
14	Altair	0.77
25	Elnath	1.66
28	Hadar	0.61
33	Miaplacidus	1.67
36	Mirzam	1.98
41	Regor	1.81
47	Sirius	−1.46

Close and Check

> ## Focus Question
> MP3, MP5
>
> How do you sample randomly? What are the advantages and disadvantages of simple random sampling?
>
> _____
>
> _____
>
> _____
>
> _____

Do you know HOW?

1. Circle the example of simple random sampling.

   A. calling the first entry for each letter of the alphabet in the phone book

   B. surveying the first 10 students to enter the classroom

   C. choosing numbers randomly assigned to the population

2. The results of a simple random sample are shown in the table. There are 207 people in the population. Based on the results, estimate how many participants have 2 siblings.

# of Siblings	# of Sample Population
None	3
One	2
Two	8
Three	5

   [____] participants

Do you UNDERSTAND?

3. **Reasoning** Could the simple random sample in Exercise 2 be biased? Explain.

   _____

   _____

   _____

4. **Error Analysis** A bag has 150 balloons. Your friend says the results of picking the first 10 balloons from the bag is an example of a simple random sample. Do you agree? Explain.

   _____

   _____

   _____

   _____

   _____

This page intentionally left blank.

Comparing Sampling Methods

CCSS: 7.SP.A.1: Understand that statistics can be used to gain information about a population by examining a sample of the population .... Understand that random sampling tends to produce representative samples and support valid inferences.

Launch

©MP4, MP6

The tumultuous town mayor decides to set an example for the town by buying recycling bins for city hall. He can choose among red, green, and blue bins but wants input from city hall workers.

Should he use convenience, systematic, or simple random sampling to get input? Tell which you would choose and describe your plan.

Reflect Which sampling method do you use most in your life? Explain.

_____

_____

_____

_____

Got It?

PART 1 Got It

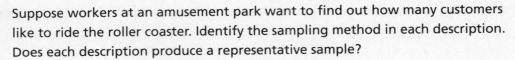

Suppose workers at an amusement park want to find out how many customers like to ride the roller coaster. Identify the sampling method in each description. Does each description produce a representative sample?

a. Survey every 8th customer waiting in line for the roller coaster.
b. Survey the customers at the food court.
c. Survey every 12th customer who enters the park.

PART 2 Got It

Suppose you want to determine how many cars exceed the speed limit on a local highway. If about 2,480 cars travel on the highway per day, tell whether you would use systematic sampling or simple random sampling to choose a sample of 100 cars. Justify your choice of sampling method.

Got It?

PART 3 Got It

You want to know how many students in your school are double-jointed. If there are 400 students in your school, tell whether you would choose a sample of 20 students using either convenience or systematic sampling. Justify your choice of sampling method.

Close and Check

Focus Question

You have studied three sampling methods. For what situations is each type of sampling most effective?

_____

_____

_____

_____

Do you know HOW?

Name the sampling method described in Exercises 1-3.

1. The drama teacher wants to audition students for a play. She assigns each student a number as they enter the room. She then draws 6 numbers from a basket to choose the students.

_____

2. The music teacher wants to know how many people support the marching band. He asks 50 people attending a football game whether they support the band.

_____

3. A marketing analyst wants to know if coupons influence the products people purchase. She asks every 3rd person entering a grocery store.

_____

Do you UNDERSTAND?

4. Reasoning You want to know how many times each year students in your school visit an amusement park. Which sampling method will you use? Explain.

_____

_____

_____

_____

5. Error Analysis A pet shop owner wants to know which tropical fish to stock. On weekday mornings, customers are asked about their favorite tropical fish. Explain why this is not the best sampling method to use.

_____

_____

_____

_____

Problem Solving

CCSS: 7.SP.A.1: Understand that … generalizations about a population from a sample are valid only if the sample is representative … . **7.SP.A.2:** Use data from a random sample to draw inferences … . Generate multiple samples … to gauge the variation in estimates or predictions … .

Launch

© MP2, MP3

To build morale, the radio station manager and the owner each separately ask station workers what special food item should be added in the cafeteria. They both systematically sample every 5th worker by last name.

Owner's Idea
Made-to-order salads
at Radio Digit

Manager's Idea
Made-to-order omelets
at Radio Digit

Explain how their recommendations could be so different.

Reflect Can a sample ever be completely free of bias? Explain.

_____

_____

_____

_____

_____

Got It?

PART 1 Got It

A researcher asked five of his dentist friends if they thought the new Brand X toothpaste that he developed was effective. Four responded "yes." The researcher used the information to write a TV advertisement claiming that "4 out of 5 dentists prefer Brand X toothpaste!" Is this a valid inference? Explain.

PART 2 Got It

Suppose you are a wildlife researcher. You want to know the total number of deer in a reservation. You catch and mark 100 deer. Then you release them into the reservation. A month later, you fly over the reservation and count 64 marked deer out of the 1,200 deer that you see. How many deer are in the reservation?

PART 3 Got It

The manager decided to buy enough bananas for half of the customers. Then a third assistant manager came on duty and decided to take a simple random sample of all the customers in the store. Should the manager change his order? Explain.

Assistant Manager 3: A simple random sample of 30 out of 50 people said yes.

Discuss with a classmate

Read your explanation to the problem out loud.
Discuss key words that you included in your explanation to make sure that you and your classmate understand the meaning of the words. Make a list of any words that you could not define so that you can discuss them with your teacher and other classmates.

Close and Check

MP2, MP6

Focus Question

If you make a judgment about a population based on a sample, how accurate is that judgment? What determines how accurate that judgment is?

_____

_____

_____

_____

Do you know HOW?

1. A researcher attaches satellite tags to 36 sea turtles. Over the next 6 months she identifies 825 sea turtles in the same area. Nine of those turtles have satellite tags. Estimate how many sea turtles are in the area.

   [_____] sea turtles

2. A bookstore owner wants to know which department to expand. Manager A surveys every 3rd teenager that comes in the store. Manager B surveys every customer on Monday evening. Manager C surveys 25% of the customers chosen at random from the store's mailing list. Identify each type of sampling and circle the one that is the least biased.

   Manager A: [_____]

   Manager B: [_____]

   Manager C: [_____]

Do you UNDERSTAND?

3. **Error Analysis** Choose one of the managers' surveys from Exercise 2. Explain how you would change the sampling technique in order to gather more accurate information.

   _____

   _____

   _____

   _____

4. **Reasoning** How might the results of the survey in Exercise 2 vary if Manager B repeated the survey every evening for a week and compared each day's results? Explain.

   _____

   _____

   _____

   _____

This page intentionally left blank.

Topic Review

New Vocabulary: bias, convenience sample, inference, population, representative sample, simple random sampling, systematic sampling

Review Vocabulary: proportional

Vocabulary Review

Identify two challenging vocabulary terms from this topic. Write one vocabulary term in the center oval, and fill in the surrounding boxes with details that will help you better understand the term.

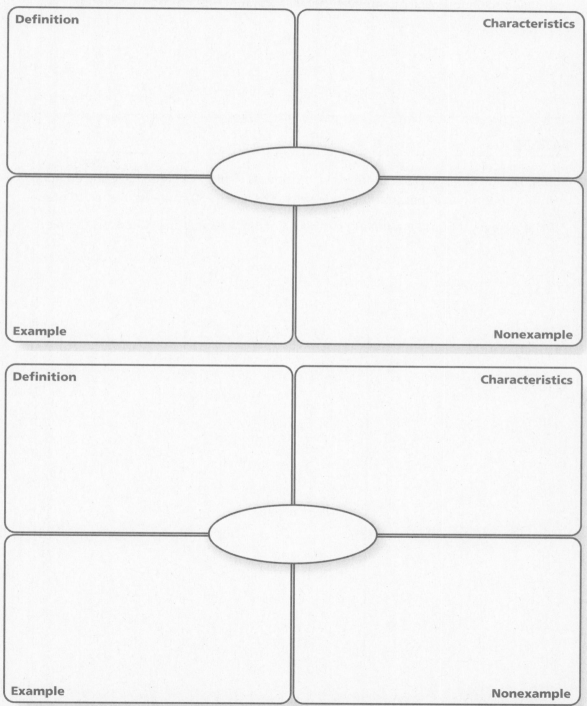

Definition

Characteristics

Example

Nonexample

Definition

Characteristics

Example

Nonexample

Pull It All Together

TASK 1

A laboratory technician places the contents of a well-mixed test tube of blood on a three-dimensional grid that holds a specified volume in each chamber. There are 25 chambers and the technician wants to count the red blood cells in 3 of them.

Decide whether the technician should use *convenience, systematic,* or *random sampling* to choose which chambers she will examine. Explain your reasoning.

TASK 2

Suppose you want to find out how many students in the 7th grade have stayed home from school this year because they were sick. There are 250 students in the 7th grade.

Write a survey. Choose a sampling method. Choose a sample size. Choose a sample.

Digital Resources

CCSS: **7.SP.A.1:** Understand that statistics can be used to gain information about a population by examining a sample of the population .... **7.SP.B.4:** Use measures of center and measures of variability for numerical data from random samples ....

Launch

© MP2, MP6

Ms. Adventure and Data Girl proposed different research studies to the local airline.

Which study should the airline fund? Explain.

> How many people flew to Puerto Rico on Tuesday?

> How many people fly to Puerto Rico on Tuesdays?

Reflect Which study could have a numerical result of 89.5? Explain.

_____

_____

_____

_____

Got It?

PART 1 Got It

During eruptions at Jewel Geyser, water soars up to various heights. What is the mean height of the geyser's eruptions?

Heights of Jewel Geyser Eruptions (feet)
15, 30, 27, 23, 28, 19, 14, 11, 22

PART 2 Got It

What is the IQR of the depths of a sample of hot spring pools in Yellowstone National Park?

Depths of Hot Springs (feet)
25, 6, 27, 23.5, 25, 32.5

Got It?

PART 3 Got It

Data Girl wants to buy a new suitcase for her next trip. She wants an unusual color to make the bag easy to spot, so she records every third suitcase that comes by on the baggage claim.

green, blue, red, green, blue

The store Data Girl shops at sells black, blue, red, and green suitcases. Which color suitcase should she buy?

Close and Check

Focus Question

MP6, MP7

What can you do to make data more useful? How does what you are looking for determine how data are best used and represented?

Do you know HOW?

Use the data set below for Exercises 1–4.

> **Monthly High Temperatures (°F)**
> **Anchorage, Alaska**
> 15, 18, 25, 36, 47, 55,
> 59, 57, 48, 35, 22, 16

1. Find the mean monthly high temperature to the nearest degree.

2. Find the median of the data set.

3. Find the range of the data set.

4. Find the IQR of the data set.

Do you UNDERSTAND?

5. **Reasoning** Is the mean or the median a better representation of the temperature data of Anchorage, Alaska? Explain.

6. **Error Analysis** Your friend uses the mean temperature to decide which clothes to buy for her move to Anchorage. Do you agree with the measure she chose? Explain.

CCSS: 7.SP.A.1: Understand that statistics can be used to gain information about a population by examining a sample ... . **7.SP.B.4:** Use measures of center and measures of variability ... to draw informal comparative inferences about two populations ... . Also, **7.SP.B.3.**

Launch

Data Girl plans out her research study for a local airline. The airline asks her to answer the following questions as part of her plan.

Provide a possible response for each question.

Who?

What?

Where?

When?

Why?

How many people fly to Puerto Rico on Tuesdays?

Tic Toc

Reflect Which "W" question was the hardest to provide an answer for? Explain.

_____

_____

_____

_____

_____

Got It?

The school nurse tested the eyesight of all the students in Grades 6, 7, and 8. To answer each question, should the nurse consider the grades as *three* populations or as *one* population?

| How many students have perfect vision in the school? | What is the mean eyesight score for each grade? | Do students' eyesight scores change more between 6th and 7th grades, or between 7th and 8th grades? |

Why can one population in a study be considered more than one population in another study?

Got It?

PART 2 Got It

A scientist is analyzing sea urchin samples taken from the ocean. For each question, how many populations should the scientist use? Describe the population(s).

Question	**Question**	**Question**
How many species of sea urchins exist?	Which continent has the greatest population of sea urchins along its coast?	Do more sea urchins live in the Atlantic Ocean or in the Pacific Ocean?

Got It?

The table shows the number of hours that a random sample of students in two classes spent on schoolwork last night.

Class A	Class B
0	0
0	0
1	0
1	0
1	1
1	1
2	1
2	1
2	1
2	1
4	2
4	2
5	2
5	2
5	2
5	2
5	3
5	3
6	3
6	3
6	4
6	4

Hours of Schoolwork

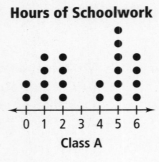

Class A

a. Make a conjecture about why there are two peaks in the dot plot of Class A.

b. Based on your conjecture, make a comparative inference about the students in each class.

Close and Check

> ### Focus Question
> MP1, MP4
>
> When does a group represent one population? When does it represent more than one population? How can you tell?
>
> _____
>
> _____
>
> _____
>
> _____

Do you know HOW?

1. The local newspaper is writing an article on the county schools. Write **S** if the question applies to a single population and **M** if the question applies to multiple populations.

    A. $\boxed{S}$ What percent of the total student population plays sports?

    B. $\boxed{M}$ What are the schools' rankings in the region?

2. The dot plots show the number of students who are in the marching band. Circle the valid inference.

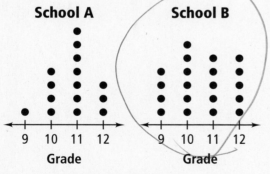

    A. School A's band is more popular.

    B. The number of band members from each grade is more evenly distributed in School B.

Do you UNDERSTAND?

3. **Writing** Write a question based on the dot plots in Exercise 2 that represents more than one population. Explain why it represents more than one population.

    _____

    _____

    _____

    _____

4. **Error Analysis** Based on the dot plots in Exercise 2, a classmate infers that School B has more students enrolled. Is this a valid inference? Explain.

    no because its band only

    _____

    _____

    _____

This page intentionally left blank.

Using Measures of Center

CCSS: 7.SP.B.4: Use measures of center ... for numerical data from random samples to draw informal comparative inferences about two populations.

Launch

© MP6, MP7

The lead local librarian and his lead assistant survey individual patrons on the number of e-books they read each week. The tablets show the survey results.

What inference should the librarians make based on the means of the data sets?

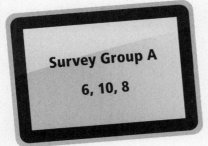

Survey Group A

6, 10, 8

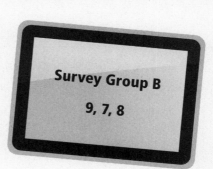

Survey Group B

9, 7, 8

Reflect Can you always draw a clear inference from data? Explain.

_____

_____

_____

_____

_____

Got It?

PART 1 Got It

A book publisher is testing two versions of a new book. A random sample of people is given 30 minutes to read each version. What is the median of each sample? Make a comparative inference based on the median values.

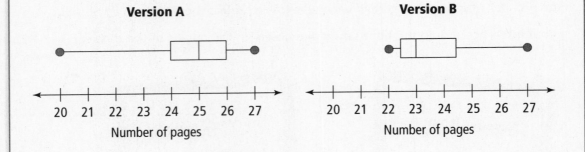

Version A   Version B

Number of pages   Number of pages

Got It?

PART 2 Got It

A book publisher is testing two versions of a new book. A random sample of people is given 30 minutes to read each version. What is the mean of each sample? Make a comparative inference based on this measure of center.

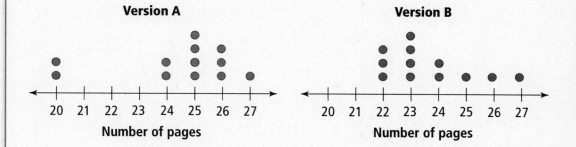

Got It?

A book publisher is testing two versions of a new book. A random sample of people is given 30 minutes to read each version. Using the data and comparing the shapes of the graphs, what might the publisher conclude about the book versions?

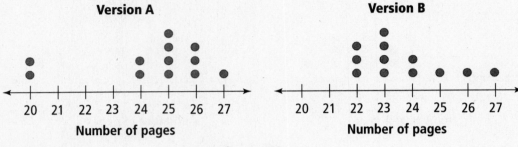

Version A

Number of pages

median = 25
mean ≈ 24.4

Version B

Number of pages

median = 23
mean ≈ 23.7

Can you make more than one comparative inference about a population using the measures of center? Explain.

Close and Check

Focus Question

How can you compare two groups using a single number from each group?

_____

_____

_____

_____

Do you know HOW?

1. A city planner records the weight of a day's garbage from a random sample of households. Find the median weight of the garbage in each neighborhood.

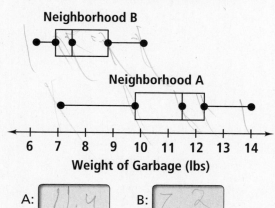

Neighborhood B

Neighborhood A

Weight of Garbage (lbs)

A: 11.4   B: 7.2

2. Next, the planner records the weight of a day's recycling from a random sample of households. Find the mean weight of recycling in each neighborhood to the nearest tenth.

Weight of Recycling (lbs)

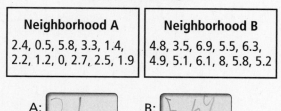

Neighborhood A	Neighborhood B
2.4, 0.5, 5.8, 3.3, 1.4, 2.2, 1.2, 0, 2.7, 2.5, 1.9	4.8, 3.5, 6.9, 5.5, 6.3, 4.9, 5.1, 6.1, 8, 5.8, 5.2

A: 2.1   B: 5.64

Do you UNDERSTAND?

3. **Writing** Make a comparative inference based on the median values in Exercise 1. Support your statement.

Neiborhood
11.4 is more
off a land fill
then neiberhood2

4. **Writing** Make a comparative inference based on the mean values in Exercise 2. Support your statement.

Nebiorhood B
reciyesmer

_____

5. **Reasoning** Based on the previous Exercises, describe one conclusion you can make about how the neighborhoods compare.

_____

_____

_____

_____

This page intentionally left blank.

Using Measures of Variability

CCSS: 7.SP.B.4: Use … measures of variability for numerical data from random samples to draw informal comparative inferences about two populations.

Launch

Ⓒ MP4, MP7

The data show a random sampling of heights in inches of female athletes in two different Olympic sports.

What inference(s) can you make about the sport each group plays?

Athlete Group A

60, 53, 54, 62,
55, 61, 63, 57

Athlete Group B

72, 70, 69, 74,
73, 71, 71, 75

Reflect Could someone else come up with a different inference on the sport of each group? Explain.

_____

_____

_____

_____

_____

Got It?

PART 1 Got It

A researcher is studying the effects of owning a cell phone on the number of hours people sleep. What is the range of hours slept for each group? Make a comparative inference about the populations based on range.

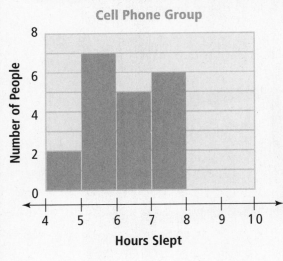

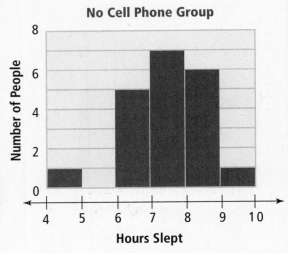

PART 2 Got It (1 of 2)

A researcher is studying the effects of owning a cell phone on the number of hours people sleep. What is the interquartile range of hours slept for each group? Make a comparative inference about the populations based on IQR.

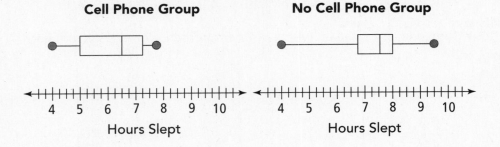

Got It?

Are the range and interquartile range by themselves enough information to determine which population sleeps more than the other? Explain.

Discuss with a classmate

Read the problem statement together.
Explain how you interpreted the problem statement in order to answer the question.
Then compare your answers to the problem.
Did you include enough detail in your answer to justify why you answered 'yes' or 'no'?

PART 3 Got It

A researcher is studying the effects of owning a cell phone on the number of hours people sleep. Using the data, what might the researcher conclude about the populations? Explain.

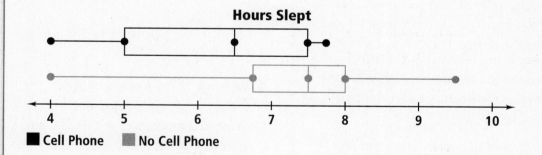

Hours Slept

■ **Cell Phone** ■ **No Cell Phone**

Close and Check

© MP3, MP4

Focus Question

How else can you compare two groups using a single number from each group?

_____

_____

_____

_____

▶ Do you know **HOW?**

1. Find the range of TV viewing time for each population.

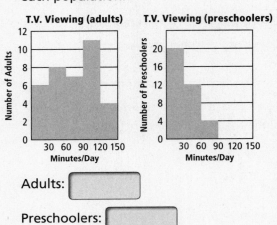

T.V. Viewing (adults)   T.V. Viewing (preschoolers)

Adults: [_____]

Preschoolers: [_____]

2. Your friend surveys dog owners with different yard sizes. Find the IQR of each population.

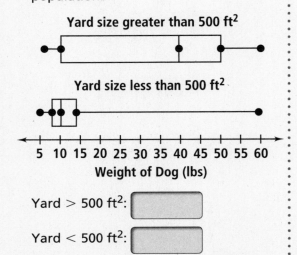

Yard size greater than 500 ft²

Yard size less than 500 ft²

Weight of Dog (lbs)

Yard > 500 ft²: [_____]

Yard < 500 ft²: [_____]

▶ Do you **UNDERSTAND?**

3. Writing Write a comparative inference that you *cannot* make about the populations in Exercise 1 based on the ranges of the data. Explain.

_____

_____

_____

_____

_____

4. Writing Make a comparative inference about the populations in Exercise 2 based on the IQR. Explain your inference.

_____

_____

_____

_____

_____

Exploring Overlap in Data Sets

Digital Resources

CCSS: 7.SP.B.3: Informally assess the degree of visual overlap of two numerical data distributions with similar variabilities, measuring the difference between the centers by expressing it as a multiple of a measure of variability .... Also, **7.SP.B.4.**

Launch

© MP2, MP6

Each tablet shows a random sampling of heights in inches of male athletes in two different Olympic sports.

What inferences can you make about the sport played by each group based on the range and mean of heights?

Athlete Group A

76, 82, 74, 80, 78, 79, 75, 86, 84, 81

Athlete Group B

81, 76, 74, 72, 78, 75, 75, 74, 77, 76

Reflect The groups have heights in common. What impact did that have in your inferences about the sports of each group?

_____

_____

_____

Got It?

PART 1 Got It (1 of 2)

Calculate the mean absolute deviation for the heights of seventh graders. The mean is about 61 inches. Round to the nearest whole number.

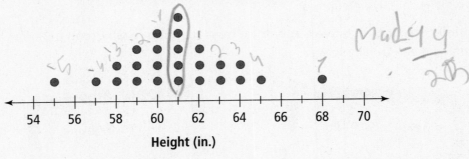

Sample of 7th Grade Students

Height (in.)

1.76

PART 1 Got It (2 of 2)

The graphs show the height distribution of samples of 2nd and 7th graders. Explain why the MADs of both samples are the same.

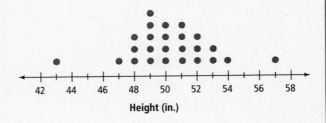

Sample of 2nd Grade Students

Height (in.)

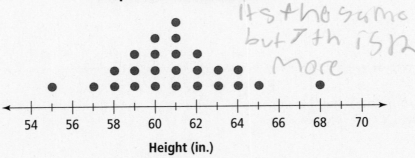

Sample of 7th Grade Students

Its the same but 7th is 12 more

Height (in.)

Got It?

PART 2 Got It (1 of 2)

How does the mean height of the 7th graders compare to the mean height of the 9th graders? Express the difference as a multiple of the mean absolute deviation of either grade.

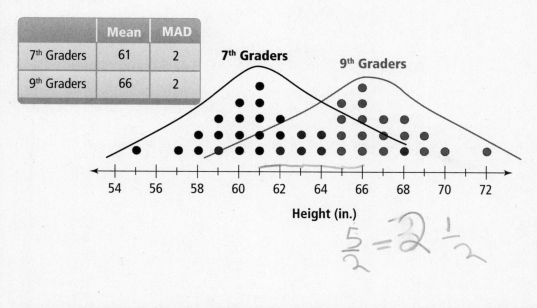

	Mean	MAD
7th Graders	61	2
9th Graders	66	2

$\frac{5}{2} = 2\frac{1}{2}$

PART 2 Got It (2 of 2)

The 2nd, 7th, and 9th grade height distributions have approximately the same mean absolute deviation. The means of the 2nd and 7th grade heights are 5.5 **MADs** apart. The means of the 7th and 9th grade heights are 2.5 **MADs** apart. How can you use the MAD to measure the degree of visual overlap of two distributions that have the same MAD?

Got It?

The curve has a mean of 6 and a MAD of 0.5. Sketch a second data distribution that is eight mean absolute deviations away from the mean of the curve.

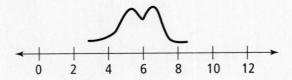

Close and Check

Focus Question

How do measures of center and variability help you determine how much two groups have in common?

_____

_____

_____

_____

_____

Do you know HOW?

1. Find the mean absolute deviation to the nearest minute for the data set.

Flight Delays

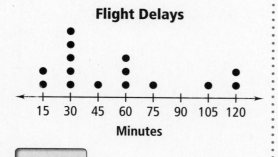

Minutes

[   ]

2. Express the difference between the grooming costs of Company A and Company B as a multiple of the mean absolute deviation of either company.

Pet Groomers

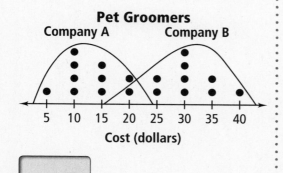

Cost (dollars)

[   ]

Do you UNDERSTAND?

3. Vocabulary Explain what the mean absolute deviation in Exercise 1 represents.

_____

_____

_____

4. Reasoning Curve 1 has a mean of 30. Your friend correctly sketches a curve three mean absolute deviations from Curve 1. How could your friend be correct?

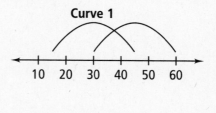

_____

_____

_____

_____

_____

This page intentionally left blank.

Problem Solving

CCSS: 7.SP.B.4: Use measures of center and measures of variability for numerical data from random samples to draw informal comparative inferences about two populations ... .

Launch

MP3, MP6

The data sets show the monthly average high temperature from January to December in degrees Fahrenheit for two U.S. cities. You must choose to live in one of the cities.

Justify your choice based on at least one measure of center (mean or median) or variability (range, interquartile range, or mean absolute deviation).

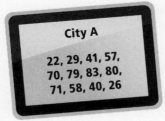

City A

22, 29, 41, 57,
70, 79, 83, 80,
71, 58, 40, 26

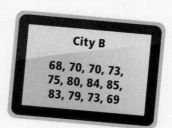

City B

68, 70, 70, 73,
75, 80, 84, 85,
83, 79, 73, 69

Reflect How did the measure(s) of center or variability you used help you decide?

_____

_____

_____

_____

_____

Got It?

PART 1 Got It

Every two months, a bicycle company gives an award to the salesperson with the best sales record. The data show the sales results of the top two bicycle salespeople. Who should get the award? Use measures of center and variability to justify your choice.

Week	Caprice	Constance
1	2650	1225
2	3989	2008
3	2698	2314
4	2160	3978
5	2073	3007
6	4875	2832
7	1690	3316
8	2178	3548

Got It?

The graphs show the number of minutes that a random sample of students from Grades 6 and 8 spend on their hair each morning. What can you infer about the relationship between the grade level and how long students spend on their hair? Explain.

Time Spent on Hair in the Morning

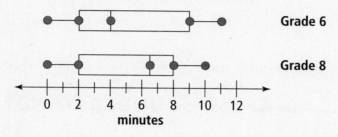

Close and Check

MP1, MP4

Focus Question

How can you use measures of center and variability of a random sample to make inferences, predictions, and decisions? Which measures work best and why?

_____

_____

_____

_____

Do you know HOW?

Use the data below to answer Exercises 1–3. Round your answers to the nearest hundredth.

Race Times (s)

Runner A: 12.52, 12.20, 8.89, 12.61

Runner B: 12.18, 12.13, 12.27, 12.15

1. Find the mean race time for each runner.

   Runner A: [   ]

   Runner B: [   ]

2. Find the median race time for each runner.

   Runner A: [   ]

   Runner B: [   ]

3. Find the IQR for each runner.

   Runner A: [   ]

   Runner B: [   ]

Do you UNDERSTAND?

4. **Reasoning** Based on the data from Exercises 1–3, which runner should be chosen to compete in the regional track meet? Explain.

   _____

   _____

   _____

   _____

5. **Writing** A study is conducted on two cities in different climates. What inference can you make? Explain.

   City 1

   City 2

   1 2 3 4 5 6 7 8 9 10 11 12
   Hours spent outside per week

   _____

   _____

   _____

   _____

New Vocabulary: comparative inference, interquartile range, mean, mean absolute deviation, median, quartile, range

Review Vocabulary: inference, measure of center, measure of variability, population, random sample

Vocabulary Review

▶ Identify two challenging vocabulary terms from this topic. Write one vocabulary term in the center oval, and fill in the surrounding boxes with details that will help you better understand the term.

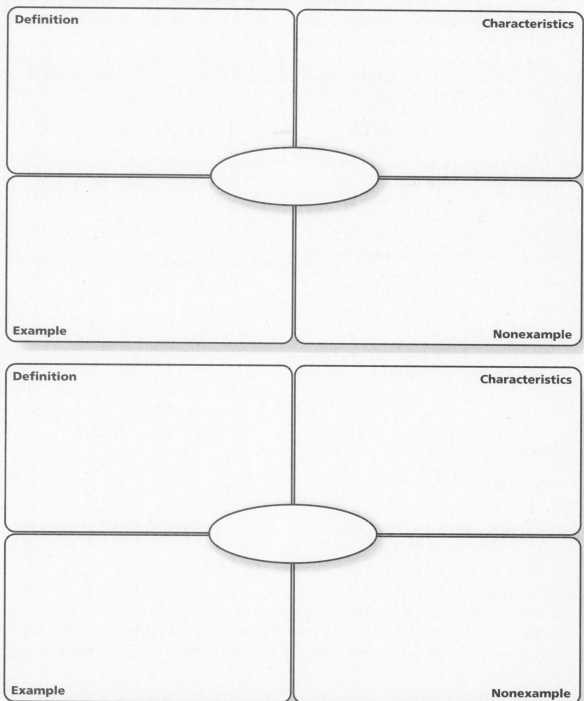

Definition

Characteristics

Example

Nonexample

Definition

Characteristics

Example

Nonexample

Pull It All Together

TASK 1

In a cooking class, students make ice cream by mixing boiling milk with sugar. An impatient student put his mixture in the freezer before waiting for the milk to cool. To his surprise, his mixture froze into ice cream before those of other students. He mentioned his observation to his friend, but was told that this was impossible.

The student decided to test his observation further using warm and cold water. The data from the student's observations when using warm and cold water are below. Find the median and range of each experiment.

Trials	Warm Water Freeze Time (min)
1	22
2	21
3	23
4	22
5	24
6	23

Trials	Cold Water Freeze Time (min)
1	$24\frac{1}{2}$
2	25
3	27
4	26
5	24
6	25

Make box plots to compare the data sets.

TASK 2

A science teacher told the student that when hot water freezes faster than cool water, it is called the Mpemba Effect. Based on the student's data and your knowledge of measures of center and variability, can the teacher infer that the student's experiment is an example of the Mpemba Effect? If not, make a valid inference.

Likelihood and Probability

Digital Resources

CCSS: 7.SP.C.5: Understand that the probability of a chance event is a number between 0 and 1 that expresses the likelihood of the event occurring ... . **7.SP.C.6:** ... predict the approximate relative frequency given the probability ... .

Launch

Ⓒ MP1, MP3

To be annoying, your friend says "probably" to every question about the future. Come up with a better way to describe the chance of each of these events happening. Describe your method.

The Earth will go around the sun.	
Tigers will fly.	
It will rain this week.	
Your team will win the big game.	
You will write a best-selling novel.	

Reflect Are all ways to describe the chance of something happening equally effective? Explain.

_____

_____

_____

Got It?

PART 1 Got It

What word best describes the likelihood that two people sitting next to each other on a bus have the same birthday?

Impossible   Unlikely   As Likely as Not   Likely   Certain

PART 2 Got It

The probability of choosing a flag with only two colors is 0.15. What is this probability written as a fraction and as a percent?

Got It?

PART 3 Got It

Based on data collected over thousands of flights, an airline believes that the probability of a passenger being a no-show on a morning flight is 12%.

If the airline overbooks a 300-seat morning flight by selling 350 tickets, how many empty seats should the airline expect to have on the flight?

Close and Check

Focus Question

What are effective ways to describe the likelihood of an event?

_____

_____

_____

_____

Do you know HOW?

1. Choose a word from the following list to best describe the likelihood that there will be 365 days in a year: _impossible, unlikely, as likely as not, likely,_ and _certain._

   [   ]

2. The probability of a U.S. resident living in a state that begins with the letter M is 0.16. Write this probability as a fraction and as a percent.

   fraction: [   ]   percent: [   ]

3. There are 2,425 participants in a national phone survey that includes residents from every state. There is an 8% probability that a participant lives in a state that begins with the letter W. How many participants are expected to live in a state that begins with W?

   [   ] participants

Do you UNDERSTAND?

4. **Reasoning** Would you rather know the likelihood of winning a prize in words or percents? Explain.

   _____

   _____

   _____

   _____

   _____

5. **Writing** Why is _maybe_ not a good term to use when describing the probability of an event?

   _____

   _____

   _____

   _____

   _____

Digital Resources

CCSS: 7.SP.C.7: Develop a probability model and use it to find probabilities of events. Compare probabilities from a model to observed frequencies; if the agreement is not good, explain possible sources of the discrepancy.

Launch

Ⓒ MP2, MP7

Your annoying friend designs a dart game for you to play. She says, "I get a point when a dart hits a composite number, and you get a point when a dart hits a prime number."

Do you like her game? Who do you think will win? Explain.

91	**64**
48	**57**

Reflect Would you change the game above? If so, how?

_____

_____

_____

_____

_____

Got It?

PART 1 Got It

Action: One spin of the spinner

What is the sample space for the action? How many outcomes are in the sample space?

PART 2 Got It (1 of 2)

Action: One spin of the spinner

Event: The spinner stops on an odd number.

Which numbers are in the event?

Got It?

Write a verbal description of the event.

Action: One spin of the spinner

Event: 3, 6, 9

List the following in the order *action, sample space, event.*

Win the game.   Play a game.   win, lose, tie

Discuss with a classmate

Think about games you have played.

How do those experiences help you make sense of this problem?

Explain how you determined the order of action, sample space, and event.

Close and Check

Topic 17   438   Lesson 17-2

Focus Question

© MP3, MP6

What is the difference between an *action* and an *event*?

_____

_____

_____

_____

Do you know HOW?

Use the picture for Exercises 1 and 2.

1. Action: Choose one card.
   How many outcomes are in the sample space?

   [7]

2. Action: Choose one card.
   Event: Choose a striped card.
   How many cards are in the event?

   [3]

3. Number the following. Use 1 for *action*, 2 for *sample space* and 3 for *event*.

   [3] Left, right, forward

   [2] Pick right.

   [1] Choose a direction.

Do you UNDERSTAND?

4. **Vocabulary** The cafeteria sells sack lunches with either a ham sandwich, turkey wrap, peanut butter sandwich, or corn dog. The lunches are not labeled. Determine the action, sample space, and event for buying a sack lunch.

   _____

   _____

   _____

   _____

5. **Error Analysis** In a certain game, players roll again if they roll a 6 on a number cube. Your friend says that rolling a 6 is an action, but you say it is an event. Explain who is correct.

   _____

   _____

   _____

   _____

Copyright © by Pearson Education, Inc., or its affiliates. All Rights Reserved.

Topic 17   438   **Lesson 17-2**

Relative Frequency and Experimental Probability

CCSS: 7.SP.C.6: Approximate the probability of a chance event by collecting data on the chance process that produces it and observing its long-run relative frequency, and predict the approximate relative frequency given the probability ... .

Launch

© MP3, MP5

Lay your Companion page flat on your desk. Hold any coin about a foot directly above the circle on the page.

What is the probability that your coin will land completely inside the circle without touching the edge? Explain how you can find out.

Reflect Could your probability be a lot different from your neighbor's? Explain why.

_____

_____

_____

_____

Got It?

PART 1 Got It (1 of 2)

The table shows one class's results for spinning the spinner 40 times. What is the relative frequency of the event "spin a number less than 4"?

Experiment Table				
Outcome	1	2	3	4
Frequency	10	12	4	14
Number of Trials: 40				

PART 1 Got It (2 of 2)

The table shows one class's results for spinning the spinner 40 times.

a. Suppose the class spins the spinner 40 more times. Do you expect the relative frequency of the event "spin a 2" to change, or to remain the same?

Experiment Table				
Outcome	1	2	3	4
Frequency	10	12	4	14
Number of Trials: 40				

b. Suppose the class spins the spinner 400 times in all. Is there a value that you expect the relative frequency of the event "spin a 2" to be close to? Explain.

Got It?

PART 2 Got It (1 of 2)

Find the experimental probability that a customer will bring reusable bags.

Answers to "What type of bag would you like?"

Type of Bag	Number of Customer Requests
Plastic	18
Paper	6
Customer's own reusable bag	8

PART 2 Got It (2 of 2)

The experimental probabilities that you found in the Example and the Got It were based on data collected from 32 customers. Do you think that these experimental probabilities are good estimates of the actual probabilities that customers will ask for these three types of bags? Explain.

Close and Check

Focus Question

For some types of events there is more than one way to determine the probability. In what situations is conducting an experiment a good way to determine the probability of an event? How can you evaluate the reasonableness of an experimental probability?

Do you know HOW?

1. The table shows the results for rolling a number cube 100 times. What is the relative frequency for the event "roll a multiple of 3?"

Outcome	1	2	3	4	5	6
Frequency	22	14	23	19	10	12

2. Write the experimental probability for the event "roll a factor of 4" from the data above as a fraction, decimal, and percent.

3. A coin is tossed 50 times. What is the expected relative frequency of the coin landing on heads?

Do you UNDERSTAND?

4. **Reasoning** Assume the number cube in Exercise 1 is rolled 500 times. For which outcome listed would you not expect the experimental probability to change much? Explain.

5. **Writing** Your friend makes 3 free throws out of 5 attempts. Then she makes 1 basket and misses 2. Will your friend definitely make the next 2 shots? Explain.

CCSS: 7.SP.C.7: Develop a probability model and use it to find probabilities of events. Compare probabilities ... to observed frequencies .... **7.SP.C.7a:** Develop a uniform probability model by assigning equal probability to all outcomes ....

Launch

© MP6, MP7

Your annoying friend devises another game. Before she puts the tiles in the bag, she says, "I get a point if a negative number is picked and you get a point if a positive number is picked."

Is this game fair? Explain why or why not.

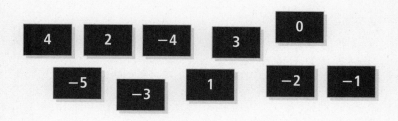

Reflect What makes a game fair? Explain.

_____

_____

_____

_____

_____

Got It?

PART 1 Got It (1 of 2)

Suppose you choose a button at random from this bag of white, gray, and black buttons.

What is the probability of choosing a gray button?

What is the probability of choosing a two-hole button?

PART 1 Got It (2 of 2)

The spinner is divided into two unequal sectors. The outcomes for red and blue are *not* equally likely.

Explain how you can use the theoretical probability formula to find the probability of spinning red.

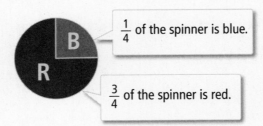

$\frac{1}{4}$ of the spinner is blue.

$\frac{3}{4}$ of the spinner is red.

Got It?

PART 2 Got It

Which probabilities are experimental?

I. An eye doctor examines 10 people and finds that 4 are color-blind.

$P(\text{color–blind}) = \frac{4}{10}$

II. A teacher chooses 1 student at random from a class of 13 boys and 12 girls.

$P(\text{boy}) = \frac{13}{25}$

III. You check 6 boxes of cereal and find that 1 box has a prize at the bottom.

$P(\text{prize}) = \frac{1}{6}$

PART 3 Got It

In one family, a child's chore for the day is chosen at random. The table shows the results of using the spinner to simulate 99 days of chores. For which chore is the number given by the simulation closest to the number predicted by the theoretical probability?

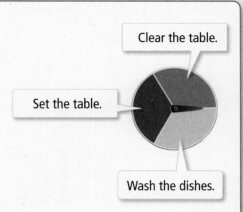

Clear the table.

Set the table.

Wash the dishes.

Chore Simulation	
Set the table (Red)	55
Clear the table (Blue)	32
Wash the dishes (Yellow)	12
Total	99

Close and Check

Focus Question

For some types of events there is more than one way to determine the probability. How do you tell the difference between a theoretical and an experimental probability?

_____

_____

_____

_____

▶ Do you know HOW?

1. Suppose you chose a card at random. What is the probability of choosing a card with an even number and a ?

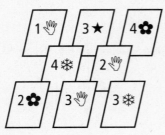

2. Circle the situation(s) that represents experimental probability.

   A. Every 100th customer receives a door prize.

   B. The gumball machine contains gumballs in six colors. You get a yellow gumball.

   C. A survey finds that 4 out of 25 people have green eyes.

▶ Do you UNDERSTAND?

3. **Vocabulary** A card from Exercise 1 is chosen at random 15 times.

   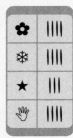

   Are the experimental probabilities and theoretical probabilities close? Explain.

   _____

   _____

   _____

4. **Reasoning** If a card were chosen at random another 100 times, what would you expect to happen to the comparisons between the theoretical and experimental probabilities?

   _____

   _____

   _____

Digital Resources

CCSS: 7.SP.C.7a: Develop a uniform probability model by assigning equal probability to all outcomes, and use the model to determine probabilities of events ... . **7.SP.C.7b:** Develop a probability model ... by observing frequencies in data ... . Also, **7.SP.C.7.**

Launch

© MP4, MP6

Your annoying friend proposes another game as you wait for the bus. She says, "I get a point for every car that passes. You get a point for every truck. We each have a 1 out of 2 probability of getting a point."

Do you agree with your friend? Are you going to play by her rules? Explain.

Reflect Can you always figure out if a game is fair before playing? Explain.

_____

_____

_____

_____

_____

Got It?

PART 1 Got It (1 of 2)

What probability statement would you add to each list to make a complete probability model of this action?

Action

The robotics team will choose one member at random to run the robot at the competition.

Sample Space

Robotics Team

Girl, age 10	Boy, age 13
Boy, age 12	Boy, age 10
Boy, age 13	Girl, age 12
Girl, age 11	Girl, age 14
Boy, age 14	Boy, age 12

List 1
$P(\text{boy}) = \frac{3}{5}$

List 2
$P(\text{younger than } 12) = \frac{3}{10}$

$P(\text{age } 12) = \frac{3}{10}$

PART 1 Got It (2 of 2)

Explain why this list of probabilities does not complete a probability model for the spinner.

$P(\text{red}) = \frac{3}{8}$ $P(\text{odd}) = \frac{1}{2}$ $P(\text{yellow}) = \frac{1}{8}$

Action: One spin of the spinner.

Sample space: Each of the eight sectors is one outcome.

Got It?

PART 2 Got It

For which situation(s) can you use a uniform probability model?

Situation A: You drop a thumbtack from a height of 1 foot. What is the probability that the thumbtack will land point up?

Situation B: This color cube has 2 red faces and 4 yellow faces. Suppose you roll the color cube. What is the probability that the cube will land with yellow facing up?

PART 3 Got It

The data in the table is from a survey of high school students with after-school jobs. Write the list of probabilities for a probability model that gives the probability that a student chosen at random from this group of high school students has each type of job.

Results of After-School Jobs Survey

Job Type	Number of Students
Store Cashier	67
Paper Route	8
Babysitting	120
Restaurant Work	55

Close and Check

Focus Question

How do you choose the best type of probability model for a situation?

_____

_____

_____

_____

_____

Do you know HOW?

1. Complete the probability model for the cards.

   Action: Choose one card at random.

   Sample space: Each card is one outcome.

   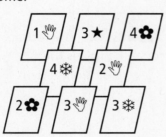

   P(❀) = ☐   P(🖐) = ☐

   P(❄) = ☐   P(prime) = ☐

2. Circle the situation(s) for which you can use a uniform probability model.

   A. A student will bring a backpack to school.

   B. Tomorrow will be a school day.

   C. The football team will win their next game.

Do you UNDERSTAND?

3. **Error Analysis** A student records the number of boys and girls who bring backpacks to school. What mistake does he make when finding probabilities?

Boys	$P(\text{yes}) = \dfrac{75}{143}$	$P(\text{no}) = \dfrac{21}{34}$
Girls	$P(\text{yes}) = \dfrac{68}{143}$	$P(\text{no}) = \dfrac{13}{34}$

   _____

   _____

   _____

4. **Vocabulary** Explain how to determine whether to use a uniform or an experimental probability model to predict outcomes.

   _____

   _____

   _____

   _____

Problem Solving

Digital Resources

CCSS: 7.SP.C.7: ... Compare probabilities from a model to observed frequencies; if the agreement is not good, explain possible sources of the discrepancy. **7.SP.C.7b:** Develop a probability model ... by observing frequencies in data ... . Also, **7.SP.C.7a.**

Launch

Ⓒ MP3, MP7

You are a basketball coach. You need to choose one player to take the shot that will determine the outcome of the game.

Which player should you choose? Support your choice by using the probability that the player chosen will make the winning shot.

Shooting Results

Player	Last Game	Last 5 Games	Last 10 Games
5	2 of 10	25 of 50	54 of 100
24	7 of 10	22 of 50	42 of 100

Reflect Did the shooting results for the last game for each player match expectations? Explain.

_____

_____

_____

_____

_____

Got It?

PART 1 Got It

A basketball team has two 6th graders, five 7th graders, and three 8th graders. Each day the coach selects one team member at random to put away the equipment.
How can you assign the numbered sectors of the spinner so that the spinner can be used to simulate this situation?

I. Assign 2 to represent 6th graders.
Assign 5 to represent 7th graders.
Assign 3 to represent 8th graders.

II. Assign 0 and 1 to represent 6th graders.
Assign 2, 3, 4, 5, and 6 to represent 7th graders.
Assign 7, 8, and 9 to represent 8th graders.

III. Assign 1 and 3 to represent 6th graders.
Assign 0, 2, 4, 6 and 8 to represent 7th graders.
Assign 5, 7, and 9 to represent 8th graders.

Got It?

PART 2 Got It

Each day, a bicycle manufacturer tests the brakes on a random sample of 50 new bikes.

New Bikes With Defective Brakes

Day	Monday	Tuesday	Wednesday	Thursday	Friday
Number	2	1	0	4	3

You want to buy a bicycle from this manufacturer only if the probability that the brakes are defective is less than 5%.

Should you buy a bike from this manufacturer?

Close and Check

Focus Question

What types of predictions and decisions can you make using probability?

_____

_____

_____

_____

Do you know HOW?

1. A dog has a litter of 6 puppies: 3 black, 2 brown, and 1 white. Circle the way you can assign the faces of a number cube to simulate randomly selecting a certain puppy.

   A. Assign 1 and 2 to black, 3 and 4 to brown, and 5 and 6 to white.

   B. Assign 1, 2, and 3 to black, 4 and 5 to brown, and 6 to white.

   C. Assign 1 to black, 3 to brown, and 5 to white. Assign 2, 4, and 6 to represent "roll again."

2. Every day, a widget company randomly samples 100 widgets and records how many are defective. Based on the week's data, write the probability that a widget will be defective as a fraction, decimal, and percent.

Day	1	2	3	4	5
Defective	2	3	3	2	2

Fraction   Decimal   Percent

Do you UNDERSTAND?

3. **Reasoning** In Exercise 1, is there an equal chance of randomly selecting a puppy of each color? Explain.

   _____

   _____

   _____

   _____

   _____

4. **Writing** Based on the percent of defective widgets you found in Exercise 2, would you feel confident buying a widget from this company? Explain.

   _____

   _____

   _____

   _____

   _____

New Vocabulary: action, event, experimental probability, outcome, probability model, probability of an event, relative frequency, sample space, simulation, theoretical probability, trial, uniform probability model
Review Vocabulary: decimal, fraction, percent

Vocabulary Review

Identify two challenging vocabulary terms from this topic. Write one vocabulary term in the center oval, and fill in the surrounding boxes with details that will help you better understand the term.

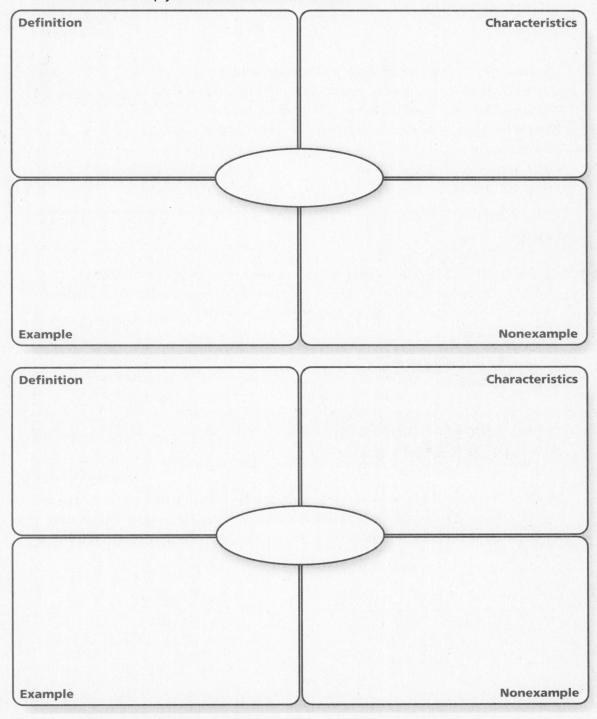

Pull It All Together

TASK 1

The list shows the new numbers of each type of song you had on your music player.

On Monday, you set your music player to select songs at random. What is the probability that the first song played will *not* be a country song?

Rock: 30
Pop: 19
Rap: 3
Country: 5
Classical: 8

The list shows the number of songs you have on your music player on Monday. On Tuesday, you download 11 new pop songs. You set your music player to play pop and rap songs at random. What is the probability that the first song played is one of your new pop songs?

TASK 2

a. The list shows the new numbers of each type of song on your music player. Write a probability model to find the probability of hearing each type of song when the music player is set to play one song at random.

b. On Thursday, you set your music player to play 100 songs at random. The table shows what you heard.

Rock: 30
Pop: 30
Rap: 3
Country: 5
Classical: 8

Thursday's Songs

Rock	Pop	Rap	Country	Classical
23	50	7	9	11

Based on Thursday's data, what is the experimental probability that you will hear a pop song when your music player selects a song at random? How does your answer compare to the theoretical probability predicted by the probability model you wrote in part (a)?

18-1 Compound Events

CCSS: 7.SP.C.8: Find probabilities of compound events using organized lists, tables, tree diagrams, and simulation. **7.SP.C.8b:** Represent sample spaces for compound events using methods such as organized lists, tables and tree diagrams ... .

Launch

© MP2, MP6

Draw lines to sort these tiles into two groups. Explain your groups.

| Pick a number from 1–9. | Toss heads then tails. | Pick a number from 10–20. |

| Toss heads. | Spin red twice. | Spin red. |

| **Group 1** | **Group 2** |

Reflect Could you sort the tiles in more than one way? Explain.

_____

_____

_____

_____

Got It?

PART 1 Got It

How many steps or choices does this action involve?

Action: Choose a sandwich filling and a type of bread.

Got It?

PART 2 Got It

Which choices show a compound event for this action?

Action: Spin the spinner four times.

I. (R, B, G)   **II.** (B, B, B, B)   **III.** (R, B, G, B)

PART 3 Got It

Which compound event is composed of independent events?

I. **Action**
Roll a standard number cube twice.

Compound Event
Get an even number on each roll.

II. **Action**
Toss a coin once and roll a standard number cube once.

Compound Event
The coin lands on tails.
The number cube lands on 5.

Close and Check

Focus Question

What makes an event a compound event? What are the different types of compound events?

_____

_____

_____

_____

Do you know HOW?

1. How many steps or choices does the action of creating a parfait cup involve?

   Action: Choose a yogurt flavor, a type of fruit, and a topping.

Yogurt	Fruit	Topping
Plain	Blueberries	Granola
Vanilla	Strawberries	Nuts
Berry	Cherries	
	Bananas	

   [   ]

2. Are the events of creating a parfait cup in Exercise 1 dependent or independent?

   [   ]

3. In gym class, two students are chosen to pick teams for a game of soccer. Is the action of choosing team members a dependent or independent event?

   [   ]

Do you UNDERSTAND?

4. **Writing** Explain your answer to Exercise 3.

   _____

   _____

   _____

5. **Error Analysis** During a game, each player rolls a number cube and moves a game piece that number of spaces. A friend says each turn is a single independent event. Do you agree? Explain.

   _____

   _____

   _____

   _____

   _____

Sample Spaces

Digital Resources

CCSS: **7.SP.C.8:** Find probabilities of compound events using organized lists, tables, tree diagrams, and simulation. **7.SP.C.8b:** Represent sample spaces for compound events using methods such as organized lists, tables and tree diagrams … .

Launch

Ⓒ MP4, MP5

A new car company allows you to design your own Car Model D online. Show all the different ways you can design the car. Explain how you know you've shown all the different ways.

> **Car Model D Options**
>
> **Color**
> ○ Red   ○ Black   ○ Silver
> _____
>
> **Doors**
> ○ Two   ○ Four
> _____
>
> **Transmission**
> ○ Automatic   ○ Manual

Reflect Does it matter what order you list the different ways to design the car? Explain.

_____

_____

_____

_____

Got It?

PART 1 Got It

Three friends buy bagels, choosing from the kinds shown. They buy three different kinds. Use an organized list to show all possible combinations for the three friends' bagels.

Show each outcome in this form:
(friend 1's bagel, friend 2's bagel, friend 3's bagel)

Plain  Sesame  Cheese  Onion

Discuss with a classmate

Compare the organized lists that you made for this problem.
Read the instructions for the problem together, paying particular attention to how to write each outcome using parentheses and commas.
Then use highlighting or color-coding to check your outcomes to see if your lists are complete. Revise your lists as needed.

PART 2 Got It

A clothing store sells sweaters in V-neck, crew neck, and cardigan styles. Each style is available in blue, gray, or red. How many different sweaters can you choose?

Got It?

PART 3 Got It (1 of 2)

On the school bus, two students sit in each seat, one by the window and one by the aisle. Make a tree diagram to show all possible arrangements of 6th, 7th, and 8th graders sharing a seat. List the possible arrangements in an outcome column.

PART 3 Got It (2 of 2)

Think about the sample spaces displayed in organized lists, tables, and tree diagrams in this lesson.

Make a conjecture about the relationship between the number of possible outcomes of each step of an action and the number of outcomes in the sample space of the action.

Close and Check

Focus Question

How do you know a sample space is complete? How do you know when you have accounted for all possibilities?

_____

_____

_____

_____

Do you know HOW?

1. How many possible combinations of parfait cups are there if one item is chosen from each list?

Yogurt	**Fruit**	**Topping**
Plain	Blueberries	Granola
Vanilla	Strawberries	Nuts
Berry	Cherries	
	Bananas	

2. A school offers three elective classes: art (a), band (b), and choir (c). Each student must choose a morning class and a different afternoon class. Make a tree diagram to show all possible class and time combinations.

Do you UNDERSTAND?

3. Reasoning The school in Exercise 2 adds an evening class time. Does the total number of combinations of classes change? Explain.

_____

_____

_____

4. Error Analysis The table displays the outcomes for a sample space involving a spinner divided into colors. Your friend says the spinner was spun four times. Is she correct? Explain.

	R	B
R	R, R	R, B
B	B, R	B, B

_____

_____

_____

Counting Outcomes

Digital Resources

CCSS: 7.SP.C.8a: Understand that … the probability of a compound event is the fraction of outcomes in the sample space for which the compound event occurs. **7.SP.C.8b:** … For an event described in everyday language … , identify the outcomes … . Also, **7.SP.C.8.**

Launch

MP4, MP6

The new car company unveils two new models. Which car can you order in more ways? Explain your reasoning.

Car Model Q Options

Color
○ Silver   ○ Black

Doors
○ Three   ○ Four   ○ Five

Transmission
○ Automatic   ○ Manual

Car Model C Options

Color
○ Silver   ○ Black   ○ White
○ Green   ○ Red   ○ Tan

Doors
○ Two   ○ Four

Transmission
○ Automatic

Reflect How would your method work for counting the different ways you could order a car with even more choices such as 12 exterior colors, 4 door options, 3 transmission options, 2 engine types, and 6 interior colors?

_____

_____

Got It?

PART 1 Got It

At Charlie's House of Chili, your chili can be mild, medium, spicy, hot, or superhot, and you can have it with or without cheese.

How many different ways can you order chili at Charlie's House of Chili?

PART 2 Got It

Use the table of possible outcomes of rolling two standard number cubes. How many outcomes are in this event?

Event: Get a sum of 7.

Sample Space for Rolling 2 Number Cubes

	1	2	3	4	5	6
1	1, 1	2, 1	3, 1	4, 1	5, 1	6, 1
2	1, 2	2, 2	3, 2	4, 2	5, 2	6, 2
3	1, 3	2, 3	3, 3	4, 3	5, 3	6, 3
4	1, 4	2, 4	3, 4	4, 4	5, 4	6, 4
5	1, 5	2, 5	3, 5	4, 5	5, 5	6, 5
6	1, 6	2, 6	3, 6	4, 6	5, 6	6, 6

PART 3 Got It

The number on your hockey jersey is 17. You decide to choose a three-character password by selecting at random two different letters, followed by one number, from the phrase below.

HOCKEY 17

How many different passwords can you make? How many of the passwords begin with the letter K?

Close and Check

Focus Question

MP2, MP7

How is the number of outcomes of a multi-step process related to the number of outcomes for each step?

_____

_____

_____

_____

Do you know **HOW?**

1. An online shoe store offers customized gym shoes. You have a choice of leather or canvas material; black, white, or gray shoe color; and red, pink, blue, green, or yellow lace color. How many different shoe choices are there?

2. Use a table to show all the possible outcomes of choosing a shape and a letter.

△   ○   □

A   B   C   D   E

3. Based on the table in Exercise 2, how many outcomes are in this event? Event: Choosing a polygon or a vowel.

Do you **UNDERSTAND?**

4. Writing Explain how you found the solution to Exercise 1.

_____

_____

_____

_____

_____

5. Reasoning Explain how the number of possible outcomes for Exercise 3 would change if the event were choosing a polygon *and* a vowel.

_____

_____

_____

_____

_____

This page intentionally left blank.

Finding Theoretical Probabilities

CCSS: **7.SP.C.8:** Find probabilities of compound events using organized lists, tables, [and] tree diagrams ... . **7.SP.C.8a:** Understand ... the probability of a compound event is the fraction of outcomes in the sample space for which the compound event occurs. Also, **7.SP.C.6.**

Launch

© MP2, MP7

An online shoe clerk unfortunately erases your order options on Shoe Model W. So, she sends you four different pairs and asks you to return any that don't match your order.

What are the chances you'll get the shoes you ordered? Explain.

Shoe Model W

Color

○ Silver ○ Black ○ Brown ○ Green

Size

○ 5   ○ 6   ○ 7   ○ 8

○ $5\frac{1}{2}$ ○ $6\frac{1}{2}$ ○ $7\frac{1}{2}$ ○ $8\frac{1}{2}$

Reflect Will the chances be the same or different depending on which four different pairs the store clerk sent?

_____

_____

_____

_____

Got It?

PART 1 Got It

The tree diagram shows the possible outcomes of choosing one card from the group shown, setting it aside, and then choosing a second card.

What is *P*(at least one fish or one apple)?

Got It?

PART 2 Got It

It is your turn to pick a Geography Fair partner and country at random. Use an organized list, a table, or a tree diagram to find the probability of choosing your best friend, Miguel, and your favorite country, Greece.

Names still in box:
Nora, Miguel, Otis, Priya, and Quincy

Countries still in box:
Ethiopia, France, and Greece

PART 3 Got It

Action: Choose one marble at random from a bag that contains one red, one green, and one blue marble. Then toss a coin.

For which compound event is the result closest to the result predicted by theoretical probability?

Results of 60 Trials

Event	Count
(R, H)	11
(R, T)	8
(G, H)	14
(G, T)	6
(B, H)	13
(B, T)	8

Discuss with a classmate

The table of results for 60 trials contains important information for this problem. Take turns choosing a row from the table and explaining what the notation in the left column and the number in the right column mean.

Then compare your answers to the problem. Revise your answers as needed.

Close and Check

Focus Question

MP2, MP5

In what situations should you use an organized list, a table, or a tree diagram to find the probability of a compound event?

_____

_____

_____

_____

Do you know HOW?

1. Find the probability of rolling sequential numbers (for example; 1 then 2) in 2 consecutive rolls of a number cube.

P(2 sequential numbers) = ☐

or about ☐ %

2. Using a number cube and 4 marbles (red, blue, yellow, and green), what is the theoretical probability of rolling a specific number and choosing a specific marble without looking?

☐

3. For which compound event is the result closest to the result predicted by theoretical probability in Exercise 2?

Results of 100 Trials				
Event	(1, R)	(3, B)	(5, Y)	(6, G)
Count	6	2	4	3

☐

Do you UNDERSTAND?

4. Writing Explain how the theoretical probability in Exercise 2 changes if the action is rolling an even number and choosing a red or yellow marble.

_____

_____

_____

_____

_____

_____

5. Reasoning If 60 trials are conducted using the compound event described in Exercise 4, how many favorable outcomes would you expect to get? Explain.

_____

_____

_____

_____

Simulation with Random Numbers

Digital Resources

CCSS: **7.SP.C.8:** Find probabilities of compound events using organized lists, tables, tree diagrams, and simulation. **7.SP.C.8c:** Design and use a simulation to generate frequencies for compound events . . . .

Launch

© MP1, MP7

Describe a pick-a-number game where contestants have a 1 in 4 chance of winning. Your game must have two rounds and use all the tiles shown.

Reflect What was most critical to you to design a game that worked?

_____

_____

_____

_____

_____

Got It?

PART 1 Got It

A grocery store finds that 30% of its customers bring their own bags. Which ways of assigning numbers to outcomes can you use to simulate the probability that a customer chosen at random brings his or her own bags?

I. own bags: 1, 2, 3
    other bags: 4, 5, 6, 7, 8, 9, 0

II. own bags: 1 to 33
    other bags: 34 to 100

III. own bags: 1 to 10
     other bags: 11 to 30

PART 2 Got It

A quarterback usually completes 60% of his passes. Use these numbers to represent possible outcomes of one pass:

Complete: 1, 2, 3, 4, 5, 6
Incomplete: 7, 8, 9, 0

Which list of random numbers simulates completing more than four passes?
I.   0 4 0 8 1 1 5 0 8 0
II. 7 0 4 0 3 0 1 1 3 9
III. 2 6 9 0 3 6 6 7 2 7

Got It?

PART 3 Got It

On a six-question multiple-choice quiz, each question has four answer choices. Only one answer choice is correct.

Use the Probability Tool to generate random numbers to simulate taking this quiz 20 times, guessing answers at random. Use your results to complete the frequency table of the results.

Six-Question Multiple-Choice Quiz

Number Correct	0	1	2	3	4	5	6
Frequency							

Close and Check

> ## Focus Question
> **MP5, MP7**
>
> How can you use random numbers to simulate real-world situations?
>
> _____
>
> _____
>
> _____
>
> _____

▶ Do you know HOW?

1. A survey finds that 49 out of 84 students ride the school bus each day. Assign numbers to simulate the outcomes that a student chosen at random rides the school bus each day.

   bus rider: [   ]

   non-bus rider: [   ]

2. Circle the list of random numbers that simulates the survey results given in Exercise 1.

   A. 3, 5, 9, 2, 11, 9, 5, 3, 8, 10, 12, 5

   B. 12, 11, 7, 9, 4, 6, 3, 5, 7, 3, 9, 10

3. Eight students take a four-question quiz. Correct answers are assigned a 1, and incorrect answers are assigned a 2. Record the results of the quiz in the frequency table.

1111	2122	1112	1122
1112	1221	1211	1112

   Quiz Results

▶ Do you UNDERSTAND?

4. **Writing** Explain how you decided which numbers to assign in Exercise 1.

   _____

   _____

   _____

   _____

   _____

5. **Reasoning** According to Exercise 3, how many students got at least 3 items on the quiz correct? Explain how you found the solution.

   _____

   _____

   _____

   _____

   _____

Finding Probabilities Using Simulation

CCSS: 7.SP.C.8: Find probabilities of compound events using organized lists, tables, tree diagrams, and simulation.

Launch

© MP1, MP5, MP6

Your friend designs a game that involves drawing *makes* and *misses* blindly out of a bag to simulate a basketball free throw. He wants his game to have *P*(making two free throws) = 0.75.

Complete and explain the possible game rules using the items shown.

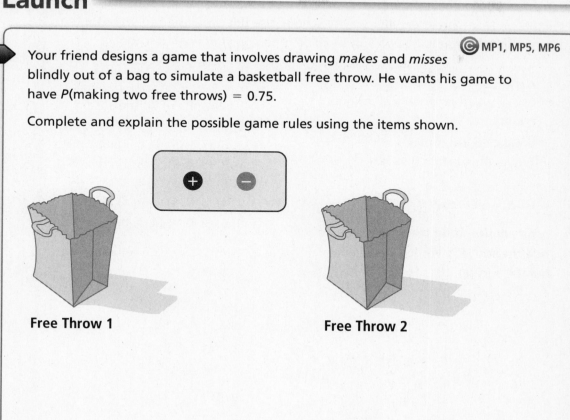

Free Throw 1   **Free Throw 2**

Reflect Does your game guarantee a 75% probability of making two free throws? Explain.

_____

_____

_____

_____

Got It?

PART 1 Got It

Traffic lights on Main Street are green 40% of the time. You travel through three lights on Main Street on your way to school. Use this simulation to estimate the probability that at least two lights will be green on your way to school.

Action
Check whether three traffic lights are green.

Simulated outcomes
Use numbers from 0 to 9.

   green: 1, 2, 3, 4
   not green: 5, 6, 7, 8, 9, 0

Simulation (one trial)
Choose three digits from 0 to 9 at random.

Results of 24 trials

(3, 3, 3) (0, 3, 5) (6, 9, 2) (7, 5, 8)
(0, 5, 6) (7, 9, 5) (0, 6, 6) (6, 0, 0)
(2, 6, 9) (5, 9, 3) (6, 6, 1) (1, 4, 5)
(0, 3, 8) (9, 6, 1) (9, 4, 9) (7, 9, 7)
(3, 7, 4) (4, 8, 5) (7, 2, 1) (2, 1, 9)
(5, 1, 6) (2, 0, 4) (4, 7, 8) (3, 3, 7)

Got It?

PART 2 Got It

Traffic lights on School Street are yellow 10% of the time. You travel through four traffic lights on School Street on your way to soccer practice. Use a simulation to predict the probability that at least one light will be yellow on your way to soccer practice.

Close and Check

Focus Question

In what situations should you use a simulation to find the probability of a compound event?

_____

_____

_____

_____

Do you know HOW?

1. A survey finds that 39% of households in a certain town own at least one dog. Assign a range of numbers to simulate each possible outcome.

   Households that own at least one dog:

   [   ]

   Households that do not own at least one dog:

   [   ]

2. Use the pairs of random numbers to find the experimental probability that exactly one of the next two people you meet will own a dog. Express the solution as a percent.

(72, 30)	(15, 38)	(67, 93)
(100, 2)	(80, 69)	(77, 89)
(88, 45)	(22, 51)	(57, 62)
(72, 59)	(74, 64)	(81, 97)

   [   ]

Do you UNDERSTAND?

3. **Writing** Describe one trial and tell what a favorable outcome would be for the simulation in Exercise 2.

   _____

   _____

   _____

   _____

   _____

4. **Reasoning** You decide to change the favorable outcome in Exercise 2 to _at least_ one of the next two people you meet owning a dog. Would you expect the experimental probability to change? Explain.

   _____

   _____

   _____

   _____

   _____

Problem Solving

CCSS: 7.SP.C.7: Develop a probability model and use it to find probabilities of events. Compare probabilities from a model to observed frequencies …. **7.SP.C.8:** Find probabilities of compound events using organized lists, tables, tree diagrams, and simulation.

Digital Resources

Launch

© MP2, MP8

Design a three-spinner game in which contestants have a 30% chance of winning. Complete the spinners and describe the rules of the game.

Reflect What was the most challenging part of designing your game? Explain.

_____

_____

_____

_____

_____

Got It?

PART 1 Got It

A class used the Probability Tool to roll two number cubes 300 times. About how many times should they expect to get either a sum or a product of 8?

Discuss with a classmate

Highlight the math terms *sum* and *product*.
Review the definitions for these terms, using the glossary in the back of the book as needed.
If you did not understand these terms when you solved the problem, revise your answer so that you use the terms correctly.

PART 2 Got It

Water flows from Start to End through a system of water pipes, as shown in the diagram. Water flows only in the direction of the arrows. At each point W, X, Y, and Z, there is a 50% chance that an obstruction prevents the flow of water.

What is the probability that there is an open path from Start to End at any given moment?

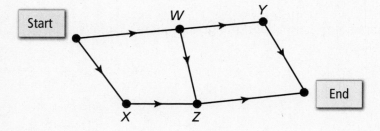

Close and Check

Focus Question

MP1, MP3

How do you choose a strategy for finding the probability of a compound event? Are there situations in which one strategy is better than another?

_____

_____

_____

_____

Do you know HOW?

1. You roll two number cubes 200 times. How many times should you expect to roll two number cubes that have an even sum?

   [_____]

2. You can travel from your house to a golf course by the roads shown. Any of the 3 intersections *A, B,* and *C* may be closed due to construction. Express the theoretical probability that there is an open path from your house to the golf course at any time as a fraction and as a percent.

   Fraction: [_____]

   Percent: [_____]

Do you UNDERSTAND?

3. **Reasoning** Explain how you found the solution to Exercise 1.

   _____

   _____

   _____

   _____

   _____

4. **Writing** Explain how you could set up a simulation to find the experimental probability for Exercise 2.

   _____

   _____

   _____

   _____

   _____

   _____

   _____

This page intentionally left blank.

New Vocabulary: compound event, counting principle, dependent events, independent events
Review Vocabulary: action, event, experimental probability, outcome, sample space, simulation, theoretical probability

Vocabulary Review

Identify two challenging vocabulary terms from this topic. Write one vocabulary term in the center oval, and fill in the surrounding boxes with details that will help you better understand the term.

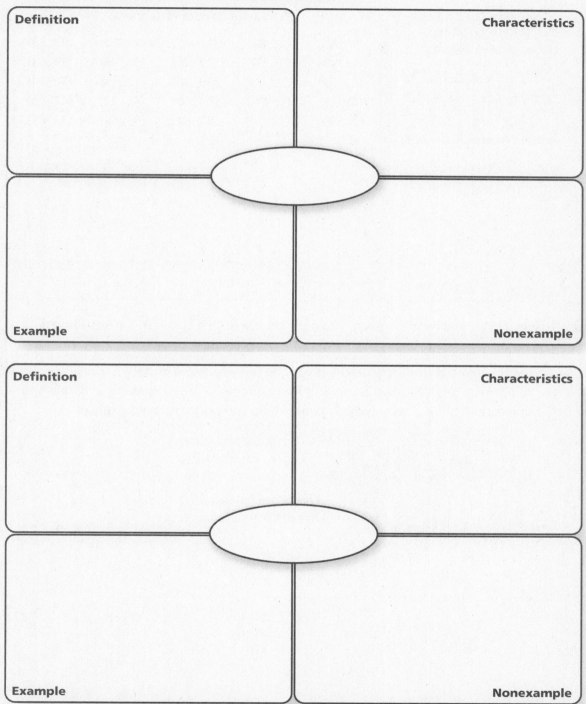

Definition

Characteristics

Example

Nonexample

Definition

Characteristics

Example

Nonexample

Pull It All Together

TASK 1

The table shows probabilities based on a town's weather records. Use the pairs of random numbers to estimate the probability of each event.

a. A partly cloudy day is followed by a clear day.

b. A cloudy day is followed by a partly cloudy day.

Sky Condition

Condition	Probability
Clear	23%
Partly Cloudy	48%
Cloudy	29%

25 Pairs of Random Numbers

(91, 96)	(28, 84)	(12, 25)	(89, 80)	(82, 93)
(15, 23)	(28, 62)	(70, 86)	(38, 56)	(99, 63)
(52, 37)	(13, 21)	(99, 38)	(12, 34)	(50, 34)
(41, 1)	(6, 99)	(64, 60)	(46, 22)	(41, 46)
(74, 94)	(73, 73)	(30, 61)	(99, 63)	(23, 81)

TASK 2

To win a prize in a carnival game, you must choose both a box with a marble and a curtain that hides a prize.

a. For the game shown, what is the probability of winning a prize?

b. A different game has two boxes and four curtains. One box contains a marble and one curtain hides a prize. Which game would you prefer to play? Explain.

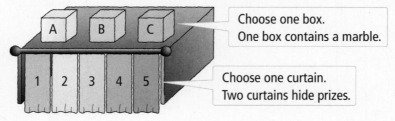

Choose one box.
One box contains a marble.

Choose one curtain.
Two curtains hide prizes.

Digital Resources

CCSS: 7.EE.B.4: Use variables to represent quantities in a real-world or mathematical problem, and construct simple equations and inequalities to solve problems by reasoning about the quantities. Also, **7.EE.B.4a** and **7.G.A.2.**

Launch

Ⓒ MP3, MP5

Compare Angle 1 and Angle 2. Tell which is greater.

1

2

Show how you know using only paper and pencil.

Reflect How does the length of the rays (or sides) in an angle relate to its measure?

_____

_____

_____

_____

_____

Got It?

PART 1 **Got It**

What is the measure of ∠CAB?

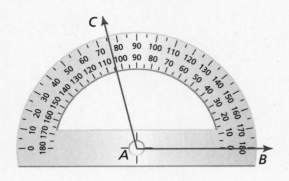

PART 2 **Got It** (1 of 2)

You can classify angles as right, acute, obtuse, or straight. Which type of angle is *not* represented in the diagram?

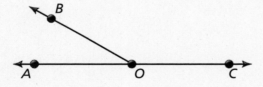

Got It?

Can the sum of the measures of two acute angles be greater than the measure of a straight angle? Explain.

PART 3 Got It

The measure of ∠ABC is 60°. Find the value of x.

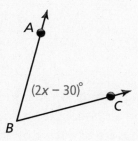

Discuss with a classmate

How did you apply what you know about solving equations to solve this problem? Describe the steps you took to set up the equation to solve.

Close and Check

Focus Question

All angles are formed by two rays. What makes angles different from each other?

_____

_____

_____

_____

▶ Do you know **HOW?**

1. What is the measure of ∠PQR?

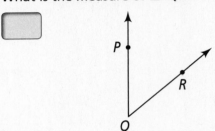

2. Label each angle *acute, right, obtuse,* or *straight.*

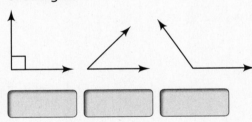

3. The measure of ∠ABC is 70°. Find the value of x.

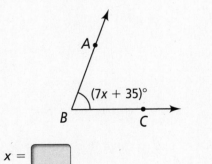

x = [ ]

▶ Do you **UNDERSTAND?**

4. Error Analysis Your friend measures the angle below and says it is 30°. Explain his mistake and find the correct angle measure.

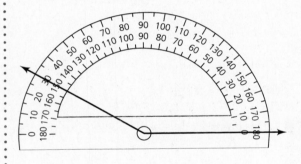

_____

_____

5. Reasoning Can the sum of an acute and a right angle be equal to the measure of a straight angle? Explain.

_____

_____

_____

_____

_____

_____

Adjacent Angles

CCSS: 7.G.B.5: Use facts about supplementary, complementary, vertical, and adjacent angles in a multi-step problem to write and solve simple equations for an unknown angle in a figure. Also, **7.G.A.2.**

Launch

MP3, MP7

∠BAC measures 100°.

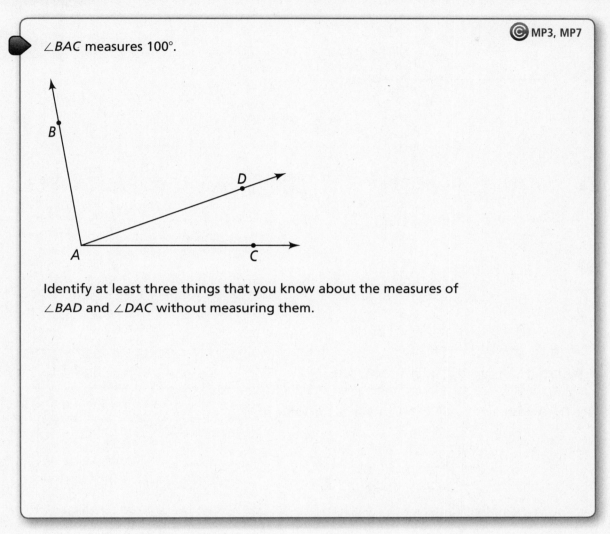

Identify at least three things that you know about the measures of ∠BAD and ∠DAC without measuring them.

Reflect Do you need to measure both ∠BAD and ∠DAC to know both of their measures? Explain.

_____

_____

_____

_____

_____

Got It?

PART 1 Got It

Which angles are adjacent to ∠*EOD*?

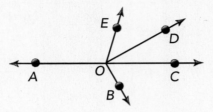

PART 2 Got It

The measure of ∠*ABC* is 100°. What is the value of *x*?

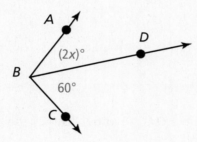

Close and Check

MP2, MP7

▶ Focus Question

A whole is the sum of its parts. How can you apply this idea to angles?

_____

_____

_____

_____

▶ Do you know HOW?

Use the diagram below for Exercises 1 and 2.

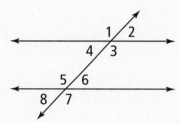

1. Name two angles adjacent to ∠2.

   [ ]   [ ]

2. Name two angles adjacent to ∠5.

   [ ]   [ ]

3. The measure of ∠ABD is 40°. What is the value of x?

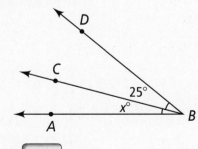

   x = [ ]

▶ Do you UNDERSTAND?

4. **Vocabulary** Explain why ∠1 and ∠3 from Exercise 1 are not adjacent angles.

   _____

   _____

   _____

   _____

   _____

5. **Error Analysis** The measure of ∠JKL is 125°. The equation $3x + 5 - 40 = 125$ was written to find the value of x. Is this correct? Explain.

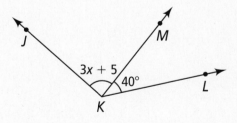

   _____

   _____

   _____

   _____

This page intentionally left blank.

Complementary Angles

CCSS: 7.G.A.2: Draw (freehand, with ruler and protractor ...) geometric shapes with given conditions .... **7.G.B.5:** Use facts about ... complementary ... angles in a multi-step problem to write and solve simple equations for an unknown angle in a figure.

Launch

MP4, MP7

You make two rectangular picture frames. Your pieces line up on the first frame but not on your second frame.

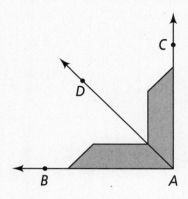
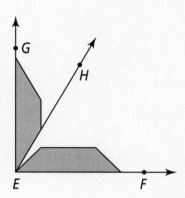

Explain why your first frame works and your second frame does not work. Explain what you know about frame angles and the adjacent angles in the frames.

Reflect If $m\angle BAD$ and $m\angle DAC$ are equal, explain how you can find the measure of each angle.

_____

_____

_____

_____

Got It?

PART 1 Got It (1 of 2)

Name two angles that are *not* complementary.

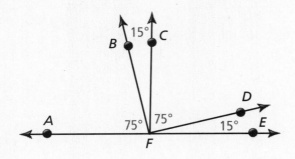

PART 1 Got It (2 of 2)

Your friend claims that all complementary angles must be acute angles. Is your friend right? Explain.

Discuss with a classmate

Read each other's explanations to this problem.
Are key words like complementary and acute part of the explanation?
Write down any key words used in the explanations that you are unfamiliar with and ask what the words mean.

Got It?

PART 2 Got It

What is the value of x?

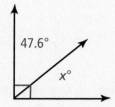

Close and Check

> **Focus Question**
>
> What do you know about the measures of two angles that form a right angle?
>
> _____
>
> _____
>
> _____

Do you know HOW?

1. What is the measure of the complement for the angle below?

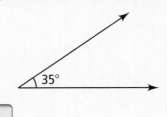

2. Name two complementary angles.

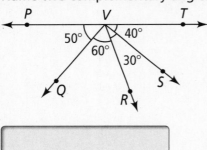

3. $\angle ABD$ and $\angle DBC$ are complementary angles. What is the value of x?

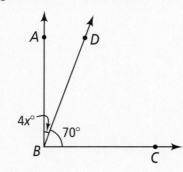

$x = \boxed{}$

Do you UNDERSTAND?

4. Reasoning Can two complementary angles form an obtuse angle? Explain.

_____

_____

_____

_____

5. Error Analysis Your friend says that the angles below are not complementary because they are not adjacent. Is she correct? Explain.

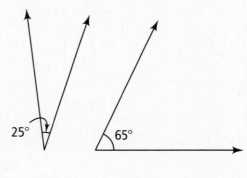

_____

_____

_____

_____

Supplementary Angles

CCSS: 7.G.A.2: Draw (freehand, with ruler and protractor ...) geometric shapes with given conditions .... **7.G.B.5:** Use facts about supplementary ... angles in a multi-step problem to write and solve simple equations for an unknown angle in a figure.

Launch

Hockey players want the blades of their sticks to lie flat on the ice.

© MP2, MP4

45°   Lie angle

If this player holds his hockey stick to the ice at a 45° angle, at what lie angle should his stick be? Explain how you know.

Reflect Will a taller player need a stick with a greater or lesser lie angle if he wants the blade to lie flat on the ice? Tell how you know.

_____

_____

_____

_____

_____

Got It?

PART 1 Got It

> Suppose $m\angle ABC = 48.4°$. Find the measure of its supplement.

PART 2 Got It (1 of 2)

> What is the value of x?

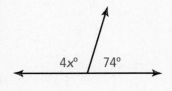

PART 2 Got It (2 of 2)

> Can the measures of supplementary angles be equal? Explain.

Close and Check

> ## ► Focus Question
>
> **MP5, MP7**
>
> What do you know about the measures of two angles that form a straight angle?
>
> _____
>
> _____
>
> _____

► Do you know HOW?

1. What is the measure of the supplement of the angle below?

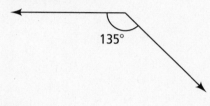

135°

[   ]

2. Suppose $m\angle PQR = 63.7°$. Find the measure of its supplement.

[   ]

3. What is the value of x?

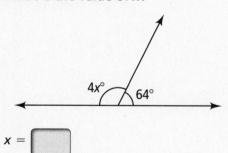

$4x°$ 64°

$x = $ [   ]

► Do you UNDERSTAND?

4. Reasoning What kinds of angles (acute, right, and obtuse) can form a pair of supplementary angles? Explain how you know.

_____

_____

_____

_____

_____

_____

_____

5. Error Analysis A friend says that a straight line is a supplementary angle because it measures 180°. Do you agree or disagree with your friend? Explain.

_____

_____

_____

_____

_____

_____

This page intentionally left blank.

Vertical Angles

CCSS: 7.G.B.5: Use facts about supplementary, complementary, vertical, and adjacent angles in a multi-step problem to write and solve simple equations for an unknown angle in a figure. Also, **7.G.A.2.**

Launch

© MP7, MP8

Your friend claims to "know all the angles." She looks at Figure 1, laughs, and says, "All the angles are 90°."

So, you show her Figure 2 and tell her Angle 1 is 80°. She laughs and says she can find the other angle measures without measuring them.

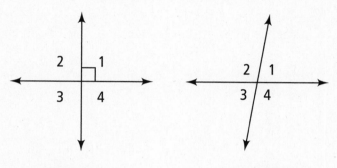

Figure 1   **Figure 2**

Explain how she could do this. Describe any patterns that you see.

Reflect Did the patterns that you found in Figure 2 apply to Figure 1? Explain.

_____

_____

_____

Got It?

Name the angle that is the vertical to ∠ABC.

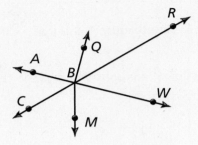

Can vertical angles be supplementary angles? Explain.

Got It?

PART 2 Got It (1 of 2)

What is the value of *x*?

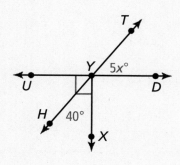

PART 2 Got It (2 of 2)

Your friend claims that vertical angles can be acute, right, or obtuse. Is your friend right? Explain.

Close and Check

> ## Focus Question
>
> ⓒ MP3, MP5
>
> Two intersecting lines form angles. How can you describe the relationship between the angles that are opposite each other?
>
> _____
>
> _____
>
> _____
>
> _____

▶ Do you know **HOW?**

1. Name the angle that is vertical to ∠*ROQ*.

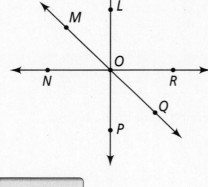

2. What is the value of *x*?

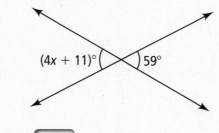

$x = \boxed{}$

▶ Do you **UNDERSTAND?**

3. Writing In the diagram, ∠1 and ∠3 are vertical angles. Why aren't ∠2 and ∠4 vertical angles?

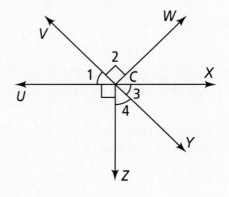

_____

_____

_____

_____

4. Reasoning If you know the measure of ∠4, how can you find the measure of ∠1?

_____

_____

_____

_____

Digital Resources

CCSS: 7.G.B.5: Use facts about supplementary, complementary, vertical, and adjacent angles in a multi-step problem to write and solve simple equations for an unknown angle in a figure.

Launch

 A dog on a leash buries bones in strategic positions in the backyard. You watch from Window 2.

© MP2, MP4

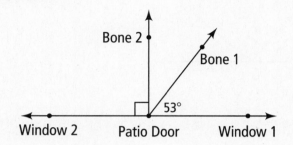

Look at the different angles formed by the leash and the house. How many degrees apart are Bones 1 and 2? How many degrees apart is Bone 1 and Window 2? Write and solve an equation for each situation.

Angle from Bone 1 to Bone 2:

Angle from Bone 1 to Window 2:

Reflect Think about the different types of angles you know about. Which ones did you use to solve the problem?

_____

_____

_____

_____

Got It?

If $m\angle 2 = 90°$, which of the following statements must always be true?

I. $m\angle 1 = m\angle 3$

II. $m\angle 1 + m\angle 3 = m\angle 2$

III. If $\angle 3$ is acute, then $\angle 1$ is obtuse.

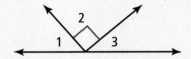

Got It?

In the following diagram, $m\angle 1 = 46°$, $m\angle 3 = (2x + 6)°$, and $m\angle 4 = (y + 8)°$. Find the values of x and y.

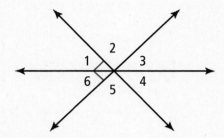

Close and Check

MP1, MP6

Focus Question

You can use relationships between angles to break complex diagrams into smaller parts. How do you decide which relationships to use?

_____

_____

_____

_____

Do you know HOW?

1. Write True or False above each statement about the diagram.

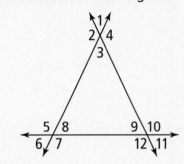

$m\angle 2 = m\angle 3$	$m\angle 1 = m\angle 3$
$m\angle 6 = m\angle 8$	$m\angle 5 + m\angle 8 = 180°$

2. What is the measure of $\angle 1$?

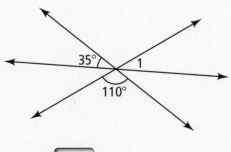

$m\angle 1 =$ ☐

Do you UNDERSTAND?

3. **Reasoning** In Exercise 1, $\angle 5$ and $\angle 12$ are congruent. Explain how to use the relationships between the angles in the triangle to find the $m\angle 1$?

_____

_____

_____

_____

_____

_____

4. **Writing** Explain how to find $m\angle 1$ in Exercise 1 if the $m\angle 5$ is 110°.

_____

_____

_____

_____

_____

_____

New Vocabulary: acute angle, adjacent angles, angle, complementary angles, obtuse angle, right angle, straight angle, supplementary angles, vertex of an angle, vertical angles

Review Vocabulary: classify, intersecting lines

Vocabulary Review

Identify two challenging vocabulary terms from this topic. Write one vocabulary term in the center oval, and fill in the surrounding boxes with details that will help you better understand the term.

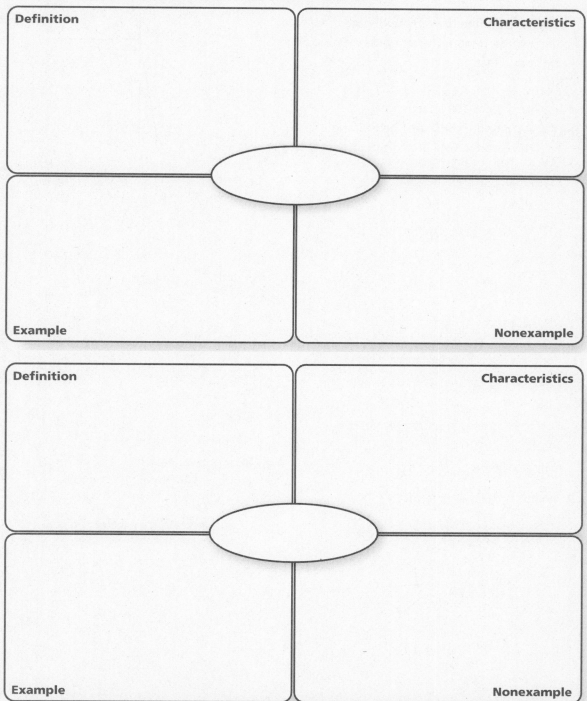

Definition	Characteristics
Example	Nonexample

Definition	Characteristics
Example	Nonexample

Pull It All Together

TASK 1

Six students (*A*, *B*, *C*, *D*, *E*, and *F*) perform a maypole dance at your school's spring festival. The positions of *A* and *C* are given. Use the clues to determine the positions of the other students around the maypole (*M*).

Then determine how many degrees separate each student from the students on his or her right and left.

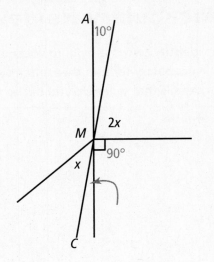

Clues:
- *A* and *B* are 10° apart.
- ∠*AMB* and ∠*CMD* are vertical angles.
- ∠*AMB* and ∠*BMF* are complementary angles.

Center, Radius, and Diameter

CCSS: 7.EE.B.4: Use variables to … construct simple equations … . **7.G.B.4:** Know the formulas for the area and circumference of a circle and use them to solve problems … . Also, **7.EE.B.4a** and **7.G.A.2.**

Launch

© MP4, MP5

A landscaper wants to build a flower garden with a fountain in the center and a path on the outside. The landscaper wants the fountain to be same distance from anywhere on the path.

Draw the garden plan. Explain how it matches what the landscaper wants.

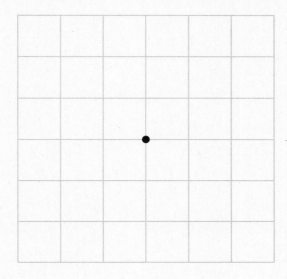

Reflect Could the garden path be any shape and still match what the landscaper wants? Explain.

_____

_____

_____

_____

_____

Got It?

PART 1 Got It

How many radii are shown?

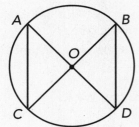

PART 2 Got It

In the diagram, $ST = 4\frac{1}{3}$ ft. What is SO?

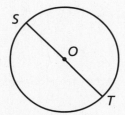

Got It?

PART 3 Got It

If $KM = 2x - 4$ and $LM = 12$, what is the value of x?

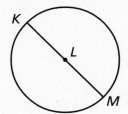

Discuss with a classmate

Name the parts of the circle that are key to solving this problem.

Identify each of these parts in the diagram.

How do you use what you know about solving equations and the parts of the circle that are given to solve the problem?

Close and Check

Focus Question

What are the relationships among the parts of a circle?

_____

_____

_____

_____

Do you know **HOW**?

1. How many radii are shown?

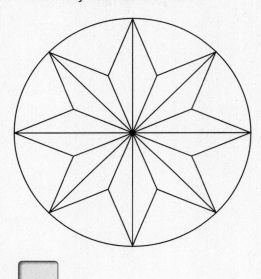

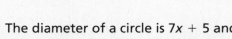

2. The radius of the circle above is 14.5 cm. Find the diameter.

3. The diameter of a circle is $7x + 5$ and the radius is 13. Find the value of x.

Do you **UNDERSTAND**?

4. Reasoning If the length of the radius of a circle is increased 3 times, what happens to the length of the diameter? Write an equation to show how you know.

_____

_____

_____

_____

5. Writing A circular path surrounds a dog park. The developers want to build a supply shed in the center of the park. How can they determine where to build the shed?

_____

_____

_____

_____

_____

Circumference of a Circle

CCSS: 7.G.A.2: Draw ... geometric shapes with given conditions ... . **7.G.B.4:** Know the formulas for the area and circumference of a circle and use them to solve problems ... .

Launch

For each circle, describe any pattern you see between the distance around the circle and the length of its diameter.

Circle 1   **Circle 2**   **Circle 3**

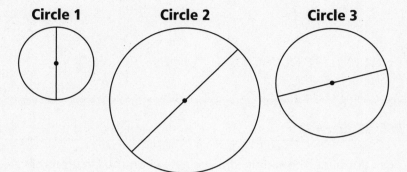

Reflect What do you think will be the distance around a circle with a diameter of 100 cm? Explain.

_____

_____

_____

_____

Got It?

PART 1 Got It (1 of 2)

> What is the circumference of a circle with a diameter of 4 in.?

PART 1 Got It (2 of 2)

> What effect does doubling the radius of a circle have on the circumference of the circle?

PART 2 Got It

> To the nearest tenth of a meter, what is the circumference of a circle with a radius of 3.4 m? Use 3.14 for π.

Got It?

PART 3 Got It (1 of 2)

What is the diameter of a circle with a circumference of 88 ft? Use $\frac{22}{7}$ for π.

PART 3 Got It (2 of 2)

Explain how you might decide whether to use $\frac{22}{7}$ or 3.14 as an approximation for π.

Close and Check

> ## Focus Question
> How is the diameter of a circle related to the distance around a circle?

_____

_____

_____

_____

Do you know HOW?

1. Find the diameter and radius of a circle with a circumference of 16π in.

Diameter: Radius:

For Exercises 2–4, use 3.14 for π.

2. The distance across a circular reflecting pool is 12 m. Find the distance around the pool.

3. Find the diameter of a circle with a circumference of 62.8 yd.

4. A roundabout is a circular road built at a traffic intersection. One city has a roundabout that is 1.5 mi long. A statue sits in the center. Find the distance from the outer edge of the roundabout to the statue to the nearest hundredth.

Do you UNDERSTAND?

5. Compare and Contrast Two students find the circumference of a circle with a diameter of 16 ft. One student says the circumference is 50.24 ft. The other says it is 50.29 ft. Can both students be correct? Explain.

_____

_____

_____

_____

_____

6. Writing Explain how to use a wheel's circumference to find its diameter.

_____

_____

_____

_____

Area of a Circle

Digital Resources

CCSS: 7.G.B.4: Know the formulas for the area and circumference of a circle and use them to solve problems; give an informal derivation of the relationship between the circumference and area of a circle. Also, **7.G.A.2.**

Launch

Each grid square represents 1 ft by 1 ft. Estimate the area of the circle. Explain how you made your estimate.

© MP2, MP5

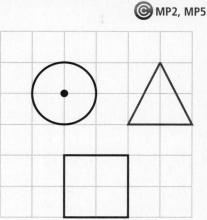

Circle	Square	Triangle

Reflect Which shapes did you find the area of first? Why?

_____

_____

_____

Got It?

PART 1 Got It (1 of 2)

> What is the area of a circle with a radius of 3.2 m? Leave your answer in terms of π.

PART 1 Got It (2 of 2)

> What is the radius of a circle that has the same numerical value for area and circumference? How do the units compare?

Got It?

PART 2 Got It

Bubble netting is a hunting technique used by humpback whales. They blow bubbles in a circular ring that drives fish toward the center of the circle. What is the area of a ring of bubbles 100 feet wide? Use 3.14 for π.

PART 3 Got It

How many smaller circles do you need to equal the area of the larger circle?

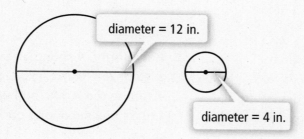

diameter = 12 in.

diameter = 4 in.

Close and Check

Focus Question

How are the areas of a circle and a parallelogram related?

_____

_____

_____

_____

_____

Do you know HOW?

1. Find the area of a circle with a radius of 6.9 m to the nearest tenth. Leave your answer in terms of π.

   [ ]

2. The average crop circle is between 100 and 300 ft in diameter. Find the area of a crop circle that is 300 ft in diameter. Use 3.14 for π.

   [ ]

3. A baker makes a giant cookie for special occasions that is 16 in. in diameter. How many 4-in. diameter cookies would it take to equal the area of one giant cookie?

   [ ] cookies

Do you UNDERSTAND?

4. **Compare and Contrast** What is the difference between the circumference and area of a circle?

   _____

   _____

   _____

   _____

   _____

5. **Reasoning** A round pizza has an area of 254.34 in.^{2}. Explain how to estimate the length and width of the square box needed to package the pizza.

   _____

   _____

   _____

   _____

   _____

   _____

Relating Circumference and Area of a Circle

CCSS: 7.G.B.4: Know the formulas for the area and circumference of a circle and use them to solve problems; give an informal derivation of the relationship between the circumference and area of a circle.

Launch

 MP3, MP5

Does a greater distance around a shape always mean a greater area?

Show one pair of rectangles and one pair of circles where greater distance around does not mean a greater area. If you can't show an example, explain why.

Rectangles

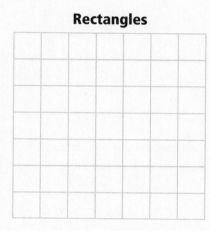

Circles

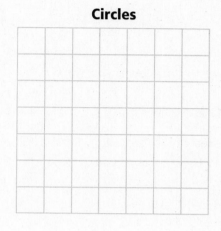

Reflect Besides size, can you change a circle's basic shape? Can you change a rectangle's basic shape? How might this relate to the problem above?

_____

_____

_____

_____

Got It?

PART 1 Got It

A circle has a circumference of 22 cm. What is the approximate area of the circle? Use 3.14 for π.

PART 1 Got It (1 of 2)

The ratio of the area of a circle to the circumference of a circle $\left(\frac{A}{C}\right)$ is $\frac{11}{1}$. What is the circumference of the circle? Leave your answer in terms of π.

Got It?

Use formulas to show why $\frac{A}{C} = \frac{1}{2}r$.

Close and Check

Focus Question

© MP3, MP8

How are the area of a circle and the circumference of a circle related?

_____

_____

_____

_____

Do you know HOW?

1. A circle has a circumference of 38 yd. Find the approximate area of the circle. Use 3.14 for π.

2. The ratio of the area of a circle to the circumference of the circle $\left(\frac{A}{C}\right)$ is $\frac{7}{1}$. Find the circumference of the circle. Leave your answer in terms of π.

3. The ratio of the area of a circle to the circumference of the circle $\left(\frac{A}{C}\right)$ is $\frac{5}{1}$. Find the area of the circle. Leave your answer in terms of π.

4. The ratio of the area of a circle to the circumference of the circle $\left(\frac{A}{C}\right)$ is $\frac{6}{1}$. Find the circumference and area of the circle. Leave your answers in terms of π.

$C = $

$A = $

Do you UNDERSTAND?

5. Reasoning The ratio $\left(\frac{A}{C}\right)$ of a circle is $\frac{3}{1}$. Explain how to use this information to find the radius and circumference of the circle.

_____

_____

_____

_____

_____

6. Error Analysis The ratio $\left(\frac{A}{C}\right)$ of a bike wheel is $\frac{4}{1}$. Your friend says $C = 8\pi$ and $A = 16\pi$. Explain and correct the error your friend made.

_____

_____

_____

_____

_____

CCSS: 7.G.B.4: Know the formulas for the area and circumference of a circle and use them to solve problems; give an informal derivation of the relationship between the circumference and area of a circle.

Digital Resources

Launch

A T-shirt company plans a logo with green circles on yellow squares. Which logo has the most green? Explain.

MP1, MP8

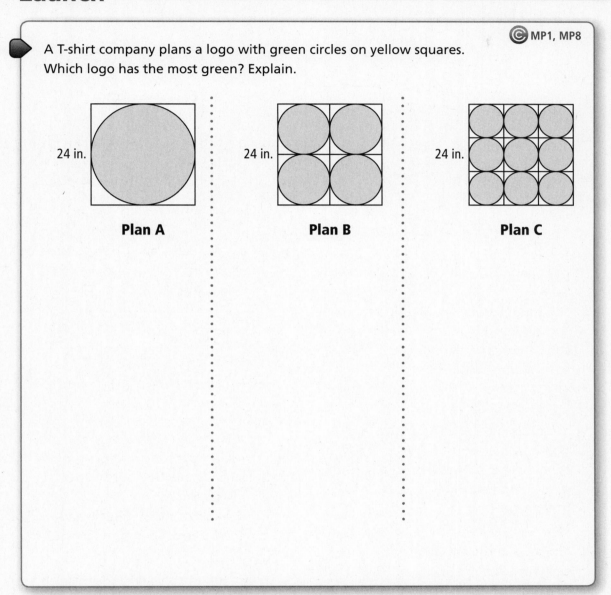

24 in.

Plan A

24 in.

Plan B

24 in.

Plan C

Reflect Which logo did you think had the most green before you found the areas? Why?

_____

_____

_____

_____

Got It?

To the nearest square inch, what is the total area of glass in the window shown? Use 3.14 for π.

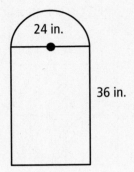

24 in.

36 in.

Got It?

PART 2 Got It

What is the area of the shaded region? The diameter of each half-circle is 1.5 in. Use 3.14 for π.

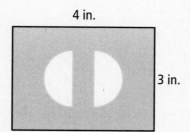

4 in.

3 in.

PART 3 Got It

The area of a rectangular skating rink with a width of 10 ft is 300 ft^2. Suppose you dismantle the surrounding fence and reuse it to surround a new circular skating rink. What is the approximate area of the new rink?

Discuss with a classmate

Draw diagrams to show the two skating rinks described in the problem.
Compare your diagrams.
Did you label the parts correctly?
How do diagrams help you to solve the problem?

Close and Check

Focus Question

When do you use circumference to measure a circle? When do you use area?

_____

_____

_____

_____

Do you know HOW?

1. You buy a square tablecloth with a side length of 5 ft. You place it on a round table with a diameter of 4 ft. Find the area of the tablecloth that is hanging off the edge of the table. Use 3.14 for π.

2. The radius of each half circle is 2 cm. The length of the figure is twice the diameter of the half circles. Find the area of the figure. Use 3.14 for π.

$r = 2$ cm

Do you UNDERSTAND?

3. **Reasoning** A fence encloses a circular area of 530.66 ft². Can the same fence be used to enclose a rectangular area with perimeter 90 ft? Explain how you know.

_____

_____

_____

_____

_____

4. **Error Analysis** Your friend says that if you double a circle's radius, the circumference and area double as well. Explain his error.

_____

_____

_____

_____

_____

New Vocabulary: area of a circle, circle, circumference, diameter, pi, radius
Review Vocabulary: segment

Vocabulary Review

Identify two challenging vocabulary terms from this topic. Write one vocabulary term in the center oval, and fill in the surrounding boxes with details that will help you better understand the term.

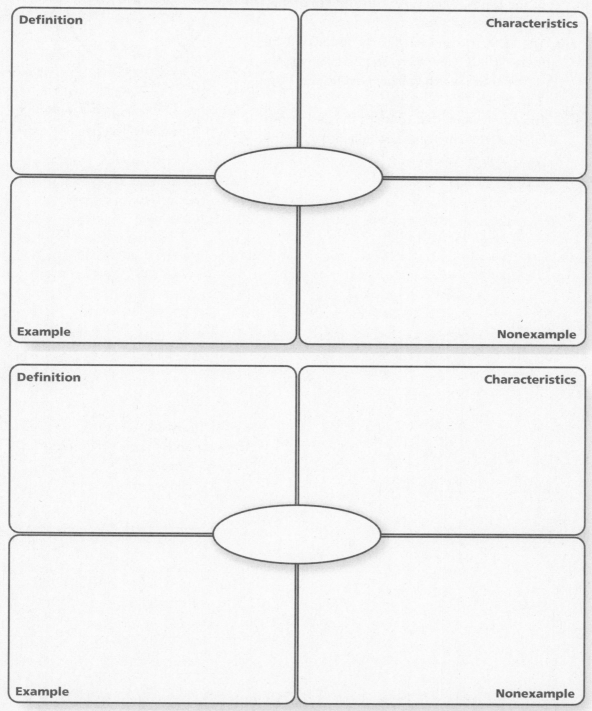

Definition

Characteristics

Example

Nonexample

Definition

Characteristics

Example

Nonexample

Pull It All Together

TASK 1

A watch designer sketched a design for a new watch. The designer needs to send a description of certain measurements to the manufacturer.

a. A purple border will surround the inner circle of the watch. What will be the length of the border? Use 3.14 for π.

b. The half-circle and small circle designs will be metallic blue. How many square millimeters of the entire watch will be metallic blue? Use 3.14 for π.

c. The outer frame that contains the designs will be silver. How many square millimeters of the watch will be silver?

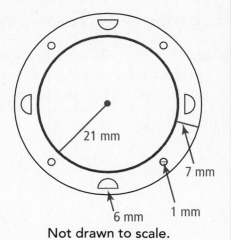

21 mm

7 mm

6 mm   1 mm

Not drawn to scale.

CCSS: 7.G.A.2: Draw (freehand, with ruler and protractor, and with technology) geometric shapes with given conditions. Focus on constructing triangles from three measures of angles or sides, noticing when the conditions determine a unique triangle ... .

Launch

© MP6, MP8

A gift-shop owner sees the eight-sided sign she ordered from the local sign maker and says, "You got it wrong. I wanted an octagon like a stop sign."

Do you think the sign maker or the gift-shop owner was to blame for the wrong sign? Explain.

Reflect If you ordered a sign for a shop, what would you do to make sure you received the correct sign?

_____

_____

_____

_____

_____

Got It?

PART 1 Got It

Sketch a quadrilateral with exactly one pair of parallel sides.

PART 2 Got It

Use a ruler and a protractor to draw a figure with two sides 1 in., two sides 3 in., and at least one right angle.

Got It?

Draw a rhombus with side lengths of 4 units and angle measures 40°, 140°, 40°, and 140°.

Close and Check

Focus Question

Which geometry drawing tools are best for drawing which types of figures?

_____

_____

_____

_____

_____

Do you know HOW?

1. Sketch a quadrilateral with one right angle and no parallel sides.

2. Use a ruler and a protractor to draw a trapezoid that has two right angles, two parallel sides, and one 55° angle. Let one side of the figure measure 3 cm and another side measure 2 cm.

Do you UNDERSTAND?

3. **Writing** You try to quickly explain the difference between equilateral and isosceles triangles to your cousin. Which geometry drawing tools should you use? Explain.

_____

_____

_____

_____

4. **Error Analysis** An architect sketches a diagram for a square room. Does the sketch provide enough information to the builders? Explain.

_____

_____

_____

Drawing Triangles with Given Conditions 1

CCSS: 7.G.A.2: Draw geometric shapes with given conditions. Focus on constructing triangles from three measures of angles or sides, noticing when the conditions determine a unique triangle, more than one triangle, or no triangle

Launch

Ⓒ MP1, MP5

The sign maker tries to sketch two possible triangle-shaped signs.
Sign 1 has side lengths 2 ft, 3 ft, and 3 ft. Sign 2 has side lengths 1 ft, 1 ft, and 3 ft.

Draw the two signs and label the side lengths. Let 1 in. = 1 ft. Can the sign maker make both signs? Explain.

Sign 1   **Sign 2**

Reflect What rule would you make about drawing triangles based on this problem?

_____

_____

_____

Got It?

Suppose the set crew receives instructions for another triangle-shaped prop that uses wood pieces of lengths 5 ft, 10 ft, and 11 ft. Your friend sketched the plan shown. Would anyone using these three wood pieces build the exact same triangle-shaped prop? Explain.

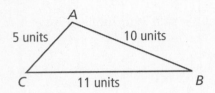

If you form a triangle from three given side lengths, do you always get a unique triangle or more than one triangle?

Got It?

Draw triangle *QRS* where $m\angle R = 40°$, *RQ* = 12 cm, and *RS* = 8 cm. Is the triangle unique? Explain.

If you form a triangle from two side lengths and the included angle measure, do you always get a unique triangle, or more than one triangle?

Got It?

PART 3 Got It (1 of 2)

Given triangle ABC, where $AB = 5$ units, $CA = 5$ units, and $m\angle ACB = 52°$, can you draw a unique triangle, more than one triangle, or no triangle? Explain.

PART 3 Got It (2 of 2)

If you form a triangle from two side lengths and the measure of an angle that is not included, do you always get a unique triangle, or more than one triangle?

Close and Check

> ## Focus Question
>
> What information do you need to draw a unique triangle?
>
> _____
>
> _____
>
> _____
>
> _____

Do you know HOW?

1. Draw triangle DEF, where $m\angle D = 45°$ and $DE = 4$ cm.

2. Given triangle XYZ, where $XZ = 10$ cm, $YZ = 7$ cm, and $m\angle XZY = 115°$, can you draw a *unique triangle, more than one triangle,* or *no triangle?*

[   ]

3. For triangle *QRS* with the given conditions, can you draw a *unique triangle, more than one triangle,* or *no triangle?*
$QR = 15$ units, $RS = 10$ units, $ST = 5$ units

[   ]

Do you UNDERSTAND?

4. Writing Is the triangle in Exercise 1 unique? Explain.

_____

_____

_____

_____

5. Error Analysis Your friend says that he can draw a unique triangle as long as he knows at least two sides and an angle. Explain the error in his reasoning.

_____

_____

_____

_____

_____

_____

This page intentionally left blank.

Drawing Triangles with Given Conditions 2

CCSS: 7.G.A.2: Draw geometric shapes with given conditions. Focus on constructing triangles from three measures of angles or sides, noticing when the conditions determine a unique triangle, more than one triangle, or no triangle.

Launch

© MP5, MP6

The sign maker again tries to sketch two triangle-shaped signs. Sign 1 has angle measures 45°, 45°, and 100°. Sign 2 has angle measures 30°, 60°, and 90°.

Draw the two signs and label the angle measures. Can the sign maker make both signs? Explain.

Sign 1

Sign 2

Reflect What rule would you make about drawing triangles based on this problem?

_____

_____

_____

_____

Got It?

Draw two different triangles with angle measures 30°, 100°, and 50°.

If you form a triangle from three given angle measures, do you always get a unique triangle, or more than one triangle?

Got It?

PART 2 Got It (1 of 2)

Given triangle ABC, where $BC = 10$ units, $m\angle ABC = 35°$, and $m\angle ACB = 80°$, can you draw a unique triangle, more than one triangle, or no triangle? Explain.

PART 2 Got It (2 of 2)

If you form a triangle from two given angle measures and the length of their included side, do you always get a unique triangle, or more than one triangle?

Got It?

PART 3 Got It (1 of 2)

Given triangle *ABC* with *BC* = 13, *m*∠*CAB* = 70°, and *m*∠*ACB* = 60°, can you draw a unique triangle, more than one triangle, or no triangle?

PART 3 Got It (2 of 2)

If you form a triangle from two given angle measures and the length of a side that is *not* included, do you always get a unique triangle, or more than one triangle?

Close and Check

Focus Question

MP2, MP6

What is the minimum number of side lengths and angle measures you need to draw a unique triangle?

_____

_____

_____

_____

Do you know HOW?

1. Given triangle DEF, where $m\angle D = 72°$, $m\angle E = 96°$, and $m\angle F = 17°$, can you draw a *unique triangle, more than one triangle,* or *no triangle?*

   [   ]

2. Given triangle *LMN*, where $LM = 23$ units, $m\angle NLM = 33°$, and $m\angle NML = 97°$, can you draw a *unique triangle, more than one triangle,* or *no triangle?*

   [   ]

3. For triangle *JKL*, two side lengths and the measure of the nonincluded angle are given. Can you draw a *unique triangle, more than one triangle,* or *no triangle?*

   [   ]

Do you UNDERSTAND?

4. **Reasoning** If you are given the length of $\overline{LN}$ instead of $\overline{LM}$ in Exercise 2, would your answer be the same?

   _____

   _____

   _____

   _____

5. **Error Analysis** A classmate says that if you know either three angle measures or three side lengths, then there is one unique triangle that can be constructed. Do you agree? Explain.

   _____

   _____

   _____

   _____

   _____

This page intentionally left blank.

2-D Slices of Right Rectangular Prisms

CCSS: 7.G.A.3: Describe the two-dimensional figures that result from slicing three-dimensional figures, as in plane sections of right rectangular prisms and right rectangular pyramids.

Launch

MP3, MP8

A chef needs a piece of cheese for a new recipe. The chef makes a straight top to bottom slice from a block of cheese.

How are the attributes of the piece of cheese and the attributes of the block of cheese alike? How are they different? Explain your reasoning.

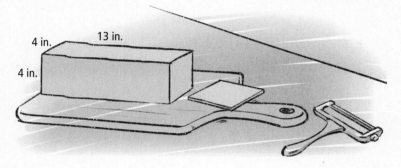

4 in.   13 in.

4 in.

Alike:

Different:

Reflect Does it matter to your solution where the chef makes the straight up and down slice? Explain.

_____

_____

_____

_____

Got It?

What are the dimensions of the cross section formed by slicing the prism as shown?

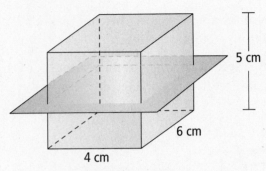

5 cm

6 cm

4 cm

Not to scale

What is one dimension of the cross section formed by slicing the prism as shown?

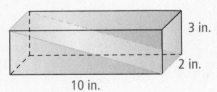

3 in.

2 in.

10 in.

Got It?

Draw and describe a cross section formed by a vertical plane that slices the front and back faces of the prism.

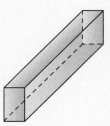

Describe a cross section formed by a plane that cuts off a corner of a cube.

Close and Check

> **Focus Question**   ⓒ MP5, MP7
>
> How can the faces of a rectangular prism determine the shape and dimensions of a slice of the prism?

> **Do you know HOW?**

1. What are the dimensions of the cross section formed by slicing the rectangular prism vertically as shown?

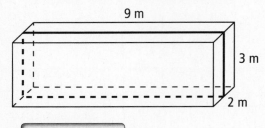

9 m   3 m   2 m

2. What are the dimensions of the cross section formed by slicing the same rectangular prism horizontally?

3. Draw the cross section that is formed by the vertical plane that intersects the front and back faces of the rectangular prism.

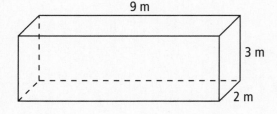

9 m   3 m   2 m

> **Do you UNDERSTAND?**

4. **Reasoning** Draw the 3-D figure that would result from slicing a corner from the prism in Exercise 1. Describe the faces of the new figure and tell its name.

5. **Writing** Explain how could you change one of the dimensions of the rectangular prism in Exercise 3 without changing the size and shape of the cross section you drew.

2-D Slices of Right Rectangular Pyramids

CCSS: 7.G.A.3: Describe the two-dimensional figures that result from slicing three-dimensional figures, as in plane sections of right rectangular prisms and right rectangular pyramids.

Launch

© MP1, MP4

A waiter slices his restaurant's world-famous meatloaf as shown for two diners to share.

Could the waiter's split be even? Is there a better way to make sure? Explain.

Waiter's Slice

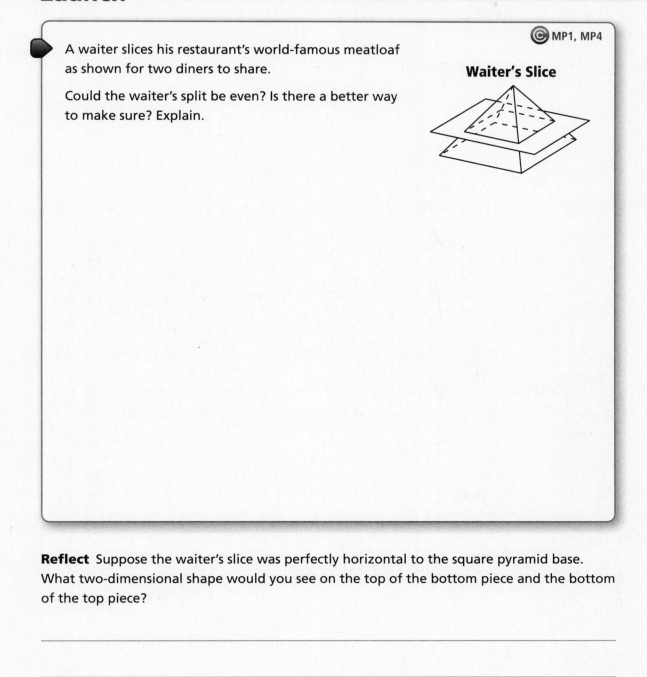

Reflect Suppose the waiter's slice was perfectly horizontal to the square pyramid base. What two-dimensional shape would you see on the top of the bottom piece and the bottom of the top piece?

_____

_____

_____

_____

Got It?

What are the shape and dimensions of the cross section formed by slicing the pyramid as shown?

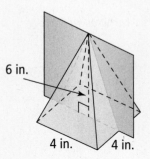

6 in.

4 in.　　4 in.

Explain how to slice a rectangular pyramid to get an isosceles trapezoid cross section.

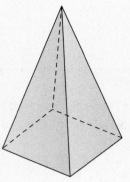

Got It?

PART 2 Got It (1 of 2)

Draw and describe two triangular cross sections, each formed by a plane that intersects the vertex and is perpendicular to the base.

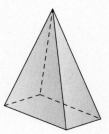

PART 2 Got It (2 of 2)

Explain how to slice a rectangular pyramid through the vertex to get triangles of many different heights.

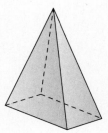

Close and Check

Focus Question

©MP2, MP7

How can the faces of a rectangular pyramid determine the shape and dimensions of a slice of the pyramid?

_____

_____

_____

_____

Do you know HOW?

1. Would the area of a slice perpendicular to the base of a rectangular pyramid that passes through the vertex be _greater than, less than,_ or _equal to_ the area of a side of the pyramid?

2. A horizontal slice is made halfway up the rectangular pyramid. What is the shape of this cross section?

5 in.

6 in.   4 in.

3. What are the dimensions of the cross section of the pyramid in Exercise 2?

Do you UNDERSTAND?

4. Reasoning Draw a slice from the rectangular pyramid that forms an isosceles trapezoid. Explain how you know your figure is correct.

_____

_____

_____

_____

_____

5. Writing Explain how you determined the answer to Exercise 3.

_____

_____

_____

_____

Problem Solving

Digital Resources

CCSS: 7.G.A.2: Draw (freehand, with ruler and protractor, and with technology) geometric shapes with given conditions ... . **7.G.A.3:** Describe the two-dimensional figures that result from slicing three-dimensional figures ... . **7.G.B.6:** Solve real-world and mathematical problems involving area ... .

Launch

Ⓒ MP3, MP6

Write detailed directions for someone else to draw a geometric figure. Test your directions by drawing the figure yourself.

Description	**Drawing**

Do you need to revise your directions? Explain.

Reflect Was the description or the drawing the most difficult part of the problem? Explain.

_____

_____

_____

_____

Got It?

The jeweler told the assistant to sketch a pendant of a blue equilateral triangle on top of a green square. The assistant drew Sketch A, but the jeweler was expecting Sketch B. What other details should the jeweler have provided?

Sketch A

Sketch B

Suppose the carpenter wants the box shown cut to have dimensions 16 in. × 6 in. × 4 in. About how many square inches of wood does the carpenter need to close the side of the new box?

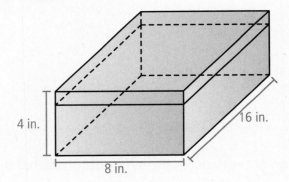

4 in.

8 in.

16 in.

Got It?

PART 3 Got It

Draw the cross section formed by a vertical slice through the vertex of the pyramid and perpendicular to the top face of each prism.

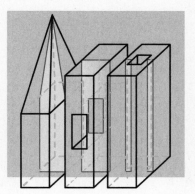

Close and Check

MP3, MP6

Focus Question

Why might it be important to have precise descriptions for drawing or making figures?

_____

_____

_____

_____

Do you know HOW?

1. Label the top cross section **T**, the middle cross section **M**, and the bottom cross section **B**.

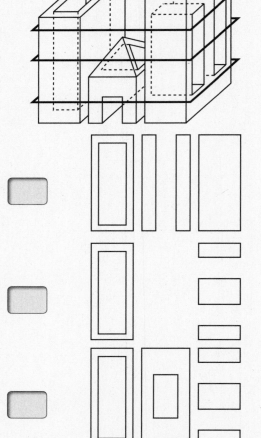

Do you UNDERSTAND?

2. **Reasoning** Two box makers want to slice the box so it has half the volume. One plans a 2 ft by 4 ft by 3 ft box. The other plans a 1 ft by 4 ft by 6 ft box. Explain which plan works.

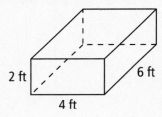

2 ft   6 ft

4 ft

_____

_____

_____

_____

3. **Writing** Write a clearer description that their boss can use to explain that he wants a 2 ft by 2 ft by 6 ft box.

_____

_____

New Vocabulary: cross section, included angle, included side
Review Vocabulary: net, parallelogram, plane, pyramid, three-dimensional figure, triangle

Vocabulary Review

Identify two challenging vocabulary terms from this topic. Write one vocabulary term in the center oval, and fill in the surrounding boxes with details that will help you better understand the term.

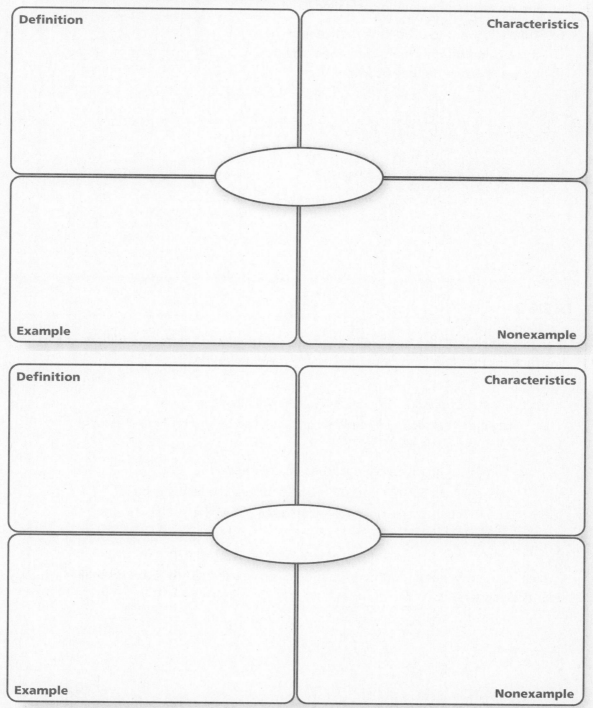

Pull It All Together

TASK 1

A team of carpenters is building bookshelves for a new library. They have completed the frames and want to install the shelves.

a. The carpenters want the bookshelves to hold six rows of books. How many additional square inches of wood do they need?

b. They also want to divide the shelves into three columns. How many additional square inches of wood do they need?

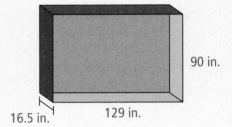

90 in.

16.5 in.   129 in.

TASK 2

The carpenters will also build rolling ladders for the bookshelves. The following are instructions that two lead carpenters wrote for the workers:

1. Construct a ladder for each bookshelf where the angle at the top is 17° and the angle at the bottom, away from the shelf, is 73°.

2. Construct a ladder for each bookshelf where the ladder leans against the shelf at 80 inches above the ground and it touches the floor 24 inches away from the shelf.

Which instruction has enough information to ensure that all the workers make identical ladders?

Surface Areas of Right Prisms

CCSS: 7.G.B.6: Solve real-world and mathematical problems involving area, volume and surface area of two- and three-dimensional objects composed of triangles, quadrilaterals, polygons, cubes, and right prisms.

Launch

© MP4, MP7

One square foot of this cube-shaped sculpture takes you 10 minutes to polish. At this rate, how long will it take you to polish the whole thing? Justify your reasoning.

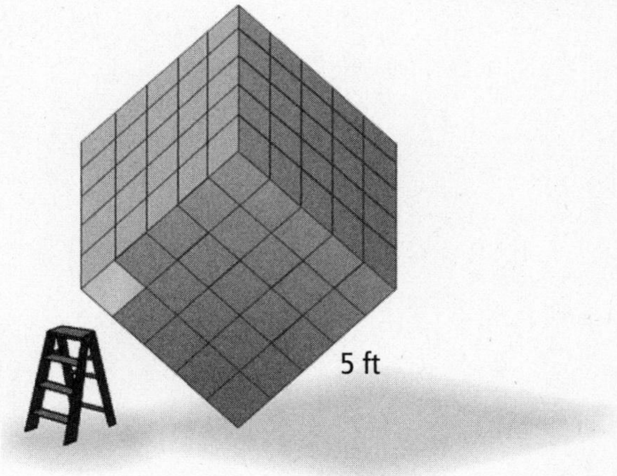

5 ft

Reflect Why do you need only the length of one edge to solve the problem?

_____

_____

_____

_____

Got It?

What is the surface area of a cube with edge length $\frac{3}{4}$ ft?

What is the surface area of the triangular prism?

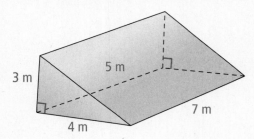

3 m

5 m

4 m

7 m

Got It?

PART 3 Got It

To the nearest square inch, what is the surface area of the regular hexagonal prism?

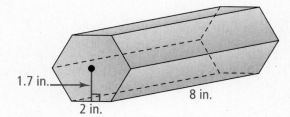

1.7 in.

2 in.

8 in.

Close and Check

Focus Question

How can you apply what you know about finding the surface area of a right rectangular prism to finding the surface area of any right prism?

_____

_____

_____

_____

Do you know **HOW?**

Find the surface area of each figure below.

1.

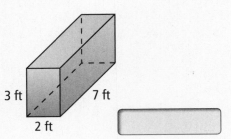

3 ft   7 ft

2 ft

2.

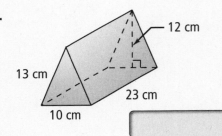

12 cm

13 cm

23 cm

10 cm

3.

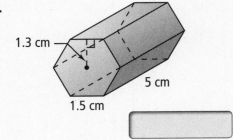

1.3 cm

5 cm

1.5 cm

Do you **UNDERSTAND?**

4. Error Analysis Explain the mistake made below. What is the correct surface area?

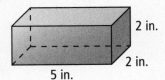

2 in.

2 in.

5 in.

S.A. = (2 + 2 + 2 + 2)(5) + 4

S.A. = (8)(5) + 4

S.A. = 40 + 4

S.A. = 44 in.^{2}

_____

_____

_____

5. Writing If you turned the rectangular prism from Exercise 1, would the surface area change? Explain.

_____

_____

_____

CCSS: 7.G.B.6: Solve real-world and mathematical problems involving area, volume and surface area of two- and three-dimensional objects composed of triangles, quadrilaterals, polygons, cubes, and right prisms.

Launch

© MP2, MP4

In Germany, Ms. Adventure packs cube-shaped candles in a box to send home. She plans to wrap the box in brown paper for shipping.

How many candles can she stack in each shipping box?

1 in.
1 in.
1 in.

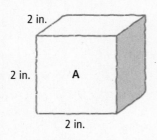

2 in.

2 in.   A

2 in.

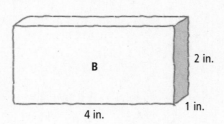

B

2 in.

1 in.

4 in.

[ ] candles   [ ] candles

. . . .

Which box should she choose? Explain your reasoning.

Reflect Do boxes with the same amount of space inside always have the same surface area? Why is this important?

_____

_____

_____

_____

Got It?

PART 1 Got It (1 of 2)

What is the volume of a cube with edge length $\frac{3}{4}$ ft?

PART 1 Got It (2 of 2)

A cube has an edge length of less then 10 units. The cube has a surface area of *x* square units and a volume of *x* cubic units. What is the edge length of the cube?

Got It?

PART 2 Got It

The triangular prism has bases that are equilateral triangles. To the nearest cubic meter, what is the volume of the prism?

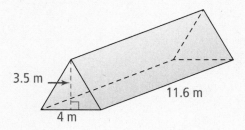

3.5 m

4 m

11.6 m

PART 3 Got It

To the nearest cubic centimeter, what is the volume of the regular hexagonal prism?

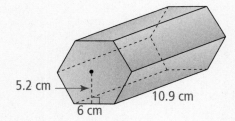

5.2 cm

6 cm

10.9 cm

Close and Check

MP2, MP7

Focus Question

How can you apply what you know about finding the volume of a right rectangular prism to finding the volume of any right prism?

_____

_____

_____

_____

Do you know HOW?

Find the volume of each figure below.

1.

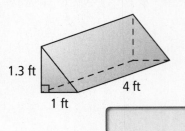

1.3 ft

1 ft

4 ft

2.

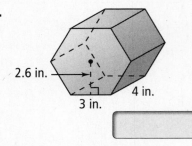

2.6 in.

3 in.

4 in.

3. A shipping company packs ornaments in cubes that have an edge length of 4 inches. How many cubes can fit in a rectangular box that is 12 inches tall, 16 inches wide, and 20 inches long?

 cubes

Do you UNDERSTAND?

4. **Compare and Contrast** Compare the volume of the triangular prism in Exercise 1 with the volume of the rectangular prism below.

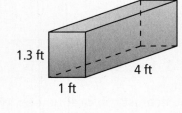

1.3 ft

1 ft

4 ft

_____

_____

_____

_____

5. **Writing** Why can the formula for the volume of a rectangular prism be written as $V = Bh$ or $V = lwh$?

_____

_____

_____

_____

22-3 | # Surface Areas of Right Pyramids

Digital Resources

CCSS: 7.G.B.6: Solve real-world and mathematical problems involving area, volume and surface area of two- and three-dimensional objects composed of triangles, quadrilaterals, polygons, cubes, and right prisms.

Launch

© MP2, MP4

Ms. Adventure plans a cardboard model of the Red Pyramid she saw in Dashur, Egypt. She only has one piece of colored construction paper to cover her pyramid.

Does she have enough construction paper? Explain your reasoning.

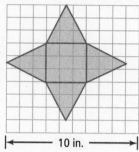

4 in.

5 in.

|← ——— 10 in. ———→|

Reflect Suppose you want to buy more than one piece of paper to cover an object. How would knowing the object's surface area help you decide how much paper to buy?

_____

_____

_____

Got It?

PART 1 Got It

What is the surface area of the square pyramid?

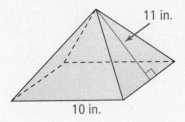

11 in.

10 in.

PART 2 Got It (1 of 2)

To the nearest square foot, what is the surface area of the regular triangular pyramid?

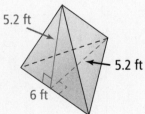

5.2 ft

5.2 ft

6 ft

Got It?

> What conclusions can you draw about a triangular pyramid if the height of the base is equal to the slant height?

> You want to make a tent that has the shape of a regular hexagonal pyramid with the dimensions shown. To the nearest square foot, how much fabric do you need?

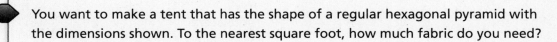
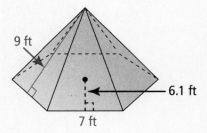

9 ft

6.1 ft

7 ft

> What are two different ways you could find the lateral area of a regular hexagonal pyramid?

Close and Check

Focus Question

How can you apply what you know about finding the surface area of one right square pyramid to finding the surface area of any right pyramid?

_____

_____

_____

_____

Do you know **HOW**?

1. Circle the pyramid that has a surface area of 52 in.²

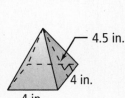
4.5 in.
4 in.
4 in.

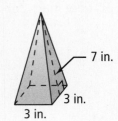
7 in.
3 in.
3 in.

2. A paperweight is in the shape of a pyramid with an equilateral triangle for a base. Find the surface area of the paperweight.

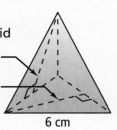
8 cm
5.2 cm
6 cm

[   ]

Do you **UNDERSTAND**?

3. **Reasoning** Is it possible to make a model of the pyramid below by using an 11-inch by 17-inch sheet of paper? Explain.

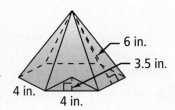
6 in.
3.5 in.
4 in.
4 in.

_____

_____

4. **Error Analysis** What mistake was made in the calculation? What is the correct surface area?

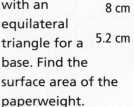
12 cm
13 cm
10 cm

S.A. = ½ (4 × 10)(12) + (10)²

S.A. = ½ (40)(12) + 100

S.A. = 240 + 100 = 340 cm²

_____

_____

Volumes of Right Pyramids

CCSS: 7.G.B.6: Solve real-world and mathematical problems involving area, volume and surface area of two- and three-dimensional objects composed of triangles, quadrilaterals, polygons, cubes, and right prisms.

Launch

Ⓒ MP1, MP8

Look for a pattern in the volumes of the prism and pyramid pairs. Then find the volume of the fourth pyramid. Explain your reasoning.

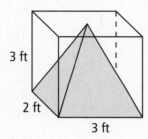

1 ft
1 ft
1 ft

Pyramid volume: $\frac{1}{3}$ ft³

Prism volume: _____

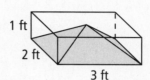

1 ft
2 ft
3 ft

Pyramid volume: 2 ft³

Prism volume: _____

3 ft
2 ft
3 ft

Pyramid volume: 6 ft³

Prism volume: _____

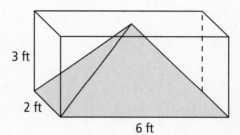

3 ft
2 ft
6 ft

Pyramid volume: _____

Prism volume: _____

Reflect Describe another situation where you can use a pattern to figure out something you don't know.

_____

_____

_____

_____

_____

Got It?

Ms. Adventure visited the Mayan pyramids in Mexico. The structure shown approximates a square pyramid with a height of 30 m. What is the approximate volume of the Mayan Pyramid?

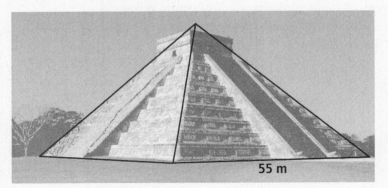

55 m

What happens to the volume of a square pyramid when you double the side length of the base?

Got It?

PART 2 Got It

To the nearest cubic foot, what is the volume of the regular triangular pyramid?

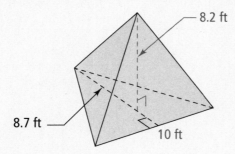

8.2 ft

8.7 ft

10 ft

PART 3 Got It

To the nearest cubic foot, what is the volume of the regular hexagonal pyramid?

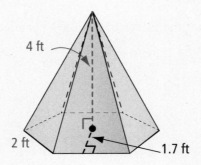

4 ft

2 ft

1.7 ft

Close and Check

MP2, MP7

Focus Question

How can you apply what you know about finding the volume of one right square pyramid to finding the volume of any right pyramid?

_____

_____

_____

_____

Do you know HOW?

1. Circle the pyramid that has the greater volume.

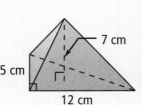

5 cm
7 cm
12 cm
15 cm
5 cm
5 cm

2. What is the volume of the pyramid below?

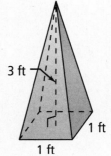

3 ft
1 ft
1 ft

Do you UNDERSTAND?

3. **Compare and Contrast** What measures of a square pyramid do you need to calculate its surface area and volume?

_____

_____

4. **Error Analysis** Describe the mistake made when calculating the volume of the pyramid. What is the correct volume?

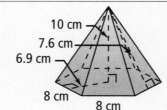

10 cm
7.6 cm
6.9 cm
8 cm
8 cm

$V = \frac{1}{3}(165.6 \cdot 7.6)$

$V = \frac{1}{3}(1258.6)$

$V = 419.5 \text{ cm}^3$

_____

_____

Problem Solving

CCSS: 7.G.B.6: Solve real-world and mathematical problems involving area, volume and surface area of two- and three-dimensional objects composed of triangles, quadrilaterals, polygons, cubes, and right prisms.

Launch

Ⓒ MP4, MP7

On her trip to Morocco, Ms. Adventure finds a tea light lantern with the glass broken. How much glass will she need to fix the lantern? Explain your reasoning.

3 in.

4 in.

4 in.

4 in.

4 in.

Reflect Describe another situation in mathematics where you can break apart a problem into simpler parts to solve.

_____

_____

_____

Got It?

PART 1 Got It

> In cubic feet, how much space is inside the doghouse?

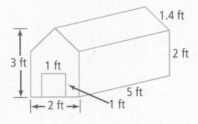

PART 2 Got It

> Ms. Adventure's friend takes home a slice of the hexagonal layer cake. The slice is one sixth of the whole cake. To the nearest cubic inch, how much cake is left?

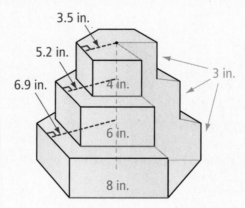

Close and Check

Focus Question

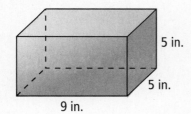

When do you use surface area to measure a three-dimensional figure? When do you use volume?

_____

_____

_____

_____

Do you know **HOW?**

1. A packaging company makes a rectangular box that is 9 inches long, 5 inches wide, and 5 inches tall. How many whole boxes can be made from a sheet of cardboard that is 20 inches by 33 inches?

5 in.

5 in.

9 in.

[   ] boxes

2. A company is redesigning a box to hold pencil erasers. The volume of the box must be 24 cubic inches. What are the dimensions of the box that uses the least amount of material?

length = [   ]

width = [   ]

height = [   ]

Do you **UNDERSTAND?**

3. Reasoning You want to find out how much wrapping you need to wrap a gift for your friend. Do you need to calculate the surface area or the volume of the gift? Explain.

_____

_____

_____

_____

4. Writing Describe how the volume and surface area change when all of the dimensions (length, width, and height) of a rectangular prism are doubled.

_____

_____

_____

_____

_____

This page intentionally left blank.

New Vocabulary: lateral area, surface area, volume
Review Vocabulary: base area, height of a prism, height of a pyramid, lateral face, prism, pyramid

Vocabulary Review

Identify two challenging vocabulary terms from this topic. Write one vocabulary term in the center oval, and fill in the surrounding boxes with details that will help you better understand the term.

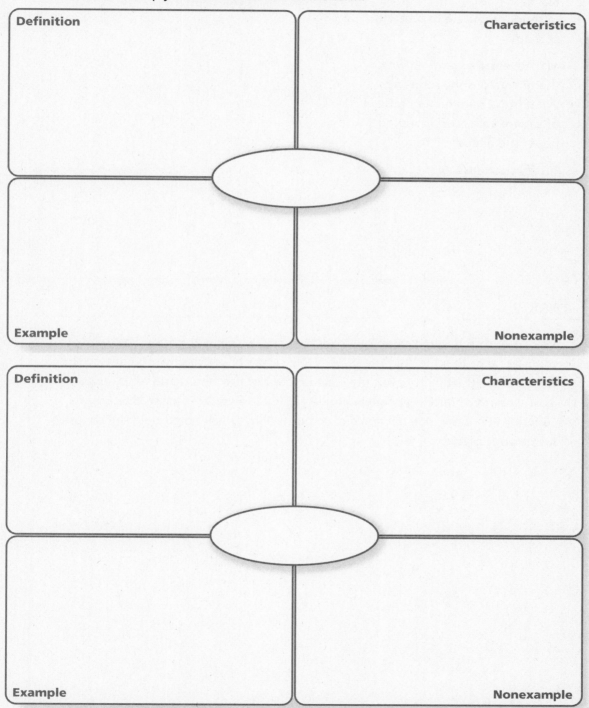

Pull It All Together

TASK 1

Ms. Adventure bought a wooden puzzle while traveling abroad. The puzzle has the shape of a regular hexagonal prism. She wants to send the puzzle to a friend as a gift.

Ms. Adventure wants to wrap the gift before she sends it. What is the minimum number of square inches of wrapping paper she needs?

Justify your answer.

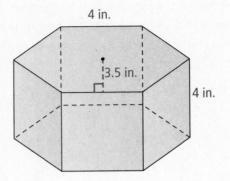

TASK 2

Ms. Adventure has two shipping boxes that are rectangular prisms. She wants to choose one of them to ship the puzzle. She cares about the environment, so she wants to use the box that has the least amount of cardboard and requires the least amount of packing peanuts. Box A has a 12-in. by 12-in. base. Box B has a 16-in. by 9-in. base. The height of each box is 8 in. Which box should she choose? Justify your answer.

Translations

CCSS: 8.G.A.1: Verify … properties of … translations: **8.G.A.1a:** Lines are taken to lines … segments to … segments … . **8.G.A.1b:** Angles … to angles … . **8.G.A.1c:** Parallel lines … to parallel lines. **8.G.A.3:** Describe the effect of dilations … and reflections … using coordinates.

Launch

Ⓒ **MP3, MP5**

Your friend begins building a figure out of shapes. He traces a trapezoid, slides it, traces one side, and then strangely stops.

Complete the tracing of the trapezoid to show your friend's slide. Explain why your tracing shows the slide.

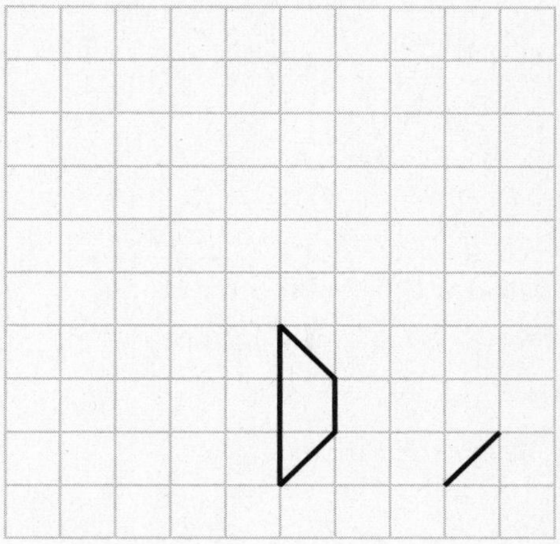

How my friend slid the trapezoid:

How my tracing shows the slide:

Reflect Were there parallel line segments in the trapezoid before the slide? What about after the slide? Tell how you know.

_____

_____

_____

_____

Got It?

PART 1 Got It

Which graph shows △DEF and △D'E'F', its image after a translation?

I.

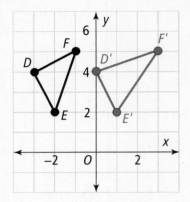

II.

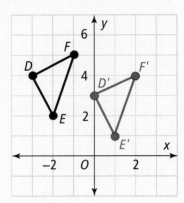

III.

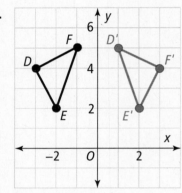

PART 2 Got It

The vertices of △JKL are J(−4, 1), K(−2, −2), and L(1, 2). If you translate △JKL 4 units right and 2 units up, what are the coordinates of K'?

Got It?

PQRS is a parallelogram. Use arrow notation to write a rule that describes the translation of *PQRS* to *P'Q'R'S'*.

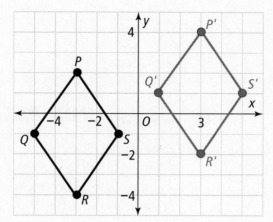

Close and Check

Focus Question

What effect does a slide have on a figure?

_____

_____

_____

Do you know HOW?

1. The vertices of △XYZ are X(−4, 1), Y(2, 2), and Z(−1, −1). If you translate △XYZ 3 units left and 1 unit down, what are the coordinates of Y'?

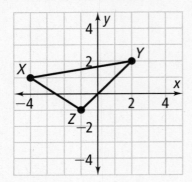

2. Use arrow notation to write a rule that describes the translation shown.

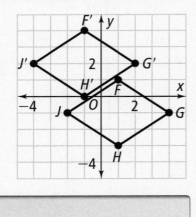

Do you UNDERSTAND?

3. **Reasoning** How do you know whether to add or subtract units from x and y when using arrow notation to describe a translation?

_____

_____

_____

_____

4. **Error Analysis** Explain the error in the translation below.

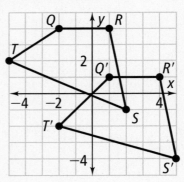

_____

_____

_____

_____

CCSS: **8.G.A.1:** Verify … properties of … reflections … : **8.G.A.1a:** Lines are taken to lines … segments to … segments … . **8.G.A.1b:** Angles … to angles … . **8.G.A.1c:** Parallel lines … to parallel lines. **8.G.A.3:** Describe the effect of dilations … and reflections … using coordinates.

Digital Resources

Launch

Your friend continues the figure. He traces a triangle, flips it over his pencil, traces one side, and then suddenly ceases.

Complete the triangle tracing to show your friend's flip. Explain why your tracing shows the flip.

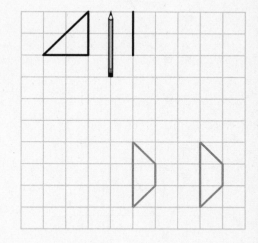

How my friend flipped the triangle:

How my tracing shows the flip:

Reflect Is there a right angle in the triangle before the flip? What about after the flip? Tell how you know.

_____

_____

_____

_____

Got It?

PART 1 Got It

Which graph shows a reflection of △DEF across the x-axis?

I.

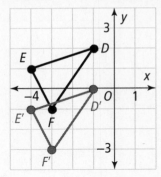

II.

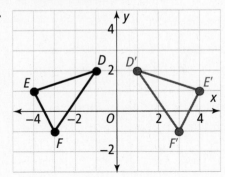

III.

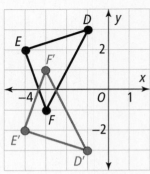

PART 2 Got It

LMNP is a parallelogram. Describe in words how to map
LMNP to its image L'M'N'P'.

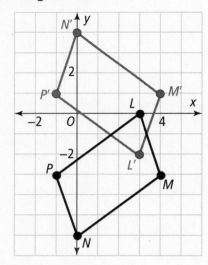

Got It?

PART 3 Got It

If you reflect △*JKL* across the *y*-axis,, what are the coordinates of *J'*?

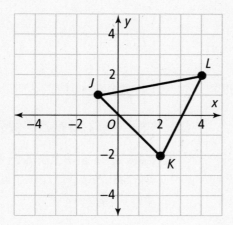

Discuss with a classmate

Circle the keyword *coordinates*.

Write a definition for this word, using the diagram from the problem as part of your definition.

Close and Check

> ## Focus Question
> What effect does a flip have on a figure?
>
> _____
>
> _____
>
> _____

▶ Do you know HOW?

1. The vertices of quadrilateral *QRST* are *Q*(−1, 3), *R*(2, 2), *S*(3, −2), *T*(1, −2). Graph quadrilateral *QRST* and quadrilateral *Q′R′S′T′*, its image after a reflection across the *x*-axis.

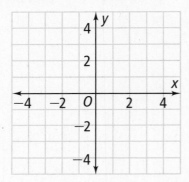

2. Use arrow notation to show how *QRST* maps to *Q′R′S′T′* from Exercise 1.

Q(⬚) → Q′(⬚)

R(⬚) → R′(⬚)

S(⬚) → S′(⬚)

T(⬚) → T′(⬚)

▶ Do you UNDERSTAND?

3. Compare and Contrast How are translations and reflections the same and different?

_____

_____

_____

_____

4. Error Analysis A classmate says that the reflection across the *x*-axis of △*PQR* is △*P′Q′R′* where *P′*(−2, 1), *Q′*(−5, −2), and *R′*(2, −4). What error did he make? What should the vertices be?

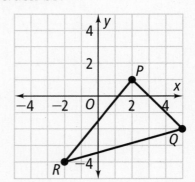

_____

_____

_____

Rotations

Digital Resources

CCSS: **8.G.A.1:** Verify ... properties of rotations ... : **8.G.A.1a:** Lines are taken to lines ... segments to ... segments ... . **8.G.A.1b:** Angles ... to angles ... . **8.G.A.1c:** Parallel lines ... to parallel lines. **8.G.A.3:** Describe the effect of dilations ... and reflections ... using coordinates.

Launch

© MP1, MP5

Your friend nearly completes his figure. He traces a square, turns it, traces one side, and then curiously quits.

Complete the turn and tracing of the square. Explain why your tracing shows your friend's turn.

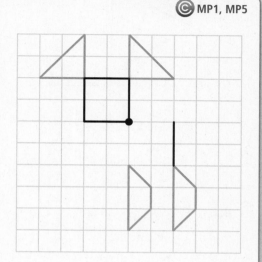

How my friend turned the square:

How my tracing shows the turn:

Reflect What other transformations could your friend have used to move the square to the same position?

_____

_____

_____

_____

_____

Got It?

PART 1 Got It

Which graph shows a rotation of △DEF about the origin?

I.

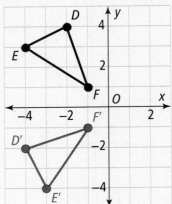

II.

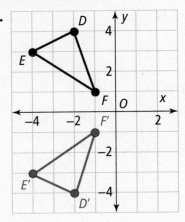

III.

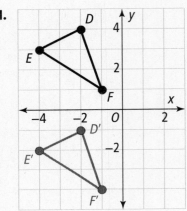

PART 2 Got It (1 of 2)

What is the angle of rotation about the origin that maps △JKO to △J'K'O'?

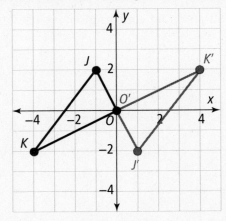

Got It?

PART 2 Got It (2 of 2)

$\triangle ABC$ maps to its image $\triangle A'B'C'$ so that $A = A'$, $B = B'$, and $C = C'$. What is the angle of rotation?

PART 3 Got It

Point P has coordinates $(3, 0)$. If you rotate P $270°$ about the origin, what are the coordinates of P'?

Close and Check

Focus Question

What effect does a turn have on a figure?

_____

_____

_____

_____

Do you know HOW?

1. Use arrow notation to show how △JKL maps to its image after a rotation 180° about the origin.

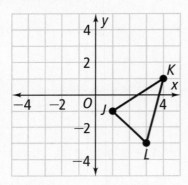

J(_____) → J'(_____)

K(_____) → K'(_____)

L(_____) → L'(_____)

2. The vertices of parallelogram WXYZ are W(−1, 1), X(3, 2), Y(3, −1), Z(−1, −2). The vertices of its image, parallelogram W'X'Y'Z', are W'(−1, 1), X'(3, 2), Y'(3, −1), Z'(−1, −2). What is the angle of rotation?

_____

Do you UNDERSTAND?

3. **Compare and Contrast** How are reflections and rotations the same and different?

_____

_____

_____

_____

4. **Reasoning** Would the relationship between the vertices of any figure rotated 360° and its image always be true regardless of the point of rotation? Explain.

_____

_____

_____

_____

_____

Digital Resources

CCSS: 8.G.A.2: Understand that a two-dimensional figure is congruent to another if the second can be obtained from the first by a sequence of rotations, reflections, and translations; given two congruent figures, describe a sequence that exhibits the congruence ... .

Launch

Your neighbor drew three kites on the grid. She said they were all exactly the same. Do you agree? Explain how you know.

MP5, MP6, MP8

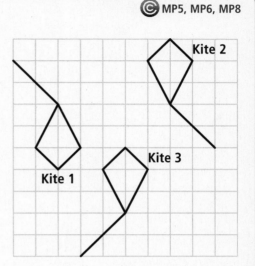

Reflect How can two shapes be exactly the same but look different?

_____

_____

_____

Got It?

PART 1 Got It (1 of 2)

Given $\triangle DEF \cong \triangle D'E'F'$, describe a sequence of rigid motions that maps $\triangle DEF$ to $\triangle D'E'F'$.

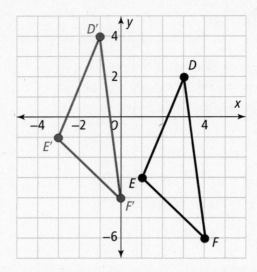

PART 1 Got It (2 of 2)

A translation followed by a translation is equivalent to which single rigid motion?

PART 2 Got It (1 of 2)

$JKLM$ is a square. Given $JKLM \cong J'K'L'M'$, describe a sequence of rigid motions that maps $JKLM$ to $J'K'L'M'$.

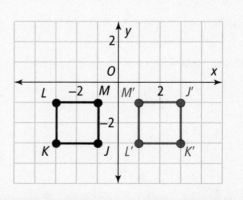

Got It?

PART 2 Got It (2 of 2)

> A reflection followed by a reflection is equivalent to which single rigid motion?

PART 3 Got It

> Which two triangles are congruent?

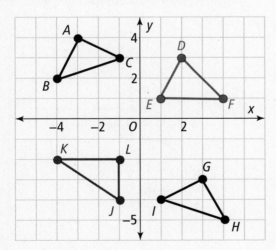

Close and Check

Focus Question

In what ways can you show that figures are identical?

_____

_____

_____

Do you know HOW?

1. Use arrow notation to show how △ABC maps to its image after a reflection across the x-axis followed by a reflection across the y-axis.

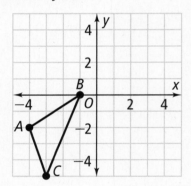

A(⬚) → A'(⬚)

B(⬚) → B'(⬚)

C(⬚) → C'(⬚)

2. What are the vertices of △DEF, the image of △ABC above, after a reflection across the y-axis followed by a 180° rotation clockwise around the origin?

D(⬚)   E(⬚)   F(⬚)

Do you UNDERSTAND?

3. **Reasoning** Assume △ABC in Problem 1 is rotated 180° about point B. What other transformation(s) could you use to map △ABC to △A'B'C'?

_____

_____

_____

_____

4. **Writing** Describe a sequence of rigid motions that maps PQRST to P'Q'R'S'T'.

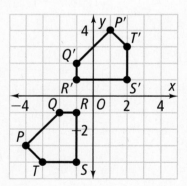

_____

_____

_____

_____

Problem Solving

CCSS: 8.G.A.2: Understand that a two-dimensional figure is congruent to another if the second can be obtained from the first by a sequence of rotations, reflections, and translations; given two congruent figures, describe a sequence that exhibits the congruence ... .

Launch

Draw and label three congruent figures. Each figure must be composed of more than one shape. Describe the moves needed to verify that the figures are congruent.

© MP2, MP8

Reflect Besides in the last two lessons, explain how you have used or could use congruence in your life.

_____

_____

_____

_____

Got It?

PART 1 Got It

Given △GHI ≅ △JKL, describe a sequence of three different rigid motions that maps △GHI to △JKL.

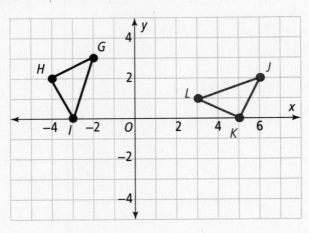

PART 2 Got It

Given that the triangle in Quadrant I is congruent to the triangle in Quadrant III, find possible coordinates for the third vertex of the triangle in Quadrant III.

I. (−1, −1)   **II.** (−1, −4)   **III.** (−5, −1)   **IV.** (−5, −4)

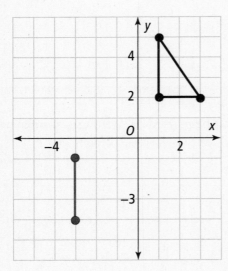

Discuss with a classmate

Define the key terms: quadrant, coordinates. Label all the quadrants and the coordinates of the given figures in the diagram at the left.

Close and Check

Focus Question

© MP1, MP4

How can you use what you know about transformations and congruence to solve problems?

_____

_____

_____

_____

Do you know HOW?

1. Given figure $ABCDEF \cong LMNPQR$, circle the sequence of rigid motions that maps $ABCDEF$ to $LMNPQR$.

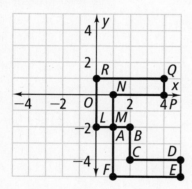

A. Reflection across x-axis, rotation 90° clockwise about point B', translation 1 unit right

B. Rotation 180° counterclockwise about point A', reflection across y-axis, translation 2 units left

C. Reflection across y-axis, rotation 180° clockwise about point A', translation 1 unit right

D. Rotation 90° counterclockwise about point C', translation 2 units left, reflection across $y = 1$

Do you UNDERSTAND?

2. **Reasoning** Given $\triangle PQR \cong \triangle STU$, explain how to find a possible coordinate for point T.

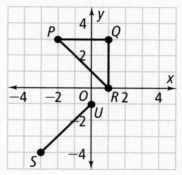

_____

_____

_____

3. **Writing** Explain why there are two possible coordinates for point T.

_____

_____

_____

_____

_____

This page intentionally left blank.

New Vocabulary: congruent figures, image, reflection, rigid motion, rotation, transformation, translation
Review Vocabulary: vertex of a polygon

Vocabulary Review

▶ Identify two challenging vocabulary terms from this topic. Write one vocabulary term in the center oval, and fill in the surrounding boxes with details that will help you better understand the term.

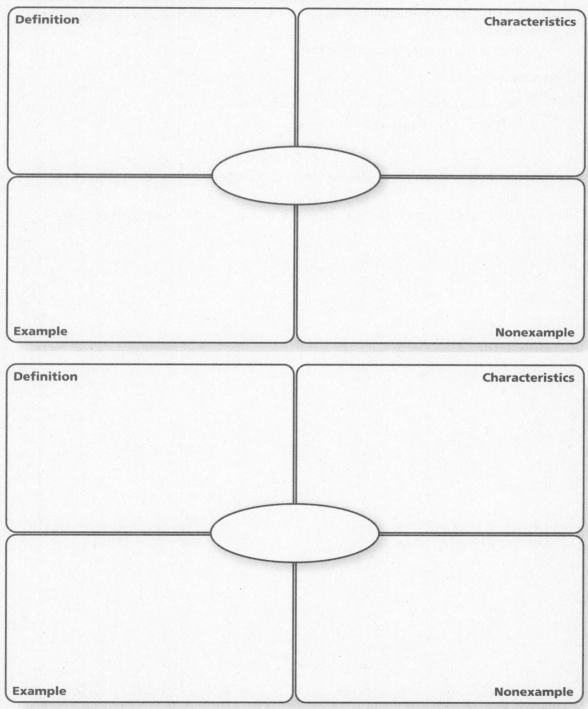

Definition

Characteristics

Example

Nonexample

Definition

Characteristics

Example

Nonexample

Pull It All Together

TASK 1

Complete all parts to solve the riddle at the right.

a. Letter One

- Start with a point at (−2, 3). Translate the point 2 units left, 1 unit down, and 2 units right. Draw segments to show the translation path.
- Reflect the segments across the line $y = 2$.

b. Letter Two

- Draw two segments: (0, −1) to (0, 0) and (0, 0) to (1, 1).
- Reflect the segments across the y-axis.

c. Letter Three

- Letter Three is congruent to Letter One. Draw Letter Three in the fourth quadrant.
- Describe a sequence of rigid motions that maps Letter One to Letter Three.

> I come in all shapes and sizes.
> I am spelled the same forward and backward.
> I sound like one letter, but I really have three. What am I?

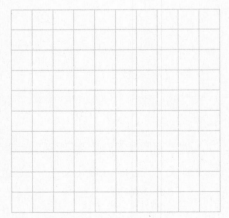

Dilations

CCSS: 8.G.A.3: Describe the effect of dilations, translations, rotations, and reflections on two-dimensional figures using coordinates.

Launch

MP2, MP6

A modern art painter used an inch-grid canvas for a figure painting.

Did the artist paint the figure to scale? Explain.

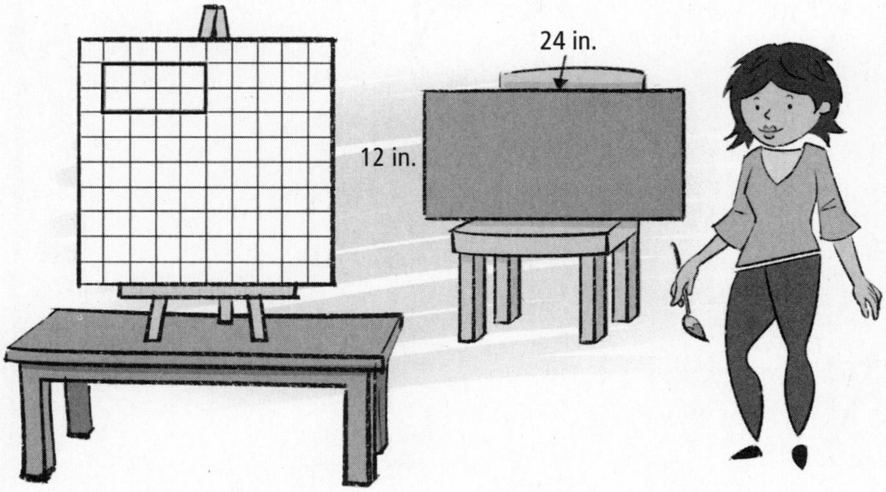

24 in.

12 in.

Reflect Why did the artist have to scale the painting?

_____

_____

_____

_____

Got It?

PART 1 Got It

Which graph shows a dilation?

I.

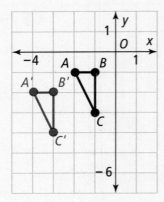

II.

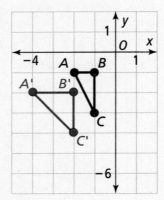

III.

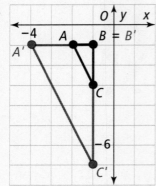

Got It?

PART 2 Got It

 For the given dilation, find the scale factor. Then decide whether the dilation is an enlargement or a reduction.

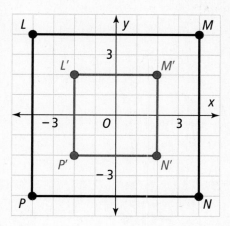

PART 3 Got It

 △MNO has vertices M(8, 4), N(4, −4), and O(0, 0). △M'N'O' is the image of △MNO after a dilation with center (0, 0) and a scale factor of $\frac{3}{4}$. What are the coordinates of M'?

Close and Check

Focus Question

©MP2, MP6

What effect does an enlargement have on a figure? What effect does a reduction have on a figure?

_____

_____

_____

_____

Do you know HOW?

1. Find the scale factor for the given dilation and tell whether the image is an enlargement or a reduction.

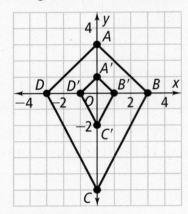

2. Parallelogram *QRST* has vertices at *Q*(−3, 1), *R*(2, 1), *S*(0, −2), and *T*(−5, −2). Find the coordinates of *Q*′ after a dilation with the center at the origin and scale factor 5.

Do you UNDERSTAND?

3. Writing △*XYZ* has vertex *Y*(0, 0). The center of the dilation is at the origin. Describe the location of *Y*′ after a dilation with scale factor $\frac{1}{5}$. Explain.

_____

_____

_____

_____

4. Error Analysis A classmate creates dilation *A″B″C″D″* for Exercise 1 with the origin at the center with scale factor 4. She says the coordinates are *A″*(0, 5), *B″*(5, 0), *C″*(0, −6), and *D″*(−5, 0). Explain her error.

_____

_____

_____

_____

Digital Resources

CCSS: 8.G.A.3: Describe the effect of dilations ... . **8.G.A.4:** Understand that a ... figure is similar to another if the second can be obtained from the first by a sequence of ... dilations; given two similar ... figures, describe a sequence that exhibits the similarity between them.

Launch

© MP3, MP5, MP6

The artist continues to paint the figure in different sizes on the inch-grid canvas. She stops and says, "One of these shapes clearly doesn't belong. I'd better start over."

Which shape does not belong? Explain your reasoning.

Reflect Do shapes have to be the same size to belong together? Explain.

_____

_____

_____

_____

Got It?

Given △ABC ~ △DEF, describe a sequence of a rigid motion followed by a dilation with center (0, 0) that maps △ABC to △DEF.

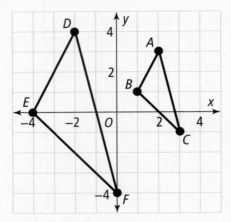

Does a given translation followed by a given dilation always map a figure to the same image as that same dilation followed by that same translation?

Got It?

JKLM and *PQRS* are squares. Given *JKLM* ~ *PQRS*, describe a sequence of a rigid motion followed by a dilation with center (0, 0) that maps square *JKLM* to square *PQRS*.

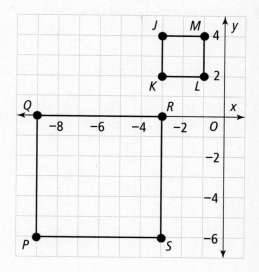

Does a given reflection followed by a given dilation always map a figure to the same image as that same dilation followed by that same reflection?

Got It?

PART 3 Got It

Which two triangles are similar?

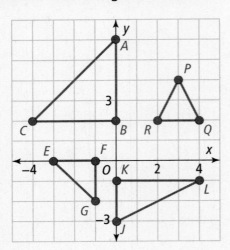

Close and Check

Focus Question

MP3, MP5

How can you show that figures are similar?

_____

_____

_____

_____

Do you know HOW?

1. Given trapezoid *QRST*, draw trapezoid *WXYZ* ~ *QRST* after a 90° clockwise rotation about the origin followed by a dilation with center (0, 0) and scale factor $\frac{1}{2}$.

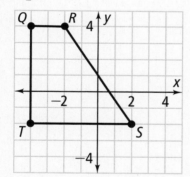

2. What would be the coordinates of *JKLM* ~ *QRST* after a reflection across the *y*-axis and a dilation with the center at the origin and scale factor 2?

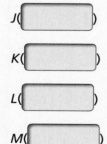

J(   )

K(   )

L(   )

M(   )

Do you UNDERSTAND?

3. **Writing** How would the figure in Exercise 1 change if trapezoid *QRST* were translated up 1 unit and right 3 units followed by a dilation with center (0, 0) and scale factor 1? Explain.

_____

_____

_____

_____

_____

4. **Compare and Contrast** How are a pair of congruent figures and a pair of similar figures alike? How are they different?

_____

_____

_____

_____

_____

This page intentionally left blank.

Relating Similar Triangles and Slope

CCSS: 8.G.A.3: Describe the effect of dilations ... . **8.G.A.4:** Understand that a ... figure is similar to another ... . **8.EE.B.6:** Use similar triangles to explain why the slope m is the same between any two distinct points on a non-vertical line in the coordinate plane ... .

Launch

© MP3, MP8

A museum displays the artist's right triangle series. The series features right triangles painted in proportion on each painting. One painting is a fake. Which is it? Explain how you know.

Painting A

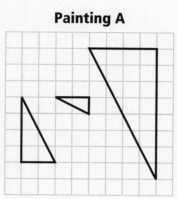

Painting B

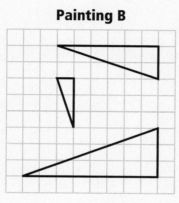

Painting C

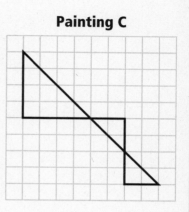

Reflect For which painting was it easiest to find equivalent ratios? Explain.

_____

_____

_____

_____

Got It?

PART 1 Got It

Consider the image of the given triangle after a dilation with center (0, 0) and scale factor of $\frac{1}{2}$. What is the ratio of the rise to the run of the image triangle?

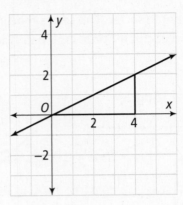

PART 2 Got It

Which slope triangles could you use to find the slope of the line with equation $y = \frac{2}{3}x - 4$?

I. 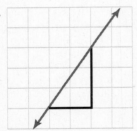   **II.**    **III.**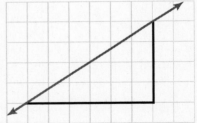

Discuss with a classmate

Choose one of the numbered graphs in this problem.

Explain the parts of the graph, including the slope triangle that is defined in the graph. Be sure to use precise math language in your explanation.

Close and Check

Focus Question

How are similar triangles and slope related?

Do you know HOW?

1. Consider the image △XYZ after a dilation with center (0, 0) and scale factor 2. What is the ratio of the rise to the run of the image triangle?

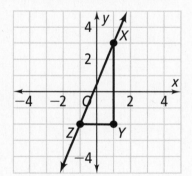

2. What is the slope of the image of △XYZ in Exercise 1 after a 180° rotation about point Y and a dilation with center (0, 0) and scale factor $\frac{1}{3}$?

Do you UNDERSTAND?

3. **Writing** Explain how you can use slope to check the accuracy of a dilation.

4. **Error Analysis** Your friend uses the slope triangle below to write the equation of the line: $y = \frac{1}{3}x + 3$. Explain his error and write the correct equation.

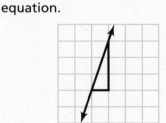

This page intentionally left blank.

Problem Solving

CCSS: **8.G.A.3:** Describe the effect of dilations … . **8.G.A.4:** Understand that a … figure is similar to another if the second can be obtained from the first by a sequence of … dilations; given two similar … figures, describe a sequence that exhibits the similarity between them.

Launch

Use the criteria to draw your own modern art figure painting on the grid. Give your painting a name. ⓒ MP1, MP5

Explain how your work of art meets the criteria.

Criteria

- Three of the figures are similar.
- Has at least one dilation.
- Has at least one translation, rotation, or reflection.

Title of Painting:

Reflect How did you choose your painting's name?

_____

_____

_____

_____

Got It?

PART 1 Got It

Given △JKL ~ △PQR, find possible coordinates for point R.

I. $\left(-\frac{1}{2}, 0\right)$ II. (1, 0)

III. (5, 0)   IV. $\left(7\frac{1}{2}, 0\right)$

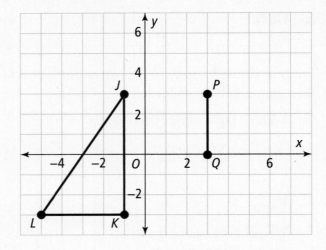

PART 2 Got It

You want to make a scale drawing of your bedroom. You decide on a scale of 3 in. = 4 ft. Your bedroom is a 12 ft-by-16 ft rectangle. What should be the dimensions of the bedroom in the scale drawing?

PART 3 Got It

A 4-ft vertical post casts a 3-ft shadow at the same time a nearby tree casts a 24-ft shadow. How tall is the tree?

Discuss with a classmate

Draw a diagram to model the problem situation.
Compare your diagrams. How are they alike? How are they different?
Is one diagram more accurate than the other? What makes it more accurate?

Close and Check

Focus Question

How can you use what you know about transformations and similarity to solve problems?

_____

_____

_____

_____

_____

Do you know HOW?

1. Given △ABC ~ △EFG, circle the possible coordinate pair(s) for point G after a dilation only.

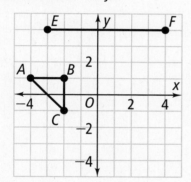

   A. (4, −3)   B. (−3, −3)

   C. (−3, 11)   D. (4, 11)

2. A landscaper makes a scale drawing of a triangular flowerbed. The side lengths of the drawing are 3 cm, 4 cm, and 5 cm. If the scale is 2 cm = 7 m, what are the dimensions of the actual flowerbed?

   3 cm = [ ]

   4 cm = [ ]

   5 cm = [ ]

Do you UNDERSTAND?

3. **Reasoning** Explain how scale drawings and indirect measurements are similar. Give an example of how one is used in real life.

_____

_____

_____

_____

4. **Error Analysis** A friend is 5.5 ft tall and her shadow is 8 ft long. The shadow of a building is 160 ft long. Explain her error in calculating the height of the building. What is the actual height?

$$\frac{5.5}{160} = \frac{8}{x}; x = 27 \text{ ft}$$

_____

_____

_____

_____

This page intentionally left blank.

New Vocabulary: dilation, scale factor, similar figures
Review Vocabulary: rigid motion, slope, transformation

Vocabulary Review

Identify two challenging vocabulary terms from this topic. Write one vocabulary term in the center oval, and fill in the surrounding boxes with details that will help you better understand the term.

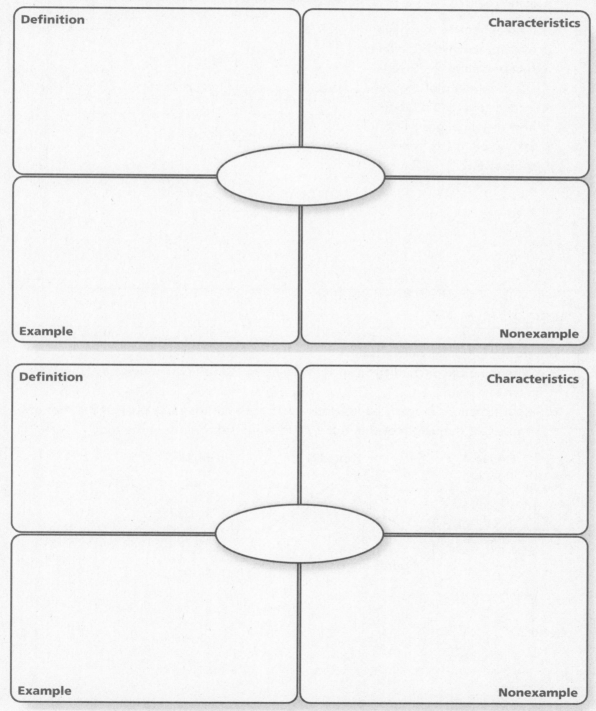

Definition

Characteristics

Example

Nonexample

Definition

Characteristics

Example

Nonexample

Pull It All Together

TASK 1

Use the scale drawing of a living room.

a. What are the length and the width of the actual living room?

b. It takes about $\frac{1}{5}$ of a gallon of paint to cover 90 square feet of wall space. Given that the height of the living room is 10 ft, about how many gallons will it take to paint the living room walls?

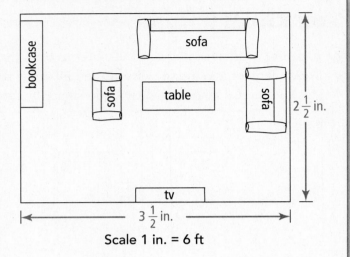

Scale 1 in. = 6 ft

TASK 2

The slope of a roof is called its pitch.

a. Determine the pitch of the roof for each house. Which two houses have the same pitch?

b. A construction company builds House D. Its roof has the same pitch as the roof of House C. If the height of the roof is 40 ft, what is the width of the roof?

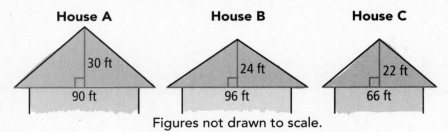

Figures not drawn to scale.

Angles, Lines, and Transversals

Digital Resources

CCSS: 8.G.A.5: Use informal arguments to establish facts about the angle sum and exterior angle of triangles, about the angles created when parallel lines are cut by a transversal, and the angle-angle criterion for similarity of triangles ...

Launch

MP5, MP6, MP8

Which angles have equal measures? Justify your reasoning.

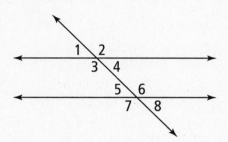

Reflect Where have you seen angles like these in the real world? Explain.

_____

_____

_____

_____

_____

Got It?

PART 1 Got It

Which pairs of angles are corresponding angles?

I. ∠3 and ∠7
II. ∠1 and ∠2
III. ∠2 and ∠6

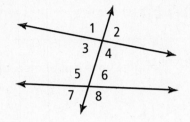

PART 2 Got It

What is $m\angle 2$?

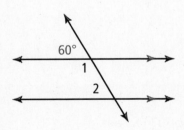

Discuss with a classmate

Compare the answers you wrote for this problem.
Discuss the steps you took to find the measure of the angle in the problem.
What key terms from the lesson did you include in your discussion?

Got It?

PART 3 Got It (1 of 2)

What is $m\angle 1$?

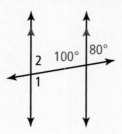

PART 3 Got It (2 of 2)

Make a conjecture about the relationship between $\angle 1$ and $\angle 4$. Justify your reasoning.

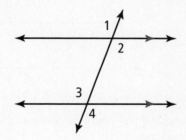

Close and Check

Focus Question

MP2, MP6

If a line intersects two parallel lines, what are the relationships among the angles formed by the lines?

_____

_____

_____

_____

Do you know HOW?

Use the diagram to complete Exercises 1–4.

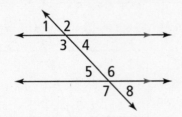

1. Name the pairs of corresponding angles.

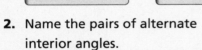

2. Name the pairs of alternate interior angles.

3. If $m\angle 4 = 50°$, what is $m\angle 8$?

4. If $m\angle 6 = 130°$, what is $m\angle 3$?

Do you UNDERSTAND?

5. **Reasoning** How many different angle measures are there in the diagram? Explain.

_____

_____

_____

_____

_____

Reasoning and Parallel Lines

CCSS: 8.G.A.5: Use informal arguments to establish facts about the angle sum and exterior angle of triangles, about the angles created when parallel lines are cut by a transversal, and the angle-angle criterion for similarity of triangles ... .

Launch

© MP3, MP5, MP7

Decide whether $\overline{AB}$ and $\overline{CD}$ are parallel. Justify your reasoning.

A •————————————————————• B

C •————————————————————• D

Reflect What tools or materials did you use to solve the problem? Explain your choice.

_____

_____

_____

_____

_____

Got It?

PART 1 Got It

> For which value of *x* is line *m* parallel to line *n*?

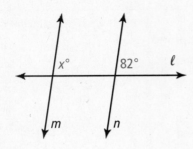

PART 2 Got It

> For which value of *x* is line *m* parallel to line *n*?

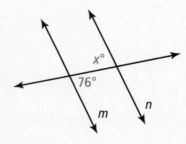

Got It?

Which lines, if any, are parallel?

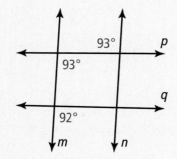

Close and Check

Focus Question

How can you use congruent angles to decide whether lines are parallel?

_____

_____

_____

_____

Do you know HOW?

Use the diagram to complete Exercises 1–3.

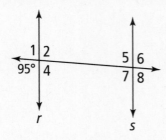

1. For what value of $m\angle 7$ is $r \parallel s$?

[ ]

2. Write **T** if the statement is true and **F** if the statement is false.

   [ ] If $m\angle 8 = 95°$, then $r \parallel s$.

   [ ] If $m\angle 5 = 85°$, then $r \parallel s$.

   [ ] If $m\angle 6 = 95°$, then $r \parallel s$.

3. If $\angle 7 \cong \angle 2$, then $r \parallel s$ because if

   [   ] angles are

   congruent, then lines are

   [   ].

Do you UNDERSTAND?

4. **Vocabulary** Explain how deductive reasoning is used to prove an argument.

_____

_____

_____

_____

_____

5. **Reasoning** Explain why two lines cannot be assumed to be parallel just because they look parallel.

_____

_____

_____

_____

_____

25-3 Interior Angles of Triangles

Digital Resources

CCSS: 8.G.A.5: Use informal arguments to establish facts about the angle sum and exterior angle of triangles, about the angles created when parallel lines are cut by a transversal, and the angle-angle criterion for similarity of triangles . . . .

Launch

MP5, MP6

Which is greater—the measure of a straight angle or the sum of the measures of the angles of a triangle?

Use copies of the triangle to justify your reasoning. You cannot use a protractor.

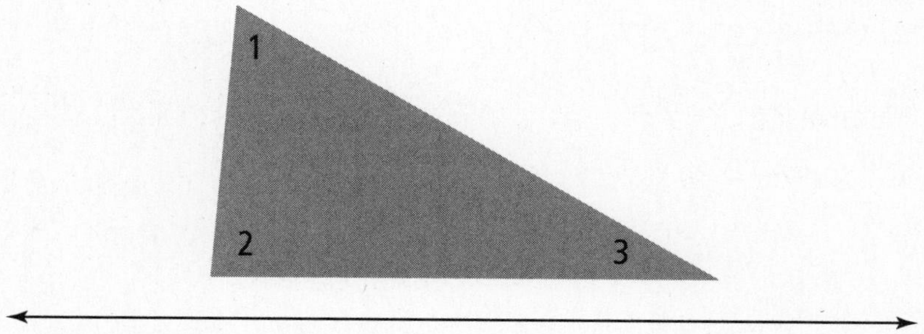

Reflect Do the angle measures of the triangle you use to compare to the straight angle matter? Explain how you could determine the answer.

Got It?

PART 1 Got It

What is $m\angle F$?

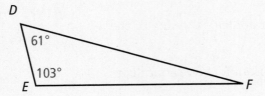

PART 2 Got It (1 of 2)

The measure of one of the acute angles in a right triangle is 42.4°. What is the measure of the other acute angle?

Discuss with a classmate

Draw a diagram to model the triangle being described in the problem.
Then, use your model to discuss how you solved the problem.
How can you check that your answer to the problem is reasonable?
Show at least one way to check your answer.

Got It?

PART 2 Got It (2 of 2)

Make a conjecture about the sum of the measures of the acute angles in a right triangle. Justify your reasoning.

PART 3 Got It

What is $m\angle F$?

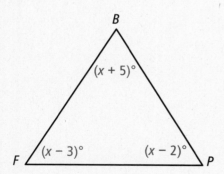

Close and Check

Focus Question

How is a straight angle related to the angles of a triangle?

_____

_____

_____

_____

Do you know HOW?

Use the diagram to answer Exercises 1–4.

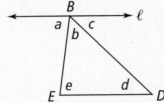

1. Find $m\angle b$, if $m\angle a = 83°$, and $m\angle c = 45°$.

   $m\angle b = \boxed{}$

2. Find $m\angle d$, given line $\ell \parallel \overline{ED}$, $m\angle a = 83°$, and $m\angle c = 45°$.

   $m\angle d = \boxed{}$

3. Find $m\angle e$, given line $\ell \parallel \overline{ED}$, $m\angle a = 83°$, and $m\angle c = 45°$.

   $m\angle e = \boxed{}$

4. What is the value of x when $m\angle b = 10x - 3$, $m\angle d = 5x + 6$, and $m\angle e = 8(x + 2)$?

   $x = \boxed{}$

Do you UNDERSTAND?

5. **Reasoning** Use deductive reasoning to justify the solution to Exercise 2.

   _____

   _____

   _____

   _____

   _____

   _____

Exterior Angles of Triangles

CCSS: 8.G.A.5: Use informal arguments to establish facts about the angle sum and exterior angle of triangles, about the angles created when parallel lines are cut by a transversal, and the angle-angle criterion for similarity of triangles … .

Launch

Ⓒ MP3, MP5

State how the sum of the measures of angles 1, 2, and 3 compares to the sum of the measures of angles 4, 5, and 6. You cannot use a protractor. Justify your reasoning.

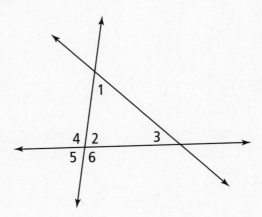

Reflect Would using a protractor make this problem easier? Explain.

_____

_____

_____

_____

_____

Got It?

PART 1 Got It

Which are the two remote interior angles of ∠6?

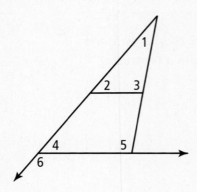

PART 2 Got It

What is the value of x?

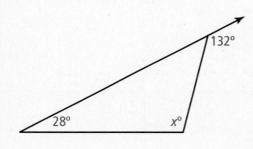

Got It?

PART 3 Got It

Given $m\angle 1 = (5x - 18)°$ and $m\angle 2 = (3x - 40)°$, what is $m\angle 1$?

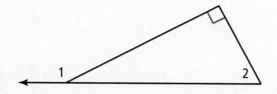

Close and Check

Focus Question

MP2, MP8

What is the relationship between the exterior and interior angles of a triangle?

_____

_____

_____

_____

Do you know HOW?

Use the diagram to solve Exercises 1–4.

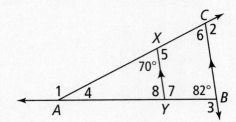

1. Find $m\angle 1$.

2. Find $m\angle 2$.

3. Find $m\angle 3$.

4. Find $m\angle 6$.

5. Given $m\angle 2 = 14x + 9$, and $m\angle 3 = 5x$, what is $m\angle 2$?

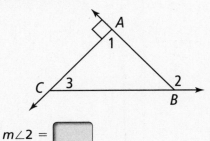

$m\angle 2 = $ ☐

Do you UNDERSTAND?

6. **Reasoning** How does the sum of the exterior angles of a triangle relate to the sum of the interior angles? Explain.

_____

_____

_____

_____

_____

_____

7. **Writing** Explain how you found the solution to Exercise 5.

_____

_____

_____

_____

_____

_____

_____

Angle-Angle Triangle Similarity

CCSS: 8.G.A.4: Understand that … figure is similar to another if the second can be obtained from the first by … dilations … . **8.G.A.5:** Use informal arguments to establish facts about … the angle-angle criterion for similarity of triangles … . Also, **8.G.A.3.**

Launch

Is there a relationship between the triangles? Explain. You can use a protractor, a ruler, and copies of the triangles.

© MP5, MP6

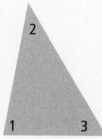

Triangle 1

Triangle 2

Reflect Could you make another triangle related to either triangle? Explain.

_____

_____

_____

_____

_____

Got It?

PART 1 Got It

Is △GHI ~ △JKL? Justify your reasoning.

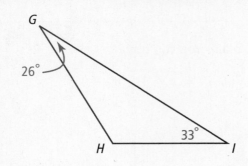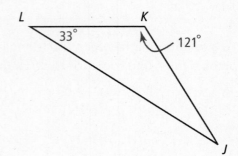

Got It?

PART 2 Got It

Can you conclude that
△*FGH* ~ △*JIH*?
Justify your reasoning.

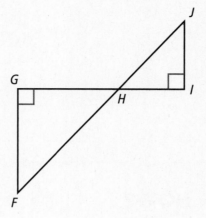

PART 3 Got It

Which statements must be true?

I. △*AZR* ~ △*AKL*
II. △*ZGL* ~ △*KGR*
III. △*AKL* ~ △*GKR*

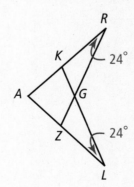

Close and Check

Focus Question

How can you use angle relationships to decide whether two triangles are similar?

_____

_____

_____

_____

Do you know HOW?

1. Which pair of triangles are similar?

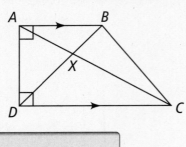

[_____]

2. Use the diagram. Write **T** if the statement is true and **F** if the statement is false.

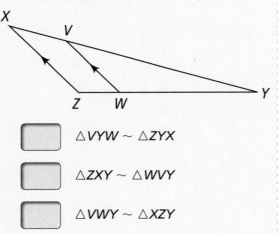

[ ] △VYW ~ △ZYX

[ ] △ZXY ~ △WVY

[ ] △VWY ~ △XZY

Do you UNDERSTAND?

3. Reasoning Given that $BD \parallel AC$, is it possible to conclude that △ABC ~ △DCB? Explain.

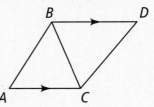

_____

_____

_____

_____

4. Error Analysis Your friend says that if two angles of one triangle are congruent to two angles of another triangle, then the triangles are congruent. Do you agree? Explain.

_____

_____

_____

_____

CCSS: 8.G.A.5: Use informal arguments to establish facts about the angle sum and exterior angle of triangles, about the angles created when parallel lines are cut by a transversal, and the angle-angle criterion for similarity of triangles ... .

Launch

© MP1, MP5

Lines 1 and 2 are parallel horizontal lines. Draw a transversal *p* that passes through point *A* and makes the greatest number of angles with equal angle measure. Justify your reasoning.

Line 1 ⟷ •*A* ⟶

Line 2 ⟷ ⟶

Reflect How many correct answers does this problem have? Why?

_____

_____

_____

_____

_____

Got It?

PART 1 Got It

In the diagram, $m \parallel n$ and $p \parallel q$. What is $m\angle 3$?

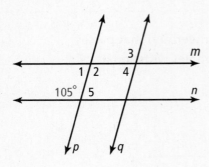

PART 2 Got It

Given $m\angle 1 = (2x + 6)°$, $m\angle 3 = (2x + 5)°$, and $m\angle 4 = (5x - 4)°$, what is $m\angle 4$?

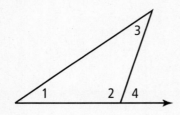

Got It?

PART 3 Got It

Which triangles are similar?

I.
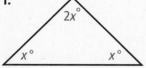

II.
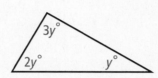

III.
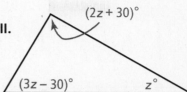

Close and Check

MP3, MP4

Focus Question

You can use relationships between angles to solve complex problems. How do you decide which relationships to use?

_____

_____

_____

_____

Do you know HOW?

Use the diagram to answer Exercises 1 and 2.

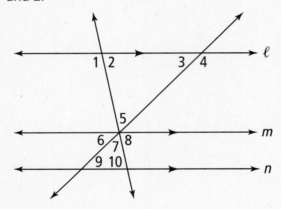

1. Given $\ell \parallel m \parallel n$, and $m\angle 3 = x$, $m\angle 5 = x + 12$, and $m\angle 8 = 2x - 12$, find the angle measures.

   $m\angle 2 = $ ☐

   $m\angle 1 = $ ☐

   $m\angle 7 = $ ☐

   $m\angle 4 = $ ☐

2. Are the triangles formed by the transversals and parallel lines similar?

   ☐

Do you UNDERSTAND?

3. **Reasoning** Is it possible to determine the measures of the remaining unlabeled angles in the diagram? Explain your strategy.

   _____

   _____

   _____

   _____

   _____

   _____

   _____

4. **Error Analysis** A classmate says $\angle 6 \cong \angle 8$. Do you agree? Explain.

   _____

   _____

   _____

   _____

   _____

New Vocabulary: alternate interior angles, corresponding angles, deductive reasoning, exterior angle of a triangle, remote interior angles, transversal
Review Vocabulary: angle, congruent, parallel lines, straight angle

Vocabulary Review

▶ Identify two challenging vocabulary terms from this topic. Write one vocabulary term in the center oval, and fill in the surrounding boxes with details that will help you better understand the term.

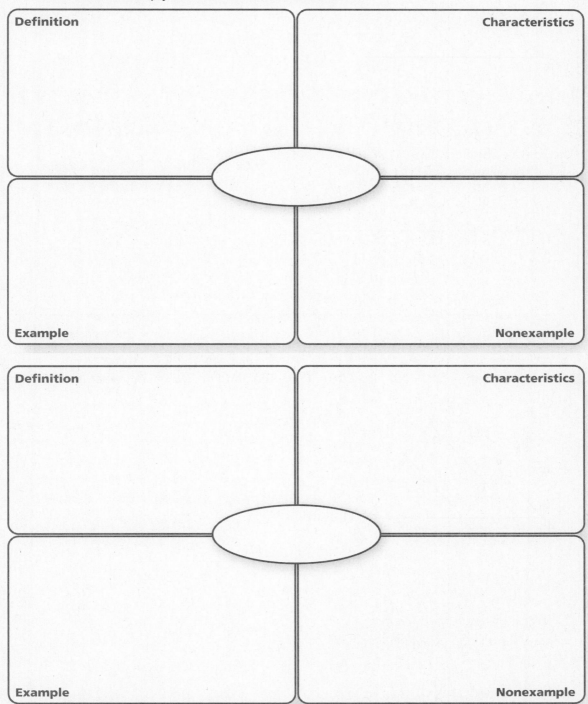

Definition

Characteristics

Example

Nonexample

Definition

Characteristics

Example

Nonexample

Pull It All Together

Name two pairs of similar triangles. Justify your reasoning.

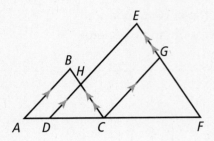

Given $m\angle BAC = (2x + 10)°$, $m\angle EDF = (5x - 35)°$, and $m\angle DEF = 7x°$, what is $m\angle EFD$?

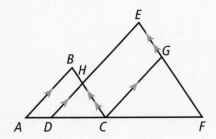

CCSS: 8.G.C.9: Know the formulas for the volumes of cones, cylinders, and spheres and use them to solve real-world and mathematical problems.

Launch

Ⓒ **MP2, MP7**

Your friend invents a new pop-up snake can. She says the height is 5 in. and traces the top of the can on an inch grid.

Draw a label that will cover the whole can except for the top and bottom. Estimate its approximate area. Explain your reasoning.

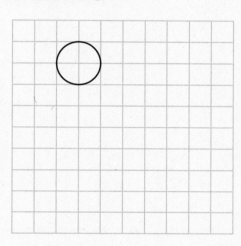

Reflect What previous mathematical knowledge did you need to solve the problem? Explain.

_____

_____

_____

Got It?

PART 1 Got It

Use the net to find the surface area of the cylindrical can. Use 3.14 for π and give the answer to the nearest tenth.

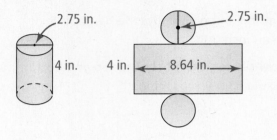

PART 2 Got It (1 of 2)

What is the surface area of the cylinder? Use 3.14 for π. Round your answer to the nearest square inch.

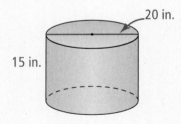

Discuss with a classmate

What is meant by a surface? Describe some familiar surfaces in your classroom. What other geometric surface areas are you familiar with?

Got It?

Use the Distributive Property to rewrite the formula for the surface area of a cylinder as a product rather than a sum. What are some advantages and disadvantages of your formula?

You plan to stain the outside of a cylindrical wooden table. You do not plan to stain the bottom. To the nearest square inch, find the area that needs staining.

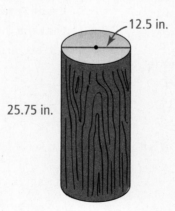

12.5 in.

25.75 in.

Close and Check

Focus Question

© MP4, MP6

What types of things can you model with a cylinder? Why might you want to find the surface area of a cylinder?

_____

_____

_____

_____

Do you know HOW?

1. Use the net to find the surface area of the cylindrical can to the nearest tenth. Use 3.14 for π.

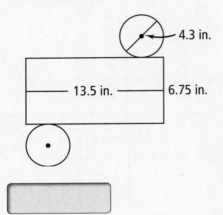

4.3 in.

13.5 in. — 6.75 in.

2. Find the surface area of the cylinder to the nearest tenth. Use 3.14 for π.

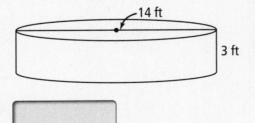

14 ft

3 ft

Do you UNDERSTAND?

3. **Writing** Explain how using the calculator key for π rather than 3.14 affects the solution to a surface area problem.

_____

_____

_____

_____

4. **Error Analysis** Your friend decides that the 2 cylinders have the same surface area. Do you agree? Explain.

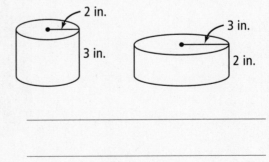

2 in.

3 in.

3 in.

2 in.

_____

_____

_____

_____

_____

Volumes of Cylinders

Digital Resources

CCSS: 8.G.C.9: Know the formulas for the volumes of cones, cylinders, and spheres and use them to solve real-world and mathematical problems.

Launch

© MP4, MP6

Your friend claims that 20 in.³ of stuffed snake will fit in her new can. Her assistant says, "She better use the box."

Will the can work? Why did the assistant say she should use the box? Explain.

2 in.

5 in.

New
Pop-Up
Snake
Can

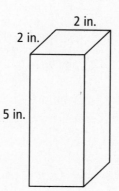

2 in.

2 in.

2 in.

5 in.

Reflect How much snake do you think the can would hold? Explain your reasoning.

_____

_____

_____

_____

Got It?

Find the volume. Leave the answer in terms of π.

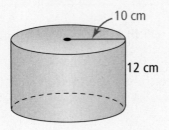

10 cm

12 cm

How does the volume of a cylinder change if its height or radius is doubled?

Got It?

PART 2 Got It

You are preparing juice from a can of liquid juice concentrate. The directions say to add three cans of water to the concentrate, and then stir. To the nearest cubic inch, how much juice will you have?

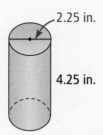

2.25 in.

4.25 in.

PART 3 Got It

What is the radius of a cylinder that has a volume of 192π cubic feet and a height of 12 feet?

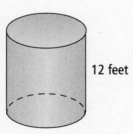

12 feet

Close and Check

Focus Question

Why might you want to find the volume of a cylinder?

_____

_____

_____

_____

Do you know HOW?

1. Find the volume. Leave the answer in terms of π.

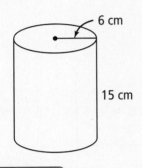

6 cm

15 cm

[blank box]

2. The volume of a can of tuna is 562.76 cm³. Find the radius of the can to the nearest tenth. Use 3.14 for π.

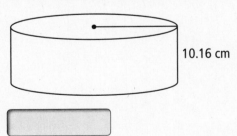

10.16 cm

[blank box]

Do you UNDERSTAND?

3. Reasoning A pitcher holds 1,614.7 in.³ of liquid. Each can of punch is 15 in. tall with a diameter of 8 in. How many full cans will the pitcher hold? Explain.

_____

_____

_____

_____

4. Error Analysis A large can of beans has twice the radius and height of a small can of beans. Your friend says that the large can has twice the volume of the small can. Is he correct? Explain.

_____

_____

_____

_____

_____

_____

CCSS: 8.G.C.9: Know the formulas for the volumes of cones, cylinders, and spheres and use them to solve real-world and mathematical problems.

Launch

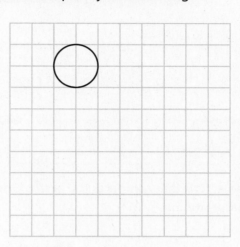

Ⓒ MP4, MP7

Your friend follows with a plan for a cone-shaped party hat. She says it is 5 in. tall and traces the bottom on the inch grid.

Draw the hat and estimate its surface area. Explain your reasoning.

Reflect Do you think drawing a net of a cone will give you a precise area? Explain.

_____

_____

_____

Got It?

PART 1 Got It (1 of 2)

Use the net to find the surface area of the cone to the nearest square centimeter. Use 3.14 for π.

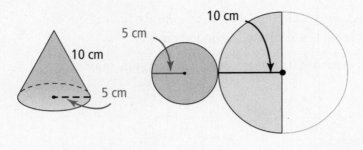

PART 1 Got It (2 of 2)

Make a conjecture that compares the area of the base with the lateral surface area. Justify your reasoning.

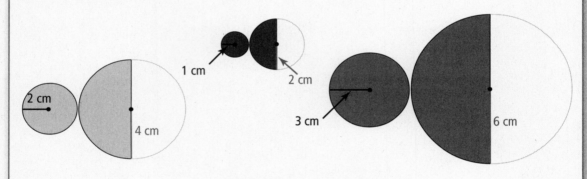

Got It?

PART 2 Got It

 Find the surface area of the model volcano to the nearest square inch. Include the base since all surfaces will be painted. Use 3.14 for π.

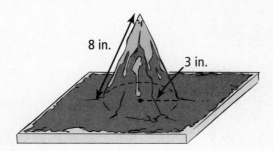

8 in.

3 in.

PART 3 Got It

 To the nearest square inch, how much cardboard is needed to make the package for the hanging decoration?

4 in.

7.5 in.

Close and Check

Focus Question

© MP4, MP6

What types of things can you model with a cone? Why might you want to find the surface area of a cone?

_____

_____

_____

Do you know HOW?

1. Use the net to find the surface area of the cone to the nearest square meter. Use 3.14 for π.

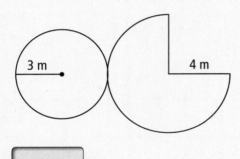

3 m   4 m

[   ]

2. Spiced pecans are sold in cone-shaped containers that include a circular lid. Find the surface area of the container to the nearest square inch. Use 3.14 for π.

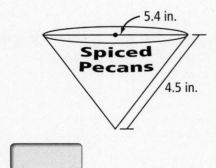

5.4 in.

Spiced Pecans

4.5 in.

[   ]

Do you UNDERSTAND?

3. **Compare and Contrast** Explain the difference between the height of a cone and the slant height of a cone. How do the measures compare?

_____

_____

_____

_____

_____

_____

_____

4. **Reasoning** Explain the differences between the surface areas of a cylinder and a cone with the same diameter.

_____

_____

_____

_____

_____

Volumes of Cones

CCSS: 8.G.C.9: Know the formulas for the volumes of cones, cylinders, and spheres and use them to solve real-world and mathematical problems.

Launch

Look for a pattern in the volumes of the cylinder and cone pairs in terms of π. Then find the volume of the fourth cone in terms of π. Explain your reasoning.

MP6, MP8

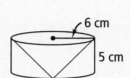

6 cm
5 cm

Cone volume: 60π cm^3

Cylinder volume:

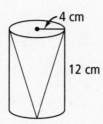

4 cm
12 cm

Cone volume: 64π cm^3

Cylinder volume:

3 cm
8 cm

Cone volume: 24π cm^3

Cylinder volume:

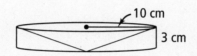

10 cm
3 cm

Cone volume:

Cylinder volume:

Reflect Describe another situation where you can use a pattern to figure out something you don't know.

_____

_____

_____

_____

Got It?

Find the approximate volume of the cone in terms of π.

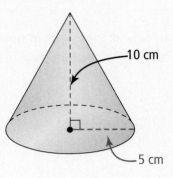

10 cm

5 cm

What happens to the volume of a cone when you double the radius?

Got It?

PART 2 Got It

Find the volume of sand in the bottom of the hourglass to the nearest cubic inch. Use 3.14 for π.

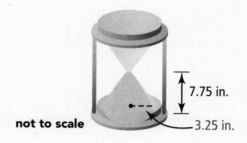

not to scale

7.75 in.

3.25 in.

PART 3 Got It

The volume of the tepee is 471 ft^3. To the nearest foot, what is the radius? Use 3.14 for π.

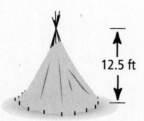

12.5 ft

Close and Check

© MP1, MP3

Focus Question

Why might you want to find the volume of a cone?

_____

_____

_____

_____

Do you know HOW?

1. Number the cones from 1 to 3 in order from least to greatest volume.

5 cm
5 cm

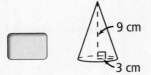
9 cm
3 cm

2 cm
7 cm

2. Find the volume of the funnel to the nearest cubic centimeter. Use 3.14 for π.

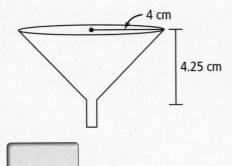
4 cm
4.25 cm

Do you UNDERSTAND?

3. Reasoning A juice company repackages individual juice cans in cone-shaped containers with the same volume. The can is 3 in. tall with a diameter of 2 in. What could be the dimensions of the cone container? Explain.

_____

_____

_____

_____

_____

4. Writing A baker pours sugar into a cylindrical jar using the funnel from Exercise 2. If the jar holds 850 cm^3, about how many times will he have to fill the funnel before the jar is full? Explain.

_____

_____

_____

Surface Areas of Spheres

CCSS: 8.G.C.9: Know the formulas for the volumes of cones, cylinders, and spheres and use them to solve real-world and mathematical problems.

Launch

© MP3, MP4

Which two-dimensional world map, Map #1 or Map #2, would you use to more accurately calculate the surface area of Earth? Explain your reasoning.

 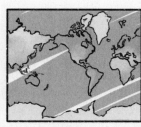 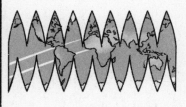

Map #1   Map #2

Reflect Which type of two-dimensional world map do you use and see more often? Why?

_____

_____

_____

_____

_____

Got It?

PART 1 Got It

To the nearest tenth of a square inch, what is the surface area of the sphere? Use 3.14 for π.

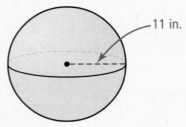

11 in.

PART 2 Got It

The new physical education instructor is 6 ft tall and his arm span is about the same as his height. When he puts his arms around the widest part of the exercise ball, his fingertips touch. What is the surface area of the exercise ball to the nearest square foot?

PART 3 Got It

The surface area of the sphere is 615.44 ft^2. What is the radius to the nearest foot?

Close and Check

▶ Focus Question

What types of things can you model with a sphere? Why might you want to find the surface area of a sphere?

_____

_____

_____

_____

▶ Do you know HOW?

1. Find the surface area of the sphere to the nearest tenth of a square centimeter. Use 3.14 for π.

15 cm

[_____]

2. The circumference of a giant beach ball is 383.08 cm. Find the surface area of the beach ball to the nearest tenth of a square centimeter. Use 3.14 for π.

[_____]

3. The surface area of a sphere is 651 ft². Find the radius of the sphere to the nearest tenth of a square foot. Use 3.14 for π.

[_____]

▶ Do you UNDERSTAND?

4. Writing Explain how to use the circumference to find the surface area of a sphere.

_____

_____

_____

_____

5. Error Analysis A classmate says it is impossible to find an exact solution for the surface area of a sphere because π is an irrational number. Do you agree? Explain.

_____

_____

_____

_____

_____

This page intentionally left blank.

Volumes of Spheres

CCSS: 8.G.C.9: Know the formulas for the volumes of cones, cylinders, and spheres and use them to solve real-world and mathematical problems.

Launch

@ MP3, MP6

Your friend claims that 40 in.^{3} of party confetti will fit in her new party globe. Her assistant says, "She better use the cylinder."

Will the party globe work? Why did the assistant say she should use the cylinder? Explain.

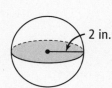

2 in.

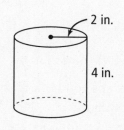

2 in.

4 in.

Reflect If you had to identify the height and width of a sphere with a radius of 2 inches what would it be?

Got It?

Find the volume of the sphere to the nearest cubic inch. Use 3.14 for π.

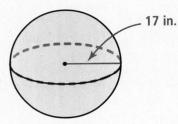

17 in.

Discuss with a classmate

Review the steps you took to solve this problem.
Are the steps clear?
Discuss the reason for each step in your solution, and make a list of the key math terms you used during your discussion.

Compare the surface area and the volume of a sphere with radius 3 ft. How are they different?

Got It?

PART 2 Got It

To the nearest tenth of a cubic millimeter, what is the volume of the sphere that appears when a nickel is spinning? Use 3.14 for π.

21.21 mm

PART 3 Got It

To the nearest foot, what is the radius of a sphere that has a volume of 523 ft^3? Use 3.14 for π.

Close and Check

MP1, MP3

> ## Focus Question
>
> Why might you want to find the volume of a sphere?
>
> _____
>
> _____
>
> _____
>
> _____

Do you know HOW?

1. To the nearest cubic inch, how much space is there inside the ball for the hamster? Use 3.14 for π.

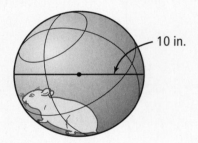

10 in.

[   ]

2. A gazing ball in the center of a garden has a volume of 904.3 cm³. To the nearest centimeter, find the diameter of the gazing ball.

[   ]

3. To the nearest tenth of a cubic foot, find the volume of a 9 ft diameter inflatable ball.

[   ]

Do you UNDERSTAND?

4. **Writing** The height and diameter of a cylinder is equal to the diameter of a sphere. Explain the relationship between the volume of the sphere and the volume of the cylinder.

_____

_____

_____

5. **Reasoning** A ball of twine has a diameter of 3.4 m. More twine is added until the diameter is 12 m. A classmate subtracts the diameters and uses the result to find the change in volume of the sphere. Is he correct? Explain.

_____

_____

_____

_____

_____

Problem Solving

CCSS: 8.G.C.9: Know the formulas for the volumes of cones, cylinders, and spheres and use them to solve real-world and mathematical problems.

Launch

MP1, MP6

The cylinder, cone, and sphere all have the same radius and height (or diameter). Describe how the volumes compare given these dimensions. State the volumes in terms of π.

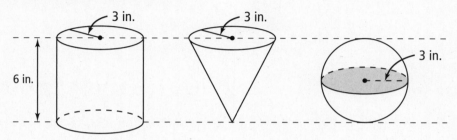

Reflect How could you use what you know about the relationships between the volumes of the shapes to make solving problems easier? Explain.

_____

_____

_____

_____

Got It?

PART 1 Got It

 You are making a teepee for your little brother. The fabric will cover only the lateral surface. To the nearest dollar, what will the fabric cost if it is $1.30 for one square foot?

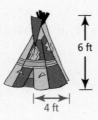

6 ft

4 ft

PART 2 Got It

To the nearest cubic inch, how much water does the watering can hold? Do not include water in the spout. Use 3.14 for π.

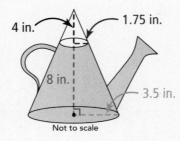

4 in.   1.75 in.

8 in.

3.5 in.

Not to scale

Close and Check

MP1, MP3

Focus Question

How can you apply what you know about surface areas and volumes of cylinders, cones, and spheres to solve problems?

_____

_____

_____

_____

Do you know HOW?

1. A greenhouse is built in the shape of half of a sphere. To the nearest tenth of a cubic foot, find the volume of the greenhouse. Use 3.14 for π.

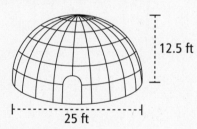

12.5 ft

25 ft

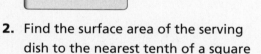

2. Find the surface area of the serving dish to the nearest tenth of a square inch. Use 3.14 for π.

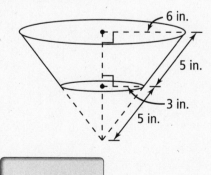

6 in.

5 in.

3 in.

5 in.

Do you UNDERSTAND?

3. **Writing** Explain how to find the total volume of the silo.

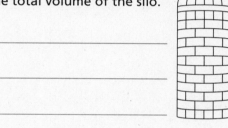

_____

_____

_____

_____

_____

4. **Reasoning** You want the container with the largest volume. If the height and diameter of each container are equal, should you choose a sphere, cylinder, or cone? Explain.

_____

_____

_____

_____

_____

This page intentionally left blank.

New Vocabulary: cone, cylinder, lateral area, sphere, surface area, volume
Review Vocabulary: net

Vocabulary Review

Identify two challenging vocabulary terms from this topic. Write one vocabulary term in the center oval, and fill in the surrounding boxes with details that will help you better understand the term.

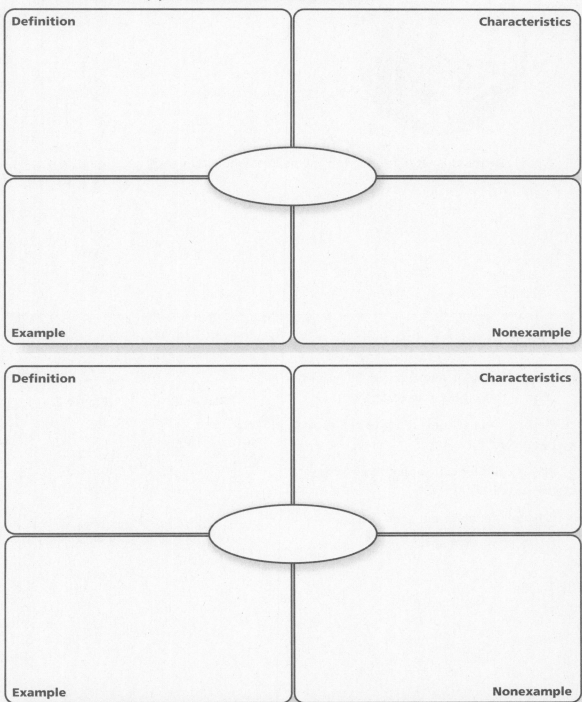

Definition

Characteristics

Example

Nonexample

Definition

Characteristics

Example

Nonexample

Pull It All Together

TASK 1

You can model Earth's shape with a sphere.

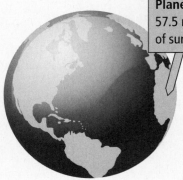

Planet Earth: 29.2%, or 57.5 million square miles of surface covered in land.

What is Earth's diameter, rounded to the nearest whole number?

TASK 2

Fun party game! Whoever can fill his or her cone with fruit juice first, wins.

Player 1 fills her cone at a rate of 3 cups per second.

Player 2 fills his cone at a rate of 2 cups per second.

Who will fill his or her cone first?

(1 cup = 14.4375 in.³)

Player 1

10 in.

12 in.

Player 2

5 in.

24 in.

English/Spanish Glossary

A

Absolute deviation from the mean Absolute deviation measures the distance that the data value is from the mean. You find the absolute deviation by taking the absolute value of the deviation of a data value. Absolute deviations are always nonnegative.

Desviación absoluta de la media La desviación absoluta mide la distancia a la que un valor se encuentra de la media. Para hallar la desviación absoluta, tomas el valor absoluto de la desviación de un valor. Las desviaciones absolutas siempre son no negativas.

Absolute value The absolute value of a number a is the distance between a and zero on a number line. The absolute value of a is written as $|a|$.

Valor absoluto El valor absoluto de un número a es la distancia entre a y cero en la recta numérica. El valor absoluto de a se escribe como $|a|$.

Accuracy The accuracy of an estimate or measurement is the degree to which it agrees with an accepted or actual value of that measurement.

Exactitud La exactitud de una estimación o medición es el grado de concordancia con un valor aceptado o real de esa medición.

Action In a probability situation, an action is a process with an uncertain result.

Acción En una situación de probabilidad, una acción es el proceso con un resultado incierto.

Acute angle An acute angle is an angle with a measure between 0° and 90°.

Ángulo agudo Un ángulo agudo es un ángulo que mide entre 0° y 90°.

Acute triangle An acute triangle is a triangle with three acute angles.

Triángulo acutángulo Un triángulo acutángulo es un triángulo que tiene tres ángulos agudos.

Addend Addends are the numbers that are added together to find a sum.

Sumando Los sumandos son los números que se suman para hallar un total.

English/Spanish Glossary

Additive inverses Two numbers that have a sum of 0.

Inversos de suma Dos números cuya suma es 0.

Adjacent angles Two angles are adjacent angles if they share a vertex and a side, but have no interior points in common.

Ángulos adyacentes Dos ángulos son adyacentes si tienen un vértice y un lado en común, pero no comparten puntos internos.

Algebraic expression An algebraic expression is a mathematical phrase that consists of variables, numbers, and operation symbols.

Expresión algebraica Una expresión algebraica es una frase matemática que consiste en variables, números y símbolos de operaciones.

Analyze To analyze is to think about and understand facts and details about a given set of information. Analyzing can involve providing a written summary supported by factual information, diagrams, charts, tables, or any combination of these.

Analizar Analizar es pensar en los datos y detalles de cierta información y comprenderlos. El análisis puede incluir la presentación de un resumen escrito sustentado por información objetiva, diagramas, tablas o una combinación de esos elementos.

Angle An angle is a figure formed by two rays with a common endpoint.

Ángulo Un ángulo es una figura formada por dos semirrectas que tienen un extremo en común.

Angle of rotation The angle of rotation is the number of degrees a figure is rotated.

Ángulo de rotación El ángulo de rotación es el número de grados que se rota una figura.

Annual salary The amount of money earned at a job in one year.

Salario annual La cantidad de dinero ganó en un trabajo en un año.

Area The area of a figure is the number of square units the figure encloses.

Área El área de una figura es el número de unidades cuadradas que ocupa.

English/Spanish Glossary

Area of a circle The formula for the area of a circle is $A = \pi r^2$, where A represents the area and r represents the radius of the circle.

Área de un círculo La fórmula del área de un círculo es $A = \pi r^2$, donde A representa el área y r representa el radio del círculo.

Area of a parallelogram The formula for the area of a parallelogram is $A = bh$, where A represents the area, b represents a base, and h is the corresponding height.

Área de un paralelogramo La fórmula del área de un paralelogramo es $A = bh$, donde A representa el área, b representa una base y h es la altura correspondiente.

Area of a rectangle The formula for the area of a rectangle is $A = bh$, where A represents the area, b represents the base, and h represents the height of the rectangle.

Área de un rectángulo La fórmula del área de un rectángulo es $A = bh$, donde A representa el área, b representa la base y h representa la altura del rectángulo.

Area of a square The formula for the area of a square is $A = s^2$, where A represents the area and s represents a side length.

Área de un cuadrado La fórmula del área de un cuadrado es $A = s^2$, donde A representa el área y l representa la longitud de un lado.

Area of a trapezoid The formula for the area of a trapezoid is $A = \frac{1}{2}h(b_1 + b_2)$, where A represents the area, b_1 and b_2 represent the bases, and h represents the height between the bases.

El área de un trapezoide La fórmula para el área de un trapezoide es $A = \frac{1}{2}h(b_1 + b_2)$, donde A representa el área, b_1 y b_2 representan las bases, y h representa la altura entre las bases.

Area of a triangle The formula for the area of a triangle is $A = \frac{1}{2}bh$, where A represents the area, b represents the length of a base, and h represents the corresponding height.

Área de un triángulo La fórmula del área de un triángulo es $A = \frac{1}{2}bh$, donde A representa el área, b representa la longitud de una base y h representa la altura correspondiente.

Asset An asset is money you have or property of value that you own.

Ventaja Una ventaja es dinero que tiene o la propiedad de valor que usted posee.

English/Spanish Glossary

Associative Property of Addition For any numbers a, b, and c:
$$(a + b) + c = a + (b + c)$$

Propiedad asociativa de la suma Para los números cualesquiera a, b y c:
$$(a + b) + c = a + (b + c)$$

Associative Property of Multiplication For any numbers a, b, and c:
$$(a \cdot b) \cdot c = a \cdot (b \cdot c)$$

Propiedad asociativa de la multiplicación Para los números cualesquiera a, b y c:
$$(a \cdot b) \cdot c = a \cdot (b \cdot c)$$

Average of two numbers The average of two numbers is the value that represents the middle of two numbers. It is found by adding the two numbers together and dividing by 2.

Promedio de dos números El promedio de dos números es el valor que está justo en el medio de esos dos números. Se halla sumando los dos números y dividiendo el resultado por 2.

B

Balance The balance in an account is the principal amount plus the interest earned.

Saldo El saldo de una cuenta es el capital más el interés ganado.

Balance of a checking account The balance of a checking account is the amount of money in the checking account.

El equilibrio de una Cuenta Corriente Bancaria El equilibrio de una cuenta corriente bancaria es la cantidad de dinero en la cuenta corriente bancaria.

Balance of a loan The balance of a loan is the remaining unpaid principal.

El equilibrio de un préstamo El equilibrio de un préstamo es el director impagado restante.

Bar diagram A bar diagram is a way to represent part to whole relationships.

Diagrama de barras Un diagrama de barras es una forma de representar una relación de parte a entero.

Base The base is the repeated factor of a number written in exponential form.

Base La base es el factor repetido de un número escrito en forma exponencial.

English/Spanish Glossary

Base area of a cone The base area of a cone is the area of a circle. Base Area = πr^2.

Área de la base de un cono El área de la base de un cono es el área de un círculo. El área de la base = πr^2.

Base of a cone The base of a cone is a circle with radius *r*.

Base de un cono La base de un cono es un círculo con radio *r*.

Base of a cylinder A base of a cylinder is one of a pair of parallel circular faces that are the same size.

Base de un cilindro Una base de un cilindro es una de dos caras circulares paralelas que tienen el mismo tamaño.

Base of a parallelogram A base of a parallelogram is any side of the parallelogram.

Base de un paralelogramo La base de un paralelogramo es cualquiera de los lados del paralelogramo.

Base of a prism A base of a prism is one of a pair of parallel polygonal faces that are the same size and shape. A prism is named for the shape of its bases.

Base de un prisma La base de un prisma es una de las dos caras poligonales paralelas que tienen el mismo tamaño y la misma forma. El nombre de un prisma depende de la forma de sus bases.

Base of a pyramid A base of a pyramid is a polygonal face that does not connect to the vertex.

Base de una pirámide La base de una pirámide es una cara poligonal que no se conecta con el vértice.

Base of a triangle The base of a triangle is any side of the triangle.

Base de un triángulo La base de un triángulo es cualquiera de los lados del triángulo.

Benchmark A benchmark is a number you can use as a reference point for other numbers.

Referencia Una referencia es un número que usted puede utilizar como un punto de referencia para otros números.

English/Spanish Glossary

Bias A bias is a tendency toward a particular perspective that is different from the overall perspective of the population.

Sesgo Un sesgo es una tendencia hacia una perspectiva particular que es diferente de la perspectiva general de la población.

Biased sample In a biased sample, the number of subjects in the sample with the trait that you are studying is not proportional to the number of members in the population with that trait. A biased sample does not accurately represent the population.

Muestra sesgada En una muestra sesgada, el número de sujetos de la muestra que tiene la característica que se está estudiando no es proporcional al número de miembros de la población que tienen esa característica. Una muestra sesgada no representa con exactitud la población.

Bivariate categorical data Bivariate categorical data pairs categorical data collected about two variables of the same population.

Datos bivariados por categorías Los datos bivariados por categorías agrupan pares de datos obtenidos acerca de dos variables de la misma población.

Bivariate data Bivariate data is comprised of pairs of linked observations about a population.

Datos bivariados Los datos bivariados se forman a partir de pares de observaciones relacionadas sobre una población.

Box plot A box plot is a statistical graph that shows the distribution of a data set by marking five boundary points where data occur along a number line. Unlike a dot plot or a histogram, a box plot does not show frequency.

Diagrama de cajas Un diagrama de cajas es un diagrama de estadísticas que muestra la distribución de un conjunto de datos al marcar cinco puntos de frontera donde se hallan los datos sobre una recta numérica. A diferencia del diagrama de puntos o el histograma, el diagrama de cajas no muestra la frecuencia.

Budget A budget is a plan for how you will spend your money.

Presupuesto Un presupuesto es un plan para cómo gastará su dinero.

English/Spanish Glossary

C

Categorical data Categorical data consist of data that fall into categories.

Datos por categorías Los datos por categorías son datos que se pueden clasificar en categorías.

Center of a circle The center of a circle is the point inside the circle that is the same distance from all points on the circle. Name a circle by its center.

Centro de un círculo El centro de un círculo es el punto dentro del círculo que está a la misma distancia de todos los puntos del círculo. Un círculo se identifica por su centro.

Center of a regular polygon The center of a regular polygon is the point that is equidistant from its vertices.

Centro de un polígono regular El centro de un polígono regular es el punto equidistante de todos sus vértices.

Center of rotation The center of rotation is a fixed point about which a figure is rotated.

Centro de rotación El centro de rotación es el punto fijo alrededor del cual se rota una figura.

Check register A record that shows all of the transactions for a bank account, including withdrawals, deposits, and transfers. It also shows the balance of the account after each transaction.

Verifique registro Un registro que muestra todas las transacciones para una cuenta bancaria, inclusive retiradas, los depósitos, y las transferencias. También muestra el equilibrio de la cuenta después de cada transacción.

Circle A circle is the set of all points in a plane that are the same distance from a given point, called the center.

Círculo Un círculo es el conjunto de todos los puntos de un plano que están a la misma distancia de un punto dado, llamado centro.

Circle graph A circle graph is a graph that represents a whole divided into parts.

Gráfica circular Una gráfica circular es una gráfica que representa un todo dividido en partes.

English/Spanish Glossary

Circumference of a circle The circumference of a circle is the distance around the circle. The formula for the circumference of a circle is $C = \pi d$, where C represents the circumference and d represents the diameter of the circle.

Circunferencia de un círculo La circunferencia de un círculo es la distancia alrededor del círculo. La fórmula de la circunferencia de un círculo es $C = \pi d$, donde C representa la circunferencia y d representa el diámetro del círculo.

Cluster A cluster is a group of points that lie close together on a scatter plot.

Grupo Un grupo es un conjunto de puntos que están agrupados en un diagrama de dispersión.

Coefficient A coefficient is the number part of a term that contains a variable.

Coeficiente Un coeficiente es la parte numérica de un término que contiene una variable.

Common denominator A common denominator is a number that is the denominator of two or more fractions.

Común denominador Un común denominador es un número que es el denominador de dos o más fracciones.

Common multiple A common multiple is a multiple that two or more numbers share.

Múltiplo común Un múltiplo común es un múltiplo que comparten dos o más números.

Commutative Property of Addition For any numbers a and b: $a + b = b + a$

Propiedad conmutativa de la suma Para los números cualesquiera a y b: $a + b = b + a$

Commutative Property of Multiplication For any numbers a and b: $a \cdot b = b \cdot a$

Propiedad conmutativa de la multiplicación Para los números cualesquiera a y b: $a \cdot b = b \cdot a$

Comparative inference A comparative inference is an inference made by interpreting and comparing two sets of data.

Inferencia comparativa Una inferencia comparativa es una inferencia que se hace al interpretar y comparar dos conjuntos de datos.

English/Spanish Glossary

Compare To compare is to tell or show how two things are alike or different.

Comparar Comparar es describir o mostrar en qué se parecen o en qué se diferencian dos cosas.

Compatible numbers Compatible numbers are numbers that are easy to compute mentally.

Números compatibles Los números compatibles son números fáciles de calcular mentalmente.

Complementary angles Two angles are complementary angles if the sum of their measures is 90°. Complementary angles that are adjacent form a right angle.

Ángulos complementarios Dos ángulos son complementarios si la suma de sus medidas es 90°. Los ángulos complementarios que son adyacentes forman un ángulo recto.

Complex fraction A complex fraction is a fraction $\frac{A}{B}$ where A and/or B are fractions and B is not zero.

Fracción compleja Una fracción compleja es una fracción $\frac{A}{B}$ donde A y/o B son fracciones y B es distinto de cero.

Compose a shape To compose a shape, join two (or more) shapes so that there is no gap or overlap.

Componer una figura Para componer una figura, debes unir dos (o más) figuras de modo que entre ellas no queden espacios ni superposiciones.

Composite figure A composite figure is the combination of two or more figures into one object.

Figura compuesta Una figura compuesta es la combinación de dos o más figuras en un objeto.

Composite number A composite number is a whole number greater than 1 with more than two factors.

Número compuesto Un número compuesto es un número entero mayor que 1 con más de dos factores.

Compound event A compound event is an event associated with a multi-step action. A compound event is composed of events that are the outcomes of the steps of the action.

Evento compuesto Un evento compuesto es un evento que se relaciona con una acción de varios pasos. Un evento compuesto se compone de eventos que son los resultados de los pasos de una acción.

English/Spanish Glossary

Compound interest Compound interest is interest paid on both the principal and the interest earned in previous interest periods. To calculate compound interest, use the formula $B = p(1 + r)^n$, where B is the balance in the account, p is the principal, r is the annual interest rate, and n is the time in years that the account earns interest.

Interés compuesto El interés compuesto es el interés que se paga sobre el capital y el interés obtenido en períodos de interés anteriores. Para calcular el interés compuesto, usa la fórmula $B = c(1 + r)^n$ donde B es el saldo de la cuenta, c es el capital, r es la tasa de interés anual y n es el tiempo en años en que la cuenta obtiene un interés.

Cone A cone is a three-dimensional figure with one circular base and one vertex.

Cono Un cono es una figura tridimensional con una base circular y un vértice.

Congruent figures Two two-dimensional figures are congruent ≅ if the second can be obtained from the first by a sequence of rotations, reflections, and translations.

Figuras congruentes Dos figuras bidimensionales son congruentes ≅ si la segunda puede obtenerse a partir de la primera mediante una secuencia de rotaciones, reflexiones y traslaciones.

Conjecture A conjecture is a statement that you believe to be true but have not yet proved to be true.

Conjetura Una conjetura es un enunciado que crees que es verdadero, pero que todavía no has comprobado que sea verdadero.

Constant A constant is a term that only contains a number.

Constante Una constante es un término que solamente contiene un número.

Constant of proportionality In a proportional relationship, one quantity y is a constant multiple of the other quantity x. The constant multiple is called the constant of proportionality. The constant of proportionality is equal to the ratio $\frac{y}{x}$.

Constante de proporcionalidad En una relación proporcional, una cantidad y es un múltiplo constante de la otra cantidad x. El múltiplo constante se llama constante de proporcionalidad. La constante de proporcionalidad es igual a la razón $\frac{y}{x}$.

English/Spanish Glossary

Construct To construct is to make something, such as an argument, by organizing ideas. Constructing an argument can involve a written response, equations, diagrams, charts, tables, or a combination of these.

Construir Construir es hacer o crear algo, como se construye un argumento al organizar ideas. Para construir un argumento puede usarse una respuesta escrita, ecuaciones, diagramas, tablas o una combinación de esos elementos.

Convenience sampling Convenience sampling is a sampling method in which a researcher chooses members of the population that are convenient and available. Many researchers use this sampling technique because it is fast and inexpensive. It does not require the researcher to keep track of everyone in the population.

Muestra de conveniencia Una muestra de conveniencia es un método de muestreo en el que un investigador escoge miembros de la población que están convenientemente disponibles. Muchos investigadores usan esta técnica de muestreo porque es rápida y no es costosa. No requiere que el investigador lleve un registro de cada miembro de la población.

Cost of attendance The cost of attendance of one year of college is the sum of all of your expenses during the year.

El costo de asistencia El costo de asistencia de un año del colegio es la suma de todos sus gastos durante el año.

Cost of credit The cost of credit for a loan is the difference between the total cost and the principal.

El costo de crédito El costo de crédito para un préstamo es la diferencia entre el coste total y el director.

Converse of the Pythagorean Theorem If the sum of the squares of the lengths of two sides of a triangle equals the square of the length of the third side, then the triangle is a right triangle. If $a^2 + b^2 = c^2$, then the triangle is a right triangle.

Expresión recíproca del Teorema de Pitágoras Si la suma del cuadrado de la longitud de dos lados de un triángulo es igual al cuadrado de la longitud del tercer lado, entonces el triángulo es un triángulo rectángulo. $a^2 + b^2 = c^2$, entonces el triángulo es un triángulo rectángulo.

Conversion factor A conversion factor is a rate that equals 1.

Factor de conversión Un factor de conversión es una tasa que es igual a 1.

English/Spanish Glossary

Coordinate plane A coordinate plane is formed by a horizontal number line called the *x*-axis and a vertical number line called the *y*-axis.

Plano de coordenadas Un plano de coordenadas está formado por una recta numérica horizontal llamada eje de las *x* y una recta numérica vertical llamada eje de las *y*.

Corresponding angles Corresponding angles lie on the same side of a transversal and in corresponding positions.

Ángulos correspondientes Los ángulos correspondientes se ubican al mismo lado de una secante y en posiciones correspondientes.

Counterexample A counterexample is a specific example that shows that a conjecture is false.

Contraejemplo Un contraejemplo es un ejemplo específico que muestra que una conjetura es falsa.

Counting Principle If there are *m* possible outcomes of one action and *n* possible outcomes of a second action, then there are $m \cdot n$ outcomes of the first action followed by the second action.

Principio de conteo Si hay *m* resultados posibles de una acción y *n* resultados posibles de una segunda acción, entonces hay $m \cdot n$ resultados de la primera acción seguida de la segunda acción.

Coupon A coupon is part of a printed or online advertisement entitling the holder to a discount at checkout.

Cupón Un cupón forma parte de un anuncio impreso o en línea que permite al poseedor a un descuento en comprueba.

Credit card A credit card is a card issued by a lender that can be used to borrow money or make purchases on credit.

Tarjeta de crédito Una tarjeta de crédito es una tarjeta publicada por un prestamista que puede ser utilizado para pedir dinero prestado o compras de marca a cuenta.

Credit history A credit history shows how a consumer has managed credit in the past.

Acredite la historia Una historia del crédito muestra cómo un consumidor ha manejado crédito en el pasado.

English/Spanish Glossary

Credit report A report that shows personal information about a consumer and details about the consumer's credit history.

Acredite reporte Un reporte que muestra información personal sobre un consumidor y detalles acerca de la historia del crédito del consumidor.

Critique A critique is a careful judgment in which you give your opinion about the good and bad parts of something, such as how a problem was solved.

Crítica Una crítica es una evaluación cuidadosa en la que das tu opinión acerca de las partes positivas y negativas de algo, como la manera en la que se resolvió un problema.

Cross section A cross section is the intersection of a three-dimensional figure and a plane.

Corte transversal Un corte transversal es la intersección de una figura tridimensional y un plano.

Cube A cube is a rectangular prism whose faces are all squares.

Cubo Un cubo es un prisma rectangular cuyas caras son todas cuadrados.

Cube root The cube root of a number, *n*, is a number whose cube equals *n*.

Raíz cúbica La raíz cúbica de un número, *n,* es un número que elevado al cubo es igual a *n.*

Cubic unit A cubic unit is the volume of a cube that measures 1 unit on each edge.

Unidad cúbica Una unidad cúbica es el volumen de un cubo en el que cada arista mide 1 unidad.

Cylinder A cylinder is a three-dimensional figure with two parallel circular bases that are the same size.

Cilindro Un cilindro es una figura tridimensional con dos bases circulares paralelas que tienen el mismo tamaño.

D

Data Data are pieces of information collected by asking questions, measuring, or making observations about the real world.

Datos Los datos son información reunida mediante preguntas, mediciones u observaciones sobre la vida diaria.

English/Spanish Glossary

Debit card A debit card is a card issued by a bank that is linked to a customer's bank account, normally a checking account. A debit card can normally be used to withdraw money from an ATM or to make a purchase.

Tarjeta de débito Una tarjeta de débito es una tarjeta publicada por un banco que es ligado la cuenta bancaria de un cliente, normalmente una cuenta corriente bancaria. Una tarjeta de débito puede ser utilizada normalmente retirar dinero de una ATM o para hacer una compra.

Decimal A decimal is a number with one or more places to the right of a decimal point.

Decimal Un decimal es un número que tiene uno o más lugares a la derecha del punto decimal.

Decimal places The digits after the decimal point are called decimal places.

Lugares decimales Los dígitos que están después del punto decimal se llaman lugares decimales.

Decompose a shape To decompose a shape, break it up to form other shapes.

Descomponer una figura Para descomponer una figura, debes separarla para formar otras figuras.

Deductive reasoning Deductive reasoning is a process of reasoning logically from given facts to a conclusion.

Razonamiento deductivo El razonamiento deductivo es un proceso de razonamiento lógico que parte de hechos dados hasta llegar a una conclusión.

Denominator The denominator is the number below the fraction bar in a fraction.

Denominador El denominador es el número que está debajo de la barra de fracción en una fracción.

Dependent events Two events are dependent events if the occurrence of the first event affects the probability of the second event.

Eventos dependientes Dos eventos son dependientes si el resultado del primer evento afecta la probabilidad del segundo evento.

Deposit A transaction that adds money to a bank account is a deposit.

Depósito Una transacción que agrega dinero a una cuenta bancaria es un depósito.

English/Spanish Glossary

Dependent variable A dependent variable is a variable whose value changes in response to another (independent) variable.

Variable dependiente Una variable dependiente es una variable cuyo valor cambia en respuesta a otra variable (independiente).

Describe To describe is to explain or tell in detail. A written description can contain facts and other information needed to communicate your answer. A diagram or a graph may also be included.

Describir Describir es explicar o indicar algo en detalle. Una descripción escrita puede incluir hechos y otra información necesaria para comunicar tu respuesta. También puede incluir un diagrama o una gráfica.

Design To design is to make using specific criteria.

Diseñar Diseñar es crear algo a partir de criterios específicos.

Determine To determine is to use the given information and any related facts to find a value or make a decision.

Determinar Determinar es usar la información dada y cualquier otro dato relacionado para hallar un valor o tomar una decisión.

Deviation from the mean Deviation indicates how far away and in which direction a data value is from the mean. Data values that are less than the mean have a negative deviation. Data values that are greater than the mean have a positive deviation.

Desviación de la media La desviación indica a qué distancia y en qué dirección un valor se aleja de la media. Los valores menores que la media tienen una desviación negativa. Los valores mayores que la media tienen una desviación positiva.

Diagonal A diagonal of a figure is a segment that connects two nonconsecutive vertices of the figure.

Diagonal La diagonal de una figura es un segmento que conecta dos vértices no consecutivos de la figura.

Diameter A diameter is a segment that passes through the center of a circle and has both endpoints on the circle. The term diameter can also mean the length of this segment.

Diámetro Un diámetro es un segmento que atraviesa el centro de un círculo y tiene sus dos extremos en el círculo. El término diámetro también puede referirse a la longitud de este segmento.

English/Spanish Glossary

Difference The difference is the answer you get when subtracting two numbers.

Diferencia La diferencia es la respuesta que obtienes cuando restas dos números.

Dilation A dilation is a transformation that moves each point along the ray through the point, starting from a fixed center, and multiplies distances from the center by a common scale factor. If a vertex of a figure is the center of dilation, then the vertex and its image after the dilation are the same point.

Dilatación Una dilatación es una transformación que mueve cada punto a lo largo de la semirrecta a través del punto, a partir de un centro fijo, y multiplica las distancias desde el centro por un factor de escala común. Si un vértice de una figura es el centro de dilatación, entonces el vértice y su imagen después de la dilatación son el mismo punto.

Direct variation A linear relationship that can be represented by an equation in the form $y = kx$, where $x \neq 0$.

Dirija variación Una relación lineal que puede ser representada por una ecuación en la forma $y = kx$, donde x no iguale 0.

Distribution (of a data set) The distribution of a data set describes the way that its data values are spread out over all possible values. This includes describing the frequencies of each data value. The shape of a data display shows the distribution of a data set.

Distribución (de un conjunto de datos) La distribución de un conjunto de datos describe la manera en que sus valores se esparcen sobre todos los valores posibles. Eso incluye la descripción de las frecuencias de cada valor. La forma de una exhibición de datos muestra la distribución de un conjunto de datos.

Distributive Property Multiplying a number by a sum or difference gives the same result as multiplying that number by each term in the sum or difference and then adding or subtracting the corresponding products.
$a \cdot (b + c) = a \cdot b + a \cdot c$ and
$a \cdot (b - c) = a \cdot b - a \cdot c$

Propiedad distributiva Multiplicar un número por una suma o una diferencia da el mismo resultado que multiplicar ese mismo número por cada uno de los términos de la suma o la diferencia y después sumar o restar los productos obtenidos.
$a \cdot (b + c) = a \cdot b + a \cdot c$ and
$a \cdot (b - c) = a \cdot b - a \cdot c$

Dividend The dividend is the number to be divided.

Dividendo El dividendo es el número que se divide.

English/Spanish Glossary

Divisible A number is divisible by another number if there is no remainder after dividing.

Divisible Un número es divisible por otro número si no hay residuo después de dividir.

Divisor The divisor is the number used to divide another number.

Divisor El divisor es el número por el cual se divide otro número.

Dot plot A dot plot is a statistical graph that shows the shape of a data set with stacked dots above each data value on a number line. Each dot represents one data value.

Diagrama de puntos Un diagrama de puntos es una gráfica estadística que muestra la forma de un conjunto de datos con puntos marcados sobre cada valor de una recta numérica. Cada punto representa un valor.

E

Earned wages Earned wages are the income you receive from an employer for doing a job. Earned wages are also called gross pay.

Sueldos ganados Los sueldos ganados son los ingresos que usted recibe de un empleador para hacer un trabajo. Los sueldos ganados también son llamados la paga bruta.

Easy-access loan The term easy-access loan refers to a wide variety of loans with a streamlined application process. Many easy-access loans are short-term loans of relatively small amounts of money. They often have high interest rates.

Préstamo de fácil-acceso El préstamo del fácil-acceso del término se refiere a una gran variedad de préstamos con un proceso simplificado de aplicación. Muchos préstamos del fácil-acceso son préstamos a corto plazo de cantidades relativamente pequeñas de dinero. Ellos a menudo tienen los tipos de interés altos.

Edge of a three-dimensional figure An edge of a three-dimensional figure is a segment formed by the intersection of two faces.

Arista de una figura tridimensional Una arista de una figura tridimensional es un segmento formado por la intersección de dos caras.

English/Spanish Glossary

Enlargement An enlargement is a dilation with a scale factor greater than 1. After an enlargement, the image is bigger than the original figure.

Aumento Un aumento es una dilatación con un factor de escala mayor que 1. Después de un aumento, la imagen es más grande que la figura original.

Equation An equation is a mathematical sentence that includes an equals sign to compare two expressions.

Ecuación Una ecuación es una oración matemática que incluye un signo igual para comparar dos expresiones.

Equilateral triangle An equilateral triangle is a triangle whose sides are all the same length.

Triángulo equilátero Un triángulo equilátero es un triángulo que tiene todos sus lados de la misma longitud.

Equivalent equations Equivalent equations are equations that have exactly the same solutions.

Ecuaciones equivalentes Las ecuaciones equivalentes son ecuaciones que tienen exactamente la misma solución.

Equivalent expressions Equivalent expressions are expressions that always have the same value.

Expresiones equivalentes Las expresiones equivalentes son expresiones que siempre tienen el mismo valor.

Equivalent fractions Equivalent fractions are fractions that name the same number.

Fracciones equivalentes Las fracciones equivalentes son fracciones que representan el mismo número.

Equivalent inequalities Equivalent inequalities are inequalities that have the same solution.

Desigualdades equivalentes Las desigualdades equivalentes son desigualdades que tienen la misma solución.

Equivalent ratios Equivalent ratios are ratios that express the same relationship.

Razones equivalentes Las razones equivalentes son razones que expresan la misma relación.

Estimate To estimate is to find a number that is close to an exact answer.

Estimar Estimar es hallar un número cercano a una respuesta exacta.

English/Spanish Glossary

Evaluate a numerical expression To evaluate a numerical expression is to follow the order of operations.

Evaluar una expresión numérica Evaluar una expresión numérica es seguir el orden de las operaciones.

Evaluate an algebraic expression To evaluate an algebraic expression, replace each variable with a number, and then follow the order of operations.

Evaluar una expresión algebraica Para evaluar una expresión algebraica, reemplaza cada variable con un número y luego sigue el orden de las operaciones.

Event An event is a single outcome or group of outcomes from a sample space.

Evento Un evento es un resultado simple o un grupo de resultados de un espacio muestral.

Expand an algebraic expression To expand an algebraic expression, use the Distributive Property to rewrite a product as a sum or difference of terms.

Desarrollar una expresión algebraica Para desarrollar una expresión algebraica, usa la propiedad distributiva para reescribir el producto como una suma o diferencia de términos.

Expected family contribution The amount of money a student's family is expected to contribute towards the student's cost of attendance for school.

Contribución familiar esperado La cantidad de dinero que la familia de un estudiante es esperada contribuir hacia el estudiante es costado de asistencia para la escuela.

Expense Money that a business or a person needs to spend to pay for or buy something.

Gasto El dinero que un negocio o una persona debe gastar para pagar por o comprar algo.

Experiment To experiment is to try to gather information in several ways.

Experimentar Experimentar es intentar reunir información de varias maneras.

English/Spanish Glossary

Experimental probability You find the experimental probability of an event by repeating an experiment many times and using this ratio: $P(\text{event}) =$

$$\frac{\text{number of times event occurs}}{\text{total number of trials}}$$

Probabilidad experimental Para hallar la probabilidad experimental de un evento, debes repetir un experimento muchas veces y usar esta razón: $P(\text{evento}) =$

$$\frac{\text{número de veces que sucede el evento}}{\text{número total de pruebas}}$$

Explain To explain is to give facts and details that make an idea easier to understand. Explaining can involve a written summary supported by a diagram, chart, table, or a combination of these.

Explicar Explicar es brindar datos y detalles para que una idea sea más fácil de comprender. Para explicar algo se puede usar un resumen escrito sustentado por un diagrama, una tabla o una combinación de esos elementos.

Exponent An exponent is a number that shows how many times a base is used as a factor.

Exponente Un exponente es un número que muestra cuántas veces se usa una base como factor.

Expression An expression is a mathematical phrase that can involve variables, numbers, and operations. See algebraic expression or numerical expression.

Expresión Una expresión es una frase matemática que puede tener variables, números y operaciones. Ver expresión algebraica o expresión numérica.

Exterior angle of a triangle An exterior angle of a triangle is an angle formed by a side and an extension of an adjacent side.

Ángulo externo de un triángulo Un ángulo externo de un triángulo es un ángulo formado por un lado y una extensión de un lado adyacente.

F

Face of a three-dimensional figure A face of a three-dimensional figure is a flat surface shaped like a polygon.

Cara de una figura tridimensional La cara de una figura tridimensional es una superficie plana con forma de polígono.

English/Spanish Glossary

Factor an algebraic expression To factor an algebraic expression, write the expression as a product.

Descomponer una expresión algebraica en factores Para descomponer una expresión algebraica en factores, escribe la expresión como un producto.

Factors Factors are numbers that are multiplied to give a product.

Factores Los factores son los números que se multiplican para obtener un producto.

False equation A false equation has values that do not equal each other on each side of the equals sign.

Ecuación falsa Una ecuación falsa tiene valores a cada lado del signo igual que no son iguales entre sí.

Financial aid Financial aid is any money offered to a student to assist with the cost of attendance.

Ayuda financiera La ayuda financiera es cualquier dinero ofreció a un estudiante para ayudar con el costo de asistencia.

Financial need A student's financial need is the difference between the student's cost of attendance and the student's expected family contribution.

Necesidad financiera Una necesidad financiera del estudiante es la diferencia entre el estudiante es costada de asistencia y la contribución esperado de familia de estudiante.

Find To find is to calculate or determine.

Hallar Hallar es calcular o determinar.

First quartile For an ordered set of data, the first quartile is the median of the lower half of the data set.

Primer cuartil Para un conjunto ordenado de datos, el primer cuartil es la mediana de la mitad inferior del conjunto de datos.

Fixed expenses Fixed expenses are expenses that do not change from one budget period to the next.

Gastos fijos Los gastos fijos son los gastos que no cambian de un período económico al próximo.

English/Spanish Glossary

Fraction A fraction is a number that can be written in the form $\frac{a}{b}$, where a is a whole number and b is a positive whole number. A fraction is formed by a parts of size $\frac{1}{b}$.

Fracción Una fracción es un número que puede expresarse de forma $\frac{a}{b}$, donde a es un entero y b es un número entero positivo. La fracción está formada por a partes de tamaño $\frac{1}{b}$.

Frequency Frequency describes the number of times a specific value occurs in a data set.

Frecuencia La frecuencia describe el número de veces que aparece un valor específico en un conjunto de datos.

Function A function is a rule for taking each input value and producing exactly one output value.

Función Una función es una regla por la cual se toma cada valor de entrada y se produce exactamente un valor de salida.

G

Gap A gap is an area of a graph that contains no data points.

Espacio vacío o brecha Un espacio vacío o brecha es un área de una gráfica que no contiene ningún valor.

Grant A type of monetary award a student can use to pay for his or her education. The student does not need to repay this money.

Grant Un tipo de premio monetario que un estudiante puede utilizar para pagar por su educación. El estudiante no debe devolver este dinero.

Greater than > The greater-than symbol shows a comparison of two numbers with the number of greater value shown first, or on the left.

Mayor que > El símbolo de mayor que muestra una comparación de dos números con el número de mayor valor que aparece primero, o a la izquierda.

Greatest common factor The greatest common factor (GCF) of two or more whole numbers is the greatest number that is a factor of all of the numbers.

Máximo común divisor El máximo común divisor (M.C.D.) de dos o más números enteros no negativos es el número mayor que es un factor de todos los números.

English/Spanish Glossary

H

Height of a cone The height of a cone, *h*, is the length of a segment perpendicular to the base that joins the vertex and the base.

Altura de un cono La altura de un cono, *h*, es la longitud de un segmento perpendicular a la base que une el vértice y la base.

Height of a cylinder The height of a cylinder is the length of a perpendicular segment that joins the planes of the bases.

Altura de un cilindro La altura de un cilindro es la longitud de un segmento perpendicular que une los planos de las bases.

Height of a parallelogram A height of a parallelogram is the perpendicular distance between opposite bases.

Altura de un paralelogramo La altura de un paralelogramo es la distancia perpendicular que existe entre las bases opuestas.

Height of a prism The height of a prism is the length of a perpendicular segment that joins the bases.

Altura de un prisma La altura de un prisma es la longitud de un segmento perpendicular que une a las bases.

Height of a pyramid The height of a pyramid is the length of a segment perpendicular to the base that joins the vertex and the base.

Altura de una pirámide La altura de una pirámide es la longitud de un segmento perpendicular a la base que une al vértice con la base.

Height of a triangle The height of a triangle is the length of the perpendicular segment from a vertex to the base opposite that vertex.

Altura de un triángulo La altura de un triángulo es la longitud del segmento perpendicular desde un vértice hasta la base opuesta a ese vértice.

Hexagon A hexagon is a polygon with six sides.

Hexágono Un hexágono es un polígono de seis lados.

English/Spanish Glossary

Histogram A histogram is a statistical graph that shows the shape of a data set with vertical bars above intervals of values on a number line. The intervals are equal in size and do not overlap. The height of each bar shows the frequency of data within that interval.

Histograma Un histograma es una gráfica de estadísticas que muestra la forma de un conjunto de datos con barras verticales encima de intervalos de valores en una recta numérica. Los intervalos tienen el mismo tamaño y no se superponen. La altura de cada barra muestra la frecuencia de los datos dentro de ese intervalo.

Hundredths One hundredth is one part of 100 equal parts of a whole.

Centésima Una centésima es 1 de las 100 partes iguales de un todo.

Hypotenuse In a right triangle, the longest side, which is opposite the right angle, is the hypotenuse.

Hipotenusa En un triángulo rectángulo, el lado más largo, que es opuesto al ángulo recto, es la hipotenusa.

I

Identify To identify is to match a definition or description to an object or to recognize something and be able to name it.

Identificar Identificar es unir una definición o una descripción con un objeto, o reconocer algo y poder nombrarlo.

Identity Property of Addition The sum of 0 and any number is that number. For any number n, $n + 0 = n$ and $0 + n = n$.

Propiedad de identidad de la suma La suma de 0 y cualquier número es ese número. Para cualquier número n, $n + 0 = n$ and $0 + n = n$.

Identity Property of Multiplication The product of 1 and any number is that number. For any number n, $n \cdot 1 = n$ and $1 \cdot n = n$.

Propiedad de identidad de la multiplicación El producto de 1 y cualquier número es ese número. Para cualquier número n, $n \cdot 1 = n$ and $1 \cdot n = n$.

Illustrate To illustrate is to show or present information, usually as a drawing or a diagram. You can also illustrate a point using a written explanation.

Ilustrar Ilustrar es mostrar o presentar información, generalmente en forma de dibujo o diagrama. También puedes usar una explicación escrita para ilustrar un punto.

English/Spanish Glossary

Image An image is the result of a transformation of a point, line, or figure.

Imagen Una imagen es el resultado de una transformación de un punto, una recta o una figura.

Improper fraction An improper fraction is a fraction in which the numerator is greater than or equal to its denominator.

Fracción impropia Una fracción impropia es una fracción en la cual el numerador es mayor que o igual a su denominador.

Included angle An included angle is an angle that is between two sides.

Ángulo incluido Un ángulo incluido es un ángulo que está entre dos lados.

Included side An included side is a side that is between two angles.

Lado incluido Un lado incluido es un lado que está entre dos ángulos.

Income Money that a business receives. The money that a person earns from working is also called income.

Ingresos El dinero que un negocio recibe. El dinero que una persona gana de trabajar también es llamado los ingresos.

Income tax Income tax is money collected by the government based on how much you earn.

Impuesto de renta El impuesto de renta es dinero completo por el gobierno basado en cuánto gana.

Independent events Two events are independent events if the occurrence of one event does not affect the probability of the other event.

Eventos independientes Dos eventos son eventos independientes cuando el resultado de un evento no altera la probabilidad del otro.

Independent variable An independent variable is a variable whose value determines the value of another (dependent) variable.

Variable independiente Una variable independiente es una variable cuyo valor determina el valor de otra variable (dependiente).

Indicate To indicate is to point out or show.

Indicar Indicar es señalar o mostrar.

English/Spanish Glossary

Indirect measurement Indirect measurement uses proportions and similar triangles to measure distances that would be difficult to measure directly.

Medición indirecta La medición indirecta usa proporciones y triángulos semejantes para medir distancias que serían difíciles de medir de forma directa.

Inequality An inequality is a mathematical sentence that uses $<$, $\leq$, $>$, $\geq$, or $\neq$ to compare two quantities.

Desigualdad Una desigualdad es una oración matemática que usa $<$, $\leq$, $>$, $\geq$, o $\neq$ para comparar dos cantidades.

Inference An inference is a judgment made by interpreting data.

Inferencia Una inferencia es una opinión que se forma al interpretar datos.

Infinitely many solutions A linear equation in one variable has infinitely many solutions if any value of the variable makes the two sides of the equation equal.

Número infinito de soluciones Una ecuación lineal en una variable tiene un número infinito de soluciones si cualquier valor de la variable hace que los dos lados de la ecuación sean iguales.

Initial value The initial value of a linear function is the value of the output when the input is 0.

Valor inicial El valor inicial de una función lineal es el valor de salida cuando el valor de entrada es 0.

Integers Integers are the set of positive whole numbers, their opposites, and 0.

Enteros Los enteros son el conjunto de los números enteros positivos, sus opuestos y 0.

Interest When you deposit money in a bank account, the bank pays you interest for the right to use your money for a period of time.

Interés Cuando depositas dinero en una cuenta bancaria, el banco te paga un interés por el derecho a usar tu dinero por un período de tiempo.

Interest period The length of time on which compound interest is based. The total number of interest periods that you keep the money in the account is represented by the variable n.

Período de interés La cantidad de tiempo sobre la que se calcula el interés compuesto. El número total de períodos de interés que mantienes el dinero en la cuenta se representa con la variable n.

English/Spanish Glossary

Interest rate Interest is calculated based on a percent of the principal. That percent is called the interest rate (*r*).

Tasa de interés El interés se calcula con base en un porcentaje del capital. Ese porcentaje se llama tasa de interés, (*r*).

Interest rate for an interest period The interest rate for an interest period is the annual interest rate divided by the number of interest periods per year.

El tipo de interés por un período de interés El tipo de interés por un período de interés es el tipo de interés anual dividido por el número de períodos de interés por año.

Interquartile range The interquartile range (IQR) is the distance between the first and third quartiles of the data set. It represents the spread of the middle 50% of the data values.

Rango intercuartil El rango intercuartil es la distancia entre el primer y el tercer cuartil del conjunto de datos. Representa la ubicación del 50% del medio de los valores.

Interval An interval is a period of time between two points of time or events.

Intervalo Un intervalo es un período de tiempo entre dos puntos en el tiempo o entre dos sucesos.

Invalid inference An invalid inference is false about the population, or does not follow from the available data. A biased sample can lead to invalid inferences.

Inferencia inválida Una inferencia inválida es una inferencia falsa acerca de una población, o no se deduce a partir de los datos disponibles. Una muestra sesgada puede llevar a inferencias inválidas.

Inverse operations Inverse operations are operations that undo each other.

Operaciones inversas Las operaciones inversas son operaciones que se cancelan entre sí.

Inverse Property of Addition Every number has an additive inverse. The sum of a number and its additive inverse is zero.

Propiedad inversa de la suma Todos los números tienen un inverso de suma. La suma de un número y su inverso de suma es cero.

English/Spanish Glossary

Irrational numbers An irrational number is a number that cannot be written in the form $\frac{a}{b}$, where a and b are integers and $b \neq 0$. In decimal form, an irrational number cannot be written as a terminating or repeating decimal.

Números irracionales Un número irracional es un número que no se puede escribir en la forma $\frac{a}{b}$ donde a y b, son enteros y $b \neq 0$. Los números racionales en forma decimal no son finitos y no son periódicos.

Isolate a variable When solving equations, to isolate a variable means to get a variable with a coefficient of 1 alone on one side of an equation. Use the properties of equality and inverse operations to isolate a variable.

Aislar una variable Cuando resuelves ecuaciones, aislar una variable significa poner una variable con un coeficiente de 1 sola a un lado de la ecuación. Usa las propiedades de igualdad y las operaciones inversas para aislar una variable.

Isosceles triangle An isosceles triangle is a triangle with at least two sides that are the same length.

Triángulo isósceles Un triángulo isósceles es un triángulo que tiene al menos dos lados de la misma longitud.

J

Justify To justify is to support your answer with reasons or examples. A justification may include a written response, diagrams, charts, tables, or a combination of these.

Justificar Justificar es apoyar tu respuesta con razones o ejemplos. Una justificación puede incluir una respuesta escrita, diagramas, tablas o una combinación de esos elementos.

L

Lateral area of a cone The lateral area of a cone is the area of its lateral surface. The formula for the lateral area of a cone is L.A. $= \pi r \ell$, where r represents the radius of the base and ℓ represents the slant height of the cone.

Área lateral de un cono El área lateral de un cono es el área de su superficie lateral. La fórmula del área lateral de un cono es A.L. $= \pi r \ell$, donde r representa el radio de la base y ℓ representa la altura inclinada del cono.

English/Spanish Glossary

Lateral area of a cylinder The lateral area of a cylinder is the area of its lateral surface. The formula for the lateral area of a cylinder is L.A. $= 2\pi rh$, where r represents the radius of a base and h represents the height of the cylinder.

Área lateral de un cilindro El área lateral de un cilindro es el área de su superficie lateral. La fórmula del área lateral de un cilindro es A.L. $= 2\pi rh$, donde r representa el radio de una base y h representa la altura del cilindro.

Lateral area of a prism The lateral area of a prism is the sum of the areas of the lateral faces of the prism. The formula for the lateral area, L.A., of a prism is L.A. $= ph$, where p represents the perimeter of the base and h represents the height of the prism.

Área lateral de un prisma El área lateral de un prisma es la suma de las áreas de las caras laterales del prisma. La fórmula del área lateral, A.L., de un prisma es A.L. $= ph$, donde p representa el perímetro de la base y h representa la altura del prisma.

Lateral area of a pyramid The lateral area of a pyramid is the sum of the areas of the lateral faces of the pyramid. The formula for the lateral area, L.A., of a pyramid is L.A. $= \frac{1}{2}p\ell$ where p represents the perimeter of the base and ℓ represents the slant height of the pyramid.

Área lateral de una pirámide El área lateral de una pirámide es la suma de las áreas de las caras laterales de la pirámide. La fórmula del área lateral, A.L., de una pirámide es A.L. $= \frac{1}{2}p\ell$ donde p representa el perímetro de la base y ℓ representa la altura inclinada de la pirámide.

Lateral face of a prism A lateral face of a prism is a face that joins the bases of the prism.

Cara lateral de un prisma La cara lateral de un prisma es la cara que une a las bases del prisma.

Lateral face of a pyramid A lateral face of a pyramid is a triangular face that joins the base and the vertex.

Cara lateral de una pirámide La cara lateral de una pirámide es una cara lateral que une a la base con el vértice.

Lateral surface of a cone The lateral surface of a cone is the curved surface that is not included in the base.

Superficie lateral de un cono La superficie lateral de un cono es la superficie curva que no está incluida en la base.

English/Spanish Glossary

Lateral surface of a cylinder The lateral surface of a cylinder is the curved surface that is not included in the bases.

Superficie lateral de un cilindro La superficie lateral de un cilindro es la superficie curva que no está incluida en las bases.

Least common multiple The least common multiple (LCM) of two or more numbers is the least multiple shared by all of the numbers.

Mínimo común múltiplo El mínimo común múltiplo (MCM) de dos o más números es el múltiplo menor compartido por todos los números.

Leg of a right triangle In a right triangle, the two shortest sides are legs.

Cateto de un triángulo rectángulo En un triángulo rectángulo, los dos lados más cortos son los catetos.

Less than $<$ The less-than symbol shows a comparison of two numbers with the number of lesser value shown first, or on the left.

Menor que $<$ El símbolo de menor que muestra una comparación de dos números con el número de menor valor que aparece primero, o a la izquierda.

Liability A liability is money that you owe.

Obligación Una obligación es dinero que usted debe.

Lifetime income The amount of money earned over a lifetime of working.

Ingresos para toda la vida La cantidad de dinero ganó sobre una vida de trabajar.

Like terms Terms that have identical variable parts are like terms.

Términos semejantes Los términos que tienen partes variables idénticas son términos semejantes.

Line of reflection A line of reflection is a line across which a figure is reflected.

Eje de reflexión Un eje de reflexión es una línea a través de la cual se refleja una figura.

Linear equation An equation is a linear equation if the graph of all of its solutions is a line.

Ecuación lineal Una ecuación es lineal si la gráfica de todas sus soluciones es una línea recta.

English/Spanish Glossary

Linear function A linear function is a function whose graph is a straight line. The rate of change for a linear function is constant.

Función lineal Una función lineal es una función cuya gráfica es una línea recta. La tasa de cambio en una función lineal es constante.

Linear function rule A linear function rule is an equation that describes a linear function.

Regla de la función lineal La ecuación que describe una función lineal es la regla de la función lineal.

Loan A loan is an amount of money borrowed for a period of time with the promise of paying it back.

Préstamo Un préstamo es una cantidad de dinero pedido prestaddo por un espacio de tiempo con la promesa de pagarlo apoya.

Loan length Loan length is the period of time set to repay a loan.

Preste longitud La longitud del préstamo es el conjunto de espacio de tiempo de devolver un préstamo.

Loan term The term of a loan is the period of time set to repay the loan.

Preste término El término de un préstamo es el conjunto de espacio de tiempo de devolver el préstamo.

Locate To locate is to find or identify a value, usually on a number line or coordinate graph.

Ubicar Ubicar es hallar o identificar un valor, generalmente en una recta numérica o en una gráfica de coordenadas.

Loss When a business's expenses are greater than the business's income, there is a loss.

Pérdida Cuando los gastos de un negocio son más que los ingresos del negocio, hay una pérdida.

English/Spanish Glossary

Mapping diagram A mapping diagram describes a relation by linking the input values to the corresponding output values using arrows.

Diagrama de correspondencia Un diagrama de correspondencia describe una relación uniendo con flechas los valores de entrada con sus correspondientes valores de salida.

Markdown Markdown is the amount of decrease from the selling price to the sale price. The markdown as a percent decrease of the original selling price is called the percent markdown.

Rebaja La rebaja es la cantidad de disminución de un precio de venta a un precio rebajado. La rebaja como una disminución porcentual del precio de venta original se llama porcentaje de rebaja.

Markup Markup is the amount of increase from the cost to the selling price. The markup as a percent increase of the original cost is called the percent markup.

Margen de ganancia El margen de ganancia es la cantidad de aumento del costo al precio de venta. El margen de ganancia como un aumento porcentual del costo original se llama porcentaje del margen de ganancia.

Mean The mean represents the center of a numerical data set. To find the mean, sum the data values and then divide by the number of values in the data set.

Media La media representa el centro de un conjunto de datos numéricos. Para hallar la media, suma los valores y luego divide por el número de valores del conjunto de datos.

Mean absolute deviation The mean absolute deviation is a measure of variability that describes how much the data values are spread out from the mean of a data set. The mean absolute deviation is the average distance that the data values are spread around the mean.

$$\text{mean absolute deviation} = \frac{\text{sum of the absolute deviations of the data values}}{\text{total number of data values}}$$

Desviación absoluta media La desviación absoluta media es una medida de variabilidad que describe cuánto se alejan los valores de la media de un conjunto de datos. La desviación absoluta media es la distancia promedio que los valores se alejan de la media.

$$\text{desviación absoluta media} = \frac{\text{suma de las desviaciones absolutas de los valores}}{\text{número total de valores}}$$

English/Spanish Glossary

Measure of variability A measure of variability describes the spread of values in a data set. There may be more than one measure of variability for a data set.

Medida de variabilidad Una medida de variabilidad describe la distribución de los valores de un conjunto de datos. Puede haber más de una medida de variabilidad para un conjunto de datos.

Measurement data Measurement data consist of data that are measures.

Datos de mediciones Los datos de mediciones son datos que son medidas.

Measures of center A measure of center is a value that represents the middle of a data set. There may be more than one measure of center for a data set.

Medida de tendencia central Una medida de tendencia central es un valor que representa el centro de un conjunto de datos. Puede haber más de una medida de tendencia central para un conjunto de datos.

Median The median represents the center of a numerical data set. For an odd number of data values, the median is the middle value when the data values are arranged in numerical order. For an even number of data values, the median is the average of the two middle values when the data values are arranged in numerical order.

Mediana La mediana representa el centro de un conjunto de datos numéricos. Para un número impar de valores, la mediana es el valor del medio cuando los valores están organizados en orden numérico. Para un número par de valores, la mediana es el promedio de los dos valores del medio cuando los valores están organizados en orden numérico.

Median-median line The median-median line, or median trend line, is a method of finding a fit line for a scatter plot that suggests a linear association. This method involves dividing the data into three subgroups and using medians to find a summary point for each subgroup. The summary points are used to find the equation of the fit line.

Recta mediana-mediana La recta mediana-mediana es un método que se usa para hallar una línea de ajuste para un diagrama de dispersión que sugiere una asociación lineal. Este método implica dividir los datos en tres subgrupos y usar medianas para hallar un punto medio para cada subgrupo. Los puntos medios se usan para hallar la ecuación de la línea de ajuste.

Million Whole numbers in the millions have 7, 8, or 9 digits.

Millón Los números enteros no negativos que están en los millones tienen 7, 8 ó 9 dígitos.

English/Spanish Glossary

Mixed number A mixed number combines a whole number and a fraction.

Número mixto Un número mixto combina un número entero no negativo con una fracción.

Mode The item, or items, in a data set that occurs most frequently.

Modo El artículo, o los artículos, en un conjunto de datos que ocurre normalmente.

Model To model is to represent a situation using pictures, diagrams, or number sentences.

Demostrar Demostrar es usar ilustraciones, diagramas o enunciados numéricos para representar una situación.

Monetary incentive A monetary incentive is an offer that might encourage customers to buy a product.

Estímulo monetario Un estímulo monetario es una oferta que quizás favorezca a clientes para comprar un producto.

Multiple A multiple of a number is the product of the number and a whole number.

Múltiplo El múltiplo de un número es el producto del número y un número entero no negativo.

N

Natural numbers The natural numbers are the counting numbers.

Números naturales Los números naturales son los números que se usan para contar.

Negative exponent property For every nonzero number a and integer n, $a^{-n} = \frac{1}{a^n}$.

Propiedad del exponente negativo Para todo número distinto de cero a y entero n, $a^{-n} = \frac{1}{a^n}$.

Negative numbers Negative numbers are numbers less than zero.

Números negativos Los números negativos son números menores que cero.

English/Spanish Glossary

Net A net is a two-dimensional pattern that you can fold to form a three-dimensional figure. A net of a figure shows all of the surfaces of that figure in one view.

Modelo plano Un modelo plano es un diseño bidimensional que puedes doblar para formar una figura tridimensional. Un modelo plano de una figura muestra todas las superficies de la figura en una vista.

Net worth Net worth is the total value of all assets minus the total value of all liabilities.

Patrimonio neto El patrimonio neto es el valor total de todas las ventajas menos el valor total de todas las obligaciones.

Net worth statement Net worth is the total value of all assets minus the total value of all liabilities.

Declaración de patrimonio neto El patrimonio neto es el valor total de todas las ventajas menos el valor total de todas las obligaciones.

No solution A linear equation in one variable has no solution if no value of the variable makes the two sides of the equation equal.

Sin solución Una ecuación lineal en una variable no tiene solución si ningún valor de la variable hace que los dos lados de la ecuación sean iguales.

Nonlinear function A nonlinear function is a function that does not have a constant rate of change.

Función no lineal Una función no lineal es una función que no tiene una tasa de cambio constante.

Numerator The numerator is the number above the fraction bar in a fraction.

Numerador El numerador es el número que está arriba de la barra de fracción en una fracción.

Numerical expression A numerical expression is a mathematical phrase that consists of numbers and operation symbols.

Expresión numérica Una expresión numérica es una frase matemática que contiene números y símbolos de operaciones.

English/Spanish Glossary

O

Obtuse angle An obtuse angle is an angle with a measure greater than 90° and less than 180°.

Ángulo obtuso Un ángulo obtuso es un ángulo con una medida mayor que 90° y menor que 180°.

Obtuse triangle An obtuse triangle is a triangle with one obtuse angle.

Triángulo obtusángulo Un triángulo obtusángulo es un triángulo que tiene un ángulo obtuso.

Octagon An octagon is a polygon with eight sides.

Octágono Un octágono es un polígono de ocho lados.

Online payment system An online payment system allows money to be exchanged electronically between buyer and seller, usually using credit card or bank account information.

Sistema en línea de pago Un sistema en línea del pago permite dinero para ser cambiado electrónicamente entre comprador y vendedor, utilizando generalmente información de tarjeta de crédito o cuenta bancaria.

Open sentence An open sentence is an equation with one or more variables.

Enunciado abierto Un enunciado abierto es una ecuación con una o más variables.

Opposites Opposites are two numbers that are the same distance from 0 on a number line, but in opposite directions.

Opuestos Los opuestos son dos números que están a la misma distancia de 0 en la recta numérica, pero en direcciones opuestas.

Order of operations The order of operations is the order in which operations should be performed in an expression. Operations inside parentheses are done first, followed by exponents. Then, multiplication and division are done in order from left to right, and finally addition and subtraction are done in order from left to right.

Orden de las operaciones El orden de las operaciones es el orden en el que se deben resolver las operaciones de una expresión. Las operaciones que están entre paréntesis se resuelven primero, seguidas de los exponentes. Luego, se multiplica y se divide en orden de izquierda a derecha, y finalmente se suma y se resta en orden de izquierda a derecha.

English/Spanish Glossary

Ordered pair An ordered pair identifies the location of a point in the coordinate plane. The *x*-coordinate shows a point's position left or right of the *y*-axis. The *y*-coordinate shows a point's position up or down from the *x*-axis.

Par ordenado Un par ordenado identifica la ubicación de un punto en el plano de coordenadas. La coordenada *x* muestra la posición de un punto a la izquierda o a la derecha del eje de las *y*. La coordenada *y* muestra la posición de un punto arriba o abajo del eje de las *x*.

Origin The origin is the point of intersection of the *x*- and *y*-axes on a coordinate plane.

Origen El origen es el punto de intersección del eje de las *x* y el eje de las *y* en un plano de coordenadas.

Outcome An outcome is a possible result of an action.

Resultado Un resultado es un desenlace posible de una acción.

Outlier An outlier is a piece of data that doesn't seem to fit with the rest of a data set.

Valor extremo Un valor extremo es un valor que parece no ajustarse al resto de los datos de un conjunto.

P

Parallel lines Parallel lines are lines in the same plane that never intersect.

Rectas paralelas Las rectas paralelas son rectas que están en el mismo plano y nunca se intersecan.

Parallelogram A parallelogram is a quadrilateral with both pairs of opposite sides parallel.

Paralelogramo Un paralelogramo es un cuadrilátero en el cual los dos pares de lados opuestos son paralelos.

Partial product A partial product is part of the total product. A product is the sum of the partial products.

Producto parcial Un producto parcial es una parte del producto total. Un producto es la suma de los productos parciales.

English/Spanish Glossary

Pay period Wages for many jobs are paid at regular intervals, such a weekly, biweekly, semimonthly, or monthly. The interval of time is called a pay period.

Pague el período Los sueldos para muchos trabajos son pagados con regularidad, tal semanal, quincenal, quincenal, o mensual. El intervalo de tiempo es llamado un período de la paga.

Payroll deductions Your employer can deduct your income taxes from your wages before you receive your paycheck. The amounts deducted are called payroll deductions.

Deducciones de nómina Su empleador puede descontar sus impuestos de renta de sus sueldos antes que reciba su cheque de pago. Las cantidades descontadas son llamadas nómina deducciones.

Percent A percent is a ratio that compares a number to 100.

Porcentaje Un porcentaje es una razón que compara un número con 100.

Percent bar graph A percent bar graph is a bar graph that shows each category as a percent of the total number of data items.

Gráfico de barras de por ciento Un gráfico de barras del por ciento es un gráfico de barras que muestra cada categoría como un por ciento del número total de artículos de datos.

Percent decrease When a quantity decreases, the percent of change is called a percent decrease. percent decrease = $\frac{\text{amount of decrease}}{\text{original quantity}}$

Disminución porcentual Cuando una cantidad disminuye, el porcentaje de cambio se llama disminución porcentual. disminución porcentual = $\frac{\text{cantidad de disminución}}{\text{cantidad original}}$

Percent equation The percent equation describes the relationship between a part and a whole. You can use the percent equation to solve percent problems. part = percent · whole

Ecuación de porcentaje La ecuación de porcentaje describe la relación entre una parte y un todo. Puedes usar la ecuación de porcentaje para resolver problemas de porcentaje. parte = por ciento · todo

Percent error Percent error describes the accuracy of a measured or estimated value compared to an actual or accepted value.

Error porcentual El error porcentual describe la exactitud de un valor medido o estimado en comparación con un valor real o aceptado.

English/Spanish Glossary

Percent increase When a quantity increases, the percent of change is called a percent increase.

Aumento porcentual Cuando una cantidad aumenta, el porcentaje de cambio se llama aumento porcentual.

Percent of change Percent of change is the percent something increases or decreases from its original measure or amount. You can find the percent of change by using the equation: percent of change $= \dfrac{\text{amount of change}}{\text{original quantity}}$

Porcentaje de cambio El porcentaje de cambio es el porcentaje en que algo aumenta o disminuye en relación a la medida o cantidad original. Puedes hallar el porcentaje de cambio con la siguiente ecuación: porcentaje de cambio $= \dfrac{\text{cantidad de cambio}}{\text{cantidad original}}$

Perfect cube A perfect cube is the cube of an integer.

Cubo perfecto Un cubo perfecto es el cubo de un entero.

Perfect square A perfect square is a number that is the square of an integer.

Cuadrado perfecto Un cuadrado perfecto es un número que es el cuadrado de un entero.

Perimeter Perimeter is the distance around a figure.

Perímetro El perímetro es la distancia alrededor de una figura.

Period A period is a group of 3 digits in a number. Periods are separated by a comma and start from the right of a number.

Período Un período es un grupo de 3 dígitos en un número. Los períodos están separados por una coma y empiezan a la derecha del número.

Periodic savings plan A periodic savings plan is a method of saving that involves making deposits on a regular basis.

Plan de ahorros periódico Un plan de ahorros periódico es un método de guardar que implica depósitos que hace con regularidad.

Perpendicular lines Perpendicular lines intersect to form right angles.

Rectas perpendiculares Las rectas perpendiculares se intersecan para formar ángulos rectos.

English/Spanish Glossary

Pi Pi (π) is the ratio of a circle's circumference, C, to its diameter, d.

Pi Pi (π) es la razón de la circunferencia de un círculo, C, a su diámetro, d.

Place value Place value is the value given to an individual digit based on its position within a number.

Valor posicional El valor posicional es el valor asignado a determinado dígito según su posición en un número.

Plane A plane is a flat surface that extends indefinitely in all directions.

Plano Un plano es una superficie plana que se extiende indefinidamente en todas direcciones.

Polygon A polygon is a closed figure formed by three or more line segments that do not cross.

Polígono Un polígono es una figura cerrada compuesta por tres o más segmentos que no se cruzan.

Population A population is the complete set of items being studied.

Población Una población es todo el conjunto de elementos que se estudian.

Positive numbers Positive numbers are numbers greater than zero.

Números positivos Los números positivos son números mayores que cero.

Power A power is a number expressed using an exponent.

Potencia Una potencia es un número expresado con un exponente.

Predict To predict is to make an educated guess based on the analysis of real data.

Predecir Predecir es hacer una estimación informada según el análisis de datos reales.

Prime factorization The prime factorization of a composite number is the expression of the number as a product of its prime factors.

Descomposición en factores primos La descomposición en factores primos de un número compuesto es la expresión del número como un producto de sus factores primos.

English/Spanish Glossary

Prime number A prime number is a whole number greater than 1 with exactly two factors, 1 and the number itself.

Número primo Un número primo es un número entero mayor que 1 con exactamente dos factores, 1 y el número mismo.

Principal The original amount of money deposited or borrowed in an account.

Capital La cantidad original de dinero que se deposita o se pide prestada en una cuenta.

Prism A prism is a three-dimensional figure with two parallel polygonal faces that are the same size and shape.

Prisma Un prisma es una figura tridimensional con dos caras poligonales paralelas que tienen el mismo tamaño y la misma forma.

Probability model A probability model consists of an action, its sample space, and a list of events with their probabilities. The events and probabilities in the list have these characteristics: each outcome in the sample space is in exactly one event, and the sum of all of the probabilities must be 1.

Modelo de probabilidad Un modelo de probabilidad consiste en una acción, su espacio muestral y una lista de eventos con sus probabilidades. Los eventos y las probabilidades de la lista tienen estas características: cada resultado del espacio muestral está exactamente en un evento, y la suma de todas las probabilidades debe ser 1.

Probability of an event The probability of an event is a number from 0 to 1 that measures the likelihood that the event will occur. The closer the probability is to 0, the less likely it is that the event will happen. The closer the probability is to 1, the more likely it is that the event will happen. You can express probability as a fraction, decimal, or percent.

Probabilidad de un evento La probabilidad de un evento es un número de 0 a 1 que mide la probabilidad de que suceda el evento. Cuanto más se acerca la probabilidad a 0, menos probable es que suceda el evento. Cuanto más se acerca la probabilidad a 1, más probable es que suceda el evento. Puedes expresar la probabilidad como una fracción, un decimal o un porcentaje.

Product A product is the value of a multiplication or an expression showing multiplication.

Producto Un producto es el valor de una multiplicación o una expresión que representa la multiplicación.

English/Spanish Glossary

Profit When a business's expenses are less than the business's income, there is a profit.

Ganancia Cuando los gastos de un negocio son menos que los ingresos del negocio, hay una ganancia.

Proof A proof is a logical, deductive argument in which every statement of fact is supported by a reason.

Comprobación Una comprobación es un argumento lógico y deductivo en el que cada enunciado de un hecho está apoyado por una razón.

Proper fraction A proper fraction has a numerator that is less than its denominator.

Fracción propia Una fracción propia tiene un numerador que es menor que su denominador.

Proportion A proportion is an equation stating that two ratios are equal.

Proporción Una proporción es una ecuación que establece que dos razones son iguales.

Proportional relationship Two quantities x and y have a proportional relationship if y is always a constant multiple of x. A relationship is proportional if it can be described by equivalent ratios.

Relación de proporción Dos cantidades x y y tienen una relación de proporción si y es siempre un múltiplo constante de x. Una relación es de proporción si se puede describir con razones equivalentes.

Pyramid A pyramid is a three-dimensional figure with a base that is a polygon and triangular faces that meet at a vertex. A pyramid is named for the shape of its base.

Pirámide Una pirámide es una figura tridimensional con una base que es un polígono y caras triangulares que se unen en un vértice. El nombre de la pirámide depende de la forma de su base.

English/Spanish Glossary

Pythagorean Theorem In any right triangle, the sum of the squares of the lengths of the legs equals the square of the length of the hypotenuse. If a triangle is a right triangle, then $a^2 + b^2 = c^2$, where a and b represent the lengths of the legs, and c represents the length of the hypotenuse.

Teorema de Pitágoras En cualquier triángulo rectángulo, la suma del cuadrado de la longitud de los catetos es igual al cuadrado de la longitud de la hipotenusa. Si un triángulo es un triángulo rectángulo, entonces $a^2 + b^2 = c^2$, donde a y b representan la longitud de los catetos, y c representa la longitud de la hipotenusa.

Q

Quadrant The x- and y-axes divide the coordinate plane into four regions called quadrants.

Cuadrante Los ejes de las x y de las y dividen el plano de coordenadas en cuatro regiones llamadas cuadrantes.

Quadrilateral A quadrilateral is a polygon with four sides.

Cuadrilátero Un cuadrilátero es un polígono de cuatro lados.

Quarter circle A quarter circle is one fourth of a circle.

Círculo cuarto Un círculo cuarto es la cuarta parte de un círculo.

Quartile The quartiles of a data set divide the data set into four parts with the same number of data values in each part.

Cuartil Los cuartiles de un conjunto de datos dividen el conjunto de datos en cuatro partes que tienen el mismo número de valores cada una.

Quotient The quotient is the answer to a division problem. When there is a remainder, "quotient" sometimes refers to the whole-number portion of the answer.

Cociente El cociente es el resultado de una división. Cuando queda un residuo, "cociente" a veces se refiere a la parte de la solución que es un número entero.

English/Spanish Glossary

R

Radius A radius of a circle is a segment that has one endpoint at the center and the other endpoint on the circle. The term radius can also mean the length of this segment.

Radio Un radio de un círculo es un segmento que tiene un extremo en el centro y el otro extremo en el círculo. El término radio también puede referirse a la longitud de este segmento.

Radius of a sphere The radius of a sphere, r, is a segment that has one endpoint at the center and the other endpoint on the sphere.

Radio de una esfera El radio de una esfera, r, es un segmento que tiene un extremo en el centro y el otro extremo en la esfera.

Random sample In a random sample, each member in the population has an equal chance of being selected.

Muestra aleatoria En una muestra aleatoria, cada miembro en la población tiene una oportunidad igual de ser seleccionado.

Range The range is a measure of variability of a numerical data set. The range of a data set is the difference between the greatest and least values in a data set.

Rango El rango es una medida de la variabilidad de un conjunto de datos numéricos. El rango de un conjunto de datos es la diferencia que existe entre el mayor y el menor valor del conjunto.

Rate A rate is a ratio involving two quantities measured in different units.

Tasa Una tasa es una razón que relaciona dos cantidades medidas con unidades diferentes.

Rate of change The rate of change of a linear function is the ratio $\frac{\text{vertical change}}{\text{horizontal change}}$ between any two points on the graph of the function.

Tasa de cambio La tasa de cambio de una función lineal es la razón del $\frac{\text{cambio vertical}}{\text{cambio horizontal}}$ que existe entre dos puntos cualesquiera de la gráfica de la función.

Ratio A ratio is a relationship in which for every x units of one quantity there are y units of another quantity.

Razón Una razón es una relación en la cual por cada x unidades de una cantidad hay y unidades de otra cantidad.

English/Spanish Glossary

Rational numbers A rational number is a number that can be written in the form $\frac{a}{b}$ or $-\frac{a}{b}$, where a is a whole number and b is a positive whole number. The rational numbers include the integers.

Números racionales Un número racional es un número que se puede escribir como $\frac{a}{b}$ or $-\frac{a}{b}$, donde a es un número entero no negativo y b es un número entero positivo. Los números racionales incluyen los enteros.

Real numbers The real numbers are the set of rational and irrational numbers.

Números reales Los números reales son el conjunto de los números racionales e irracionales.

Reason To reason is to think through a problem using facts and information.

Razonar Razonar es usar hechos e información para estudiar detenidamente un problema.

Rebate A rebate returns part of the purchase price of an item after the buyer provides proof of purchase through a mail-in or online form.

Reembolso Un reembolso regresa la parte del precio de compra de un artículo después de que el comprador proporcione comprobante de compra por un correo-en o forma en línea.

Recall To recall is to remember a fact quickly.

Recordar Recordar es traer a la memoria un hecho rápidamente.

Reciprocals Two numbers are reciprocals if their product is 1. If a nonzero number is named as a fraction, $\frac{a}{b}$, then its reciprocal is $\frac{b}{a}$.

Recíprocos Dos números son recíprocos si su producto es 1. Si un número distinto de cero se expresa como una fracción, $\frac{a}{b}$, entonces su recíproco es $\frac{b}{a}$.

Rectangle A rectangle is a quadrilateral with four right angles.

Rectángulo Un rectángulo es un cuadrilátero que tiene cuatro ángulos rectos.

Rectangular prism A rectangular prism is a prism with bases in the shape of a rectangle.

Prisma rectangular Un prisma rectangular es un prisma cuyas bases tienen la forma de un rectángulo.

English/Spanish Glossary

Reduction A reduction is a dilation with a scale factor less than 1. After a reduction, the image is smaller than the original figure.

Reducción Una reducción es una dilatación con un factor de escala menor que 1. Después de una reducción, la imagen es más pequeña que la figura original.

Reflection A reflection, or flip, is a transformation that flips a figure across a line of reflection.

Reflexión Una reflexión, o inversión, es una transformación que invierte una figura a través de un eje de reflexión.

Regular polygon A regular polygon is a polygon with all sides of equal length and all angles of equal measure.

Polígono regular Un polígono regular es un polígono que tiene todos los lados de la misma longitud y todos los ángulos de la misma medida.

Relate To relate two different things, find a connection between them.

Relacionar Para relacionar dos cosas diferentes, halla una conexión entre ellas.

Relation Any set of ordered pairs is called a relation.

Relación Todo conjunto de pares ordenados se llama relación.

Relative frequency relative frequency

of an event $= \dfrac{\text{number of times event occurs}}{\text{total number of trials}}$

Frecuencia relativa frecuencia relativa de un evento $=$
$\dfrac{\text{número de veces que sucede el evento}}{\text{número total de pruebas}}$

Relative frequency table A relative frequency table shows the ratio of the number of data in each category to the total number of data items. The ratio can be expressed as a fraction, decimal, or percent.

Mesa relativa de frecuencia Una mesa relativa de la frecuencia muestra la proporción del número de datos en cada categoría al número total de artículos de datos. La proporción puede ser expresada como una fracción, el decimal, o el por ciento.

Remainder In division, the remainder is the number that is left after the division is complete.

Residuo En una división, el residuo es el número que queda después de terminar la operación.

English/Spanish Glossary

Remote interior angles Remote interior angles are the two nonadjacent interior angles corresponding to each exterior angle of a triangle.

Ángulos internos no adyacentes Los ángulos internos no adyacentes son los dos ángulos internos de un triángulo que se corresponden con el ángulo externo que está más alejado de ellos.

Repeating decimal A repeating decimal has a decimal expansion that repeats the same digit, or block of digits, without end.

Decimal periódico Un decimal periódico tiene una expansión decimal que repite el mismo dígito, o grupo de dígitos, sin fin.

Represent To represent is to stand for or take the place of something else. Symbols, equations, charts, and tables are often used to represent particular situations.

Representar Representar es sustituir u ocupar el lugar de otra cosa. A menudo se usan símbolos, ecuaciones y tablas para representar determinadas situaciones.

Representative sample A representative sample is a sample of a population in which the number of subjects in the sample with the trait that you are studying is proportional to the number of members in the population with that trait. A representative sample accurately represents the population and does not have bias.

Muestra representativa Una muestra representativa es una muestra de una población en la que el número de sujetos de la muestra que tiene la característica que se estudia es proporcional al número de miembros de la población que tienen esa característica. Una muestra representativa representa la población con exactitud y no está sesgada.

Rhombus A rhombus is a parallelogram whose sides are all the same length.

Rombo Un rombo es un paralelogramo que tiene todos sus lados de la misma longitud.

Right angle A right angle is an angle with a measure of 90°.

Ángulo recto Un ángulo recto es un ángulo que mide 90°.

Right cone A right cone is a cone in which the segment representing the height connects the vertex and the center of the base.

Cono recto Un cono recto es un cono en el que el segmento que representa la altura une el vértice y el centro de la base.

English/Spanish Glossary

Right cylinder A right cylinder is a cylinder in which the height joins the centers of the bases.

Cilindro recto Un cilindro recto es un cilindro en el que la altura une los centros de las bases.

Right prism In a right prism, all lateral faces are rectangles.

Prisma recto En un prisma recto, todas las caras laterales son rectángulos.

Right pyramid In a right pyramid, the segment that represents the height intersects the base at its center.

Pirámide recta En una pirámide recta, el segmento que representa la altura interseca la base en el centro.

Right triangle A right triangle is a triangle with one right angle.

Triángulo rectángulo Un triángulo rectángulo es un triángulo que tiene un ángulo recto.

Rigid motion A rigid motion is a transformation that changes only the position of a figure.

Movimiento rígido Un movimiento rígido es una transformación que sólo cambia la posición de una figura.

Rotation A rotation is a rigid motion that turns a figure around a fixed point, called the center of rotation.

Rotación Una rotación es un movimiento rígido que hace girar una figura alrededor de un punto fijo, llamado centro de rotación.

Rounding Rounding a number means replacing the number with a number that tells about how much or how many.

Redondear Redondear un número significa reemplazar ese número por un número que indica más o menos cuánto o cuántos.

S

Sale A sale is a discount offered by a store. A sale does not require the customer to have a coupon.

Venta Una venta es un descuento ofreció por una tienda. Una venta no requiere al cliente a tener un cupón.

English/Spanish Glossary

Sales tax A tax added to the price of goods and services.

Las ventas tasan Un impuesto añadió al precio de bienes y servicios.

Sample of a population A sample of a population is part of the population. A sample is useful when you want to find out about a population but you do not have the resources to study every member of the population.

Muestra de una población Una muestra de una población es una parte de la población. Una muestra es útil cuando quieres saber algo acerca de una población, pero no tienes los recursos para estudiar a cada miembro de esa población.

Sample space The sample space for an action is the set of all possible outcomes of that action.

Espacio muestral El espacio muestral de una acción es el conjunto de todos los resultados posibles de esa acción.

Sampling method A sampling method is the method by which you choose members of a population to sample.

Método de muestreo Un método de muestreo es el método por el cual escoges miembros de una población para muestrear.

Savings Savings is money that a person puts away for use at a later date.

Ahorros Los ahorros son dinero que una persona guarda para el uso en una fecha posterior.

Scale A scale is a ratio that compares a length in a scale drawing to the corresponding length in the actual object.

Escala Una escala es una razón que compara una longitud en un dibujo a escala con la longitud correspondiente en el objeto real.

Scale drawing A scale drawing is an enlarged or reduced drawing of an object that is proportional to the actual object.

Dibujo a escala Un dibujo a escala es un dibujo ampliado o reducido de un objeto que es proporcional al objeto real.

English/Spanish Glossary

Scale factor The scale factor is the ratio of a length in the image to the corresponding length in the original figure.

Factor de escala El factor de escala es la razón de una longitud de la imagen a la longitud correspondiente en la figura original.

Scalene triangle A scalene triangle is a triangle in which no sides have the same length.

Triángulo escaleno Un triángulo escaleno es un triángulo que no tiene lados de la misma longitud.

Scatter plot A scatter plot is a graph that uses points to display the relationship between two different sets of data. Each point can be represented by an ordered pair.

Diagrama de dispersión Un diagrama de dispersión es una gráfica que usa puntos para mostrar la relación entre dos conjuntos de datos diferentes. Cada punto se puede representar con un par ordenado.

Scholarship A type of monetary award a student can use to pay for his or her education. The student does not need to repay this money.

Beca Un tipo de premio monetario que un estudiante puede utilizar para pagar por su educación. El estudiante no debe devolver este dinero.

Scientific notation A number in scientific notation is written as the product of two factors, one greater than or equal to 1 and less than 10, and the other a power of 10.

Notación científica Un número en notación científica está escrito como el producto de dos factores, uno mayor que o igual a 1 y menor que 10, y el otro una potencia de 10.

Segment A segment is part of a line. It consists of two endpoints and all of the points on the line between the endpoints.

Segmento Un segmento es una parte de una recta. Está formado por dos extremos y todos los puntos de la recta que están entre los extremos.

Semicircle A semicircle is one half of a circle.

Semicírculo Un semicírculo es la mitad de un círculo.

English/Spanish Glossary

Similar figures A two-dimensional figure is similar (~) to another two-dimensional figure if you can map one figure to the other by a sequence of rotations, reflections, translations, and dilations.

Figuras semejantes Una figura bidimensional es semejante (~) a otra figura bidimensional si puedes hacer corresponder una figura con otra mediante una secuencia de rotaciones, reflexiones, traslaciones y dilataciones.

Simple interest Simple interest is interest paid only on an original deposit. To calculate simple interest, use the formula $I = prt$ where I is the simple interest, p is the principal, r is the annual interest rate, and t is the number of years that the account earns interest.

Interés simple El interés simple es el interés que se paga sobre un depósito original solamente. Para calcular el interés simple, usa la fórmula $I = crt$ donde I es el interés simple, c es el capital, r es la tasa de interés anual y t es el número de años en que la cuenta obtiene un interés.

Simple random sampling Simple random sampling is a sampling method in which every member of the population has an equal chance of being chosen for the sample.

Muestreo aleatorio simple El muestreo aleatorio simple es un método de muestreo en el que cada miembro de la población tiene la misma probabilidad de ser seleccionado para la muestra.

Simpler form A fraction is in simpler form when it is equivalent to a given fraction and has smaller numbers in the numerator and denominator.

Forma simplificada Una fracción está en su forma simplificada cuando es equivalente a otra fracción dada, pero tiene números más pequeños en el numerador y el denominador.

Simplest form A fraction is in simplest form when the only common factor of the numerator and denominator is one.

Mínima expresión Una fracción está en su mínima expresión cuando el único factor común del numerador y el denominador es 1.

Simplify an algebraic expression To simplify an algebraic expression, combine the like terms of the expression.

Simplificar una expresión algebraica Para simplificar una expresión algebraica, combina los términos semejantes de la expresión.

English/Spanish Glossary

Simulation A simulation is a model of a real-world situation that is used to find probabilities.

Simulación Una simulación es un modelo de una situación de la vida diaria que se usa para hallar probabilidades.

Sketch To sketch a figure, draw a rough outline. When a sketch is asked for, it means that a drawing needs to be included in your response.

Bosquejo Para hacer un bosquejo, dibuja un esquema simple. Si se pide un bosquejo, tu respuesta debe incluir un dibujo.

Slant height of a cone The slant height of a cone, ℓ, is the length of its lateral surface from base to vertex.

Altura inclinada de un cono La altura inclinada de un cono, ℓ, es la longitud de su superficie lateral desde la base hasta el vértice.

Slant height of a pyramid The slant height of a pyramid is the height of a lateral face.

Altura inclinada de una pirámide La altura inclinada de una pirámide es la altura de una cara lateral.

Slope Slope is a ratio that describes steepness.

$$\text{slope} = \frac{\text{vertical change}}{\text{horizontal change}} = \frac{\text{rise}}{\text{run}}$$

Pendiente La pendiente es una razón que describe la inclinación.

$$\text{pendiente} = \frac{\text{cambio vertical}}{\text{cambio horizontal}}$$
$$= \frac{\text{distancia vertical}}{\text{distancia horizontal}}$$

Slope of a line slope =

$$\frac{\text{change in } y\text{-coordinates}}{\text{change in } x\text{-coordinates}} = \frac{\text{rise}}{\text{run}}$$

Pendiente de una recta pendiente =
$$\frac{\text{cambio en las coordenadas } y}{\text{cambio en las coordenadas } x}$$
$$= \frac{\text{distancia vertical}}{\text{distancia horizontal}}$$

Slope-intercept form An equation written in the form $y = mx + b$ is in slope-intercept form. The graph is a line with slope m and y-intercept b.

Forma pendiente-intercepto Una ecuación escrita en la forma $y = mx + b$ está en forma de pendiente-intercepto. La gráfica es una línea recta con pendiente m e intercepto en y b.

English/Spanish Glossary

Solution of a system of linear equations A solution of a system of linear equations is any ordered pair that makes all the equations of that system true.

Solución de un sistema de ecuaciones lineales Una solución de un sistema de ecuaciones lineales es cualquier par ordenado que hace que todas las ecuaciones de ese sistema sean verdaderas.

Solution of an equation A solution of an equation is a value of the variable that makes the equation true.

Solución de una ecuación Una solución de una ecuación es un valor de la variable que hace que la ecuación sea verdadera.

Solution of an inequality The solutions of an inequality are the values of the variable that make the inequality true.

Solución de una desigualdad Las soluciones de una desigualdad son los valores de la variable que hacen que la desigualdad sea verdadera.

Solution set A solution set contains all of the numbers that satisfy an equation or inequality.

Conjunto solución Un conjunto solución contiene todos los números que satisfacen una ecuación o desigualdad.

Solve To solve a given statement, determine the value or values that make the statement true. Several methods and strategies can be used to solve a problem, including estimating, isolating the variable, drawing a graph, or using a table of values.

Resolver Para resolver un enunciado dado, determina el valor o los valores que hacen que ese enunciado sea verdadero. Para resolver un problema se pueden usar varios métodos y estrategias, como estimar, aislar la variable, dibujar una gráfica o usar una tabla de valores.

Sphere A sphere is the set of all points in space that are the same distance from a center point.

Esfera Una esfera es el conjunto de todos los puntos en el espacio que están a la misma distancia de un punto central.

Square A square is a quadrilateral with four right angles and all sides the same length.

Cuadrado Un cuadrado es un cuadrilátero que tiene cuatro ángulos rectos y todos los lados de la misma longitud.

English/Spanish Glossary

Square root A square root of a number is a number that, when multiplied by itself, equals the original number.

Raíz cuadrada La raíz cuadrada de un número es un número que, cuando se multiplica por sí mismo, es igual al número original.

Square unit A square unit is the area of a square that has sides that are 1 unit long.

Unidad cuadrada Una unidad cuadrada es el área de un cuadrado en el que cada lado mide 1 unidad de longitud.

Standard form A number written using digits and place value is in standard form.

Forma estándar Un número escrito con dígitos y valor posicional está escrito en forma estándar.

Statistical question A statistical question is a question that investigates an aspect of the real world and can have variety in the responses.

Pregunta estadística Una pregunta estadística es una pregunta que investiga un aspecto de la vida diaria y puede tener varias respuestas.

Statistics Statistics is the study of collecting, organizing, graphing, and analyzing data to draw conclusions about the real world.

Estadística La estadística es el estudio de la recolección, organización, representación gráfica y análisis de datos para sacar conclusiones sobre la vida diaria.

Stem-and-leaf plot A stem-and-leaf plot is a graph that uses the digits of each number to show the data distribution. Each data item is broken into a stem and into a leaf. The leaf is the last digit of the data value. The stem is the other digit or digits of the data value.

Complot de tallo y hoja Un complot del tallo y la hoja es un gráfico que utiliza los dígitos de cada número para mostrar la distribución de datos. Cada artículo de datos es roto en un tallo y en una hoja. La hoja es el último dígito de los datos valora. El tallo es el otro dígito o los dígitos de los datos valoran.

Stored-value card A stored-value card is a prepaid card electronically coded to be worth a specified amount of money.

Tarjeta de almacenado-valor Una tarjeta del almacenado-valor es una tarjeta pagada por adelantado codificó electrónicamente valer una cantidad especificado de dinero.

English/Spanish Glossary

Straight angle A straight angle is an angle with a measure of 180°.

Ángulo llano Un ángulo llano es un ángulo que mide 180°.

Student loan A student loan provides money to a student to pay for college. The student needs to repay the loan after leaving college. Often the student will need to pay interest on the amount of the loan.

Crédito personal para estudiantes Un crédito personal para estudiantes le proporciona dinero a un estudiante para pagar por el colegio. El estudiante debe devolver el préstamo después de dejar el colegio. A menudo el estudiante deberá pagar interés en la cantidad del préstamo.

Subject Each member in a sample is a subject.

Sujeto Cada miembro de una muestra es un sujeto.

Sum The sum is the answer to an addition problem.

Suma o total La suma o total es el resultado de una operación de suma.

Summarize To summarize an explanation or solution, go over or review the most important points.

Resumir Para resumir una explicación o solución, revisa o repasa los puntos más importantes.

Supplementary angles Two angles are supplementary angles if the sum of their measures is 180°. Supplementary angles that are adjacent form a straight angle.

Ángulos suplementarios Dos ángulos son suplementarios si la suma de sus medidas es 180°. Los ángulos suplementarios que son adyacentes forman un ángulo llano.

Surface area of a cone The surface area of a cone is the sum of the lateral area and the area of the base. The formula for the surface area of a cone is S.A. = L.A. + B.

Área total de un cono El área total de un cono es la suma del área lateral y el área de la base. La fórmula del área total de un cono es A.T. = A.L. + B.

English/Spanish Glossary

Surface area of a cube The surface area of a cube is the sum of the areas of the faces of the cube. The formula for the surface area, S.A., of a cube is S.A. $= 6s^2$, where s represents the length of an edge of the cube.

Área total de un cubo El área total de un cubo es la suma de las áreas de las caras del cubo. La fórmula del área total, A.T., de un cubo es A.T. $= 6s^2$, donde s representa la longitud de una arista del cubo.

Surface area of a cylinder The surface area of a cylinder is the sum of the lateral area and the areas of the two circular bases. The formula for the surface area of a cylinder is S.A. $=$ L.A. $+ 2B$, where L.A. represents the lateral area of the cylinder and B represents the area of a base of the cylinder.

Área total de un cilindro El área total de un cilindro es la suma del área lateral y las áreas de las dos bases circulares. La fórmula del área total de un cilindro es A.T. $=$ A.L. $+ 2B$, donde A.L. representa el área lateral del cilindro y B representa el área de una base del cilindro.

Surface area of a pyramid The surface area of a pyramid is the sum of the areas of the faces of the pyramid. The formula for the surface area, S.A., of a pyramid is S.A. $=$ L.A. $+ B$, where L.A. represents the lateral area of the pyramid and B represents the area of the base of the pyramid.

Área total de una pirámide El área total de una pirámide es la suma de las áreas de las caras de la pirámide. La fórmula del área total, A.T., de una pirámide es A.T. $=$ A.L. $+ B$, donde A.L. representa el área lateral de la pirámide y B representa el área de la base de la pirámide.

Surface area of a sphere The surface area of a sphere is equal to the lateral area of a cylinder that has the same radius, r, and height $2r$. The formula for the surface area of a sphere is S.A. $= 4\pi r^2$, where r represents the radius of the sphere.

Área total de una esfera El área total de una esfera es igual al área lateral de un cilindro que tiene el mismo radio, r, y una altura de $2r$. La fórmula del área total de una esfera es A.T. $= 4\pi r^2$, donde r representa el radio de la esfera.

Surface area of a three-dimensional figure The surface area of a three-dimensional figure is the sum of the areas of its faces. You can find the surface area by finding the area of the net of the three-dimensional figure.

Área total de una figura tridimensional El área total de una figura tridimensional es la suma de las áreas de sus caras. Puedes hallar el área total si hallas el área del modelo plano de la figura tridimensional.

English/Spanish Glossary

System of linear equations A system of linear equations is formed by two or more linear equations that use the same variables.

Sistema de ecuaciones lineales Un sistema de ecuaciones lineales está formado por dos o más ecuaciones lineales que usan las mismas variables.

Systematic sampling Systematic sampling is a sampling method in which you choose every nth member of the population, where *n* is a predetermined number. A systematic sample is useful when the researcher is able to approach the population in a systematic, or methodical, way.

Muestreo sistemático El muestreo sistemático es un método de muestreo en el que se escoge cada enésimo miembro de la población, donde *n* es un número predeterminado. Una muestra sistemática es útil cuando el investigador puede enfocarse en la población de manera sistemática o metódica.

T

Taxable wages For federal income tax purposes, your taxable wages are the difference between your earned wages and your withholding allowance. Your employer divides your withholding allowance equally among the pay periods of one year.

Sueldos imponibles Para propósitos federales de impuesto de renta, sus sueldos imponibles son la diferencia entre sus sueldos ganados y su concesión que retienen. Su empleador divide su concesión que retiene igualmente entre los períodos de paga de un año.

Tenths One tenth is one out of ten equal parts of a whole.

Décimas Una décima es 1 de 10 partes iguales de un todo.

Term A term is a number, a variable, or the product of a number and one or more variables.

Término Un término es un número, una variable o el producto de un número y una o más variables.

Terminating decimal A terminating decimal has a decimal expansion that terminates in 0.

Decimal finito Un decimal finito tiene una expansión decimal que termina en 0.

English/Spanish Glossary

Terms of a ratio The terms of a ratio are the quantities *x* and *y* in the ratio.

Términos de una razón Los términos de una razón son la cantidad *x* y la cantidad *y* de la razón.

Theorem A theorem is a conjecture that is proven.

Teorema Un teorema es una conjetura que se ha comprobado.

Theoretical probability When all outcomes of an action are equally likely, $P(\text{event}) = \dfrac{\text{number of favourable outcomes}}{\text{number of possible outcomes}}$.

Probabilidad teórica Cuando todos los resultados de una acción son igualmente probables, $P(\text{evento}) = \dfrac{\text{número de resultados favorables}}{\text{número de resultados posibles}}$.

Third quartile For an ordered set of data, the third quartile is the median of the upper half of the data set.

Tercer cuartil Para un conjunto de datos ordenados, el tercer cuartil es la mediana de la mitad superior del conjunto de datos.

Thousandths One thousandth is one part of 1,000 equal parts of a whole.

Milésimas Una milésima es 1 de 1,000 partes iguales de un todo.

Three-dimensional figure A three-dimensional (3-D) figure is a figure that does not lie in a plane.

Figura tridimensional Una figura tridimensional es una figura que no está en un plano.

Total cost of a loan The total cost of a loan is the total amount spent to repay the loan. Total cost includes the principal and all interest paid over the length of the loan. Total cost also includes any fees charged.

El coste total de un préstamo El coste total de un préstamo es el cantidad total que es gastado para devolver el préstamo. El coste total incluye al director y todo el interés pagó sobre la longitud del préstamo. El coste total también incluye cualquier honorario cargado.

Transaction A banking transaction moves money into or out of a bank account.

Transacción Una transacción bancaria mueve dinero en o fuera de una cuenta bancaria.

English/Spanish Glossary

Transfer A transaction that moves money from one bank account to another is a transfer. The balance of one account increases by the same amount the other account decreases.

Transferencia Una transacción que mueve dinero de una cuenta bancaria a otro es una transferencia. El equilibrio de un aumentos de cuenta por la misma cantidad que la otra cuenta disminuye.

Transformation A transformation is a change in position, shape, or size of a figure. Three types of transformations that change position only are translations, reflections, and rotations.

Transformación Una transformación es un cambio en la posición, la forma o el tamaño de una figura. Tres tipos de transformaciones que cambian sólo la posición son las traslaciones, las reflexiones y las rotaciones.

Translation A translation, or slide, is a rigid motion that moves every point of a figure the same distance and in the same direction.

Traslación Una traslación, o deslizamiento, es un movimiento rígido que mueve cada punto de una figura a la misma distancia y en la misma dirección.

Transversal A transversal is a line that intersects two or more lines at different points.

Transversal o secante Una transversal o secante es una línea que interseca dos o más líneas en distintos puntos.

Trapezoid A trapezoid is a quadrilateral with exactly one pair of parallel sides.

Trapecio Un trapecio es un cuadrilátero que tiene exactamente un par de lados paralelos.

Trend line A trend line is a line on a scatter plot, drawn near the points, that approximates the association between the data sets.

Línea de tendencia Una línea de tendencia es una línea en un diagrama de dispersión, trazada cerca de los puntos, que se aproxima a la relación entre los conjuntos de datos.

Trial In a probability experiment, you carry out or observe an action repeatedly. Each observation of the action is a trial.

Prueba En un experimento de probabilidad, realizas u observas una acción varias veces. Cada observación de la acción es una prueba.

Triangle A triangle is a polygon with three sides.

Triángulo Un triángulo es un polígono de tres lados.

English/Spanish Glossary

Triangular prism A triangular prism is a prism with bases in the shape of a triangle.

Prisma triangular Un prisma triangular es un prisma cuyas bases tienen la forma de un triángulo.

True equation A true equation has equal values on each side of the equals sign.

Ecuación verdadera En una ecuación verdadera, los valores a ambos lados del signo igual son iguales.

Two-way frequency table A two-way frequency table displays the counts of the data in each group.

Tabla de frecuencia con dos variables Una tabla de frecuencia con dos variables muestra el conteo de los datos de cada grupo.

Two-way relative frequency table A two-way relative frequency table shows the ratio of the number of data in each group to the size of the population. The relative frequencies can be calculated with respect to the entire population, the row populations, or the column populations. The relative frequencies can be expressed as fractions, decimals, or percents.

Tabla de frecuencias relativas con dos variables Una tabla de frecuencias relativas con dos variables muestra la razón del número de datos de cada grupo al tamaño de la población. Las frecuencias relativas se pueden calcular respecto de la población entera, las poblaciones de las filas o las poblaciones de las columnas. Las frecuencias relativas se pueden expresar como fracciones, decimales o porcentajes.

Two-way table A two-way table shows bivariate categorical data for a population.

Tabla con dos variables Una tabla con dos variables muestra datos bivariados por categorías de una población.

U

Uniform probability model A uniform probability model is a probability model based on using the theoretical probability of equally likely outcomes.

Modelo de probabilidad uniforme Un modelo de probabilidad uniforme es un modelo de probabilidad que se basa en el uso de la probabilidad teórica de resultados igualmente probables.

English/Spanish Glossary

Unit fraction A unit fraction is a fraction with a numerator of 1 and a denominator that is a whole number greater than 1.

Fracción unitaria Una fracción unitaria es una fracción con un numerador 1 y un denominador que es un número entero mayor que 1.

Unit price A unit price is a unit rate that gives the price of one item.

Precio por unidad El precio por unidad es una tasa por unidad que muestra el precio de un artículo.

Unit rate The rate for one unit of a given quantity is called the unit rate.

Tasa por unidad Se llama tasa por unidad a la tasa que corresponde a 1 unidad de una cantidad dada.

Use To use given information, draw on it to help you determine something else.

Usar Para usar una información dada, apóyate en ella para determinar otra cosa.

V

Valid inference A valid inference is an inference that is true about the population. Valid inferences can be made when they are based on data from a representative sample.

Inferencia válida Una inferencia válida es una inferencia verdadera acerca de una población. Se pueden hacer inferencias válidas si están basadas en los datos de una muestra representativa.

Variability Variability describes how much the items in a data set differ (or vary) from each other. On a data display, variability is shown by how much the data on the horizontal scale are spread out.

Variabilidad La variabilidad describe qué diferencia (o variación) existe entre los elementos de un conjunto de datos. Al exhibir datos, la variabilidad queda representada por la distancia que separa los datos en la escala horizontal.

Variable A variable is a letter that represents an unknown value.

Variable Una variable es una letra que representa un valor desconocido.

Variable expenses Variable expenses are expenses that change from one budget period to the next.

Gastos variables Los gastos variables son los gastos que cambian de un período económico al próximo.

English/Spanish Glossary

Vertex of a cone The vertex of a cone is the point farthest from the base.

Vértice de un cono El vértice de un cono es el punto más alejado de la base.

Vertex of a polygon The vertex of a polygon is any point where two sides of a polygon meet.

Vértice de un polígono El vértice de un polígono es cualquier punto donde se encuentran dos lados de un polígono.

Vertex of a three-dimensional figure A vertex of a three-dimensional figure is a point where three or more edges meet.

Vértice de una figura tridimensional El vértice de una figura tridimensional es un punto donde se unen tres o más aristas.

Vertex of an angle The vertex of an angle is the point of intersection of the rays that make up the sides of the angle.

Vértice de un ángulo El vértice de un ángulo es el punto de intersección de las semirrectas que forman los lados del ángulo.

Vertical angles Vertical angles are formed by two intersecting lines and are opposite each other. Vertical angles have equal measures.

Ángulos opuestos por el vértice Los ángulos opuestos por el vértice están formados por dos rectas secantes y están uno frente a otro. Los ángulos opuestos por el vértice tienen la misma medida.

Vertical-line test The vertical-line test is a method used to determine if a relation is a function or not. If a vertical line passes through a graph more than once, the graph is not the graph of a function.

Prueba de recta vertical La prueba de recta vertical es un método que se usa para determinar si una relación es una función o no. Si una recta vertical atraviesa la gráfica más de una vez, la gráfica no es la gráfica de una función.

Volume Volume is the number of cubic units needed to fill a solid figure.

Volumen El volumen es el número de unidades cúbicas que se necesitan para llenar un cuerpo geométrico.

English/Spanish Glossary

Volume of a cone The volume of a cone is the number of unit cubes, or cubic units, needed to fill the cone. The formula for the volume of a cone is $V = \frac{1}{3}Bh$, where B represents the area of the base and h represents the height of the cone.

Volumen de un cono El volumen de un cono es el número de bloques de unidades, o unidades cúbicas, que se necesitan para llenar el cono. La fórmula del volumen de un cono $V = \frac{1}{3}Bh$, donde B representa el área de la base y h representa la altura del cono.

Volume of a cube The volume of a cube is the number of unit cubes, or cubic units, needed to fill the cube. The formula for the volume V of a cube is $V = s^3$, where s represents the length of an edge of the cube.

Volumen de un cubo El volumen de un cubo es el número de bloques de unidades, o unidades cúbicas, que se necesitan para llenar el cubo. La fórmula del volumen, V, de un cubo es $V = s^3$, donde s representa la longitud de una arista del cubo.

Volume of a cylinder The volume of a cylinder is the number of unit cubes, or cubic units, needed to fill the cylinder. The formula for the volume of a cylinder is $V = \pi r^2 h$, where r represents the radius of a base and h represents the height of the cylinder.

Volumen de un cilindro El volumen de un cilindro es el número de bloques de unidades, o unidades cúbicas, que se necesitan para llenar el cilindro. La fórmula del volumen de un cilindro es $V = \pi r^2 h$, donde r representa el radio de una base y h representa la altura del cilindro.

Volume of a prism The volume of a prism is the number of unit cubes, or cubic units, needed to fill the prism. The formula for the volume V of a prism is $V = Bh$, where B represents the area of a base and h represents the height of the prism.

Volumen de un prisma El volumen de un prisma es el número de bloques de unidades, o unidades cúbicas, que se necesitan para llenar el prisma. La fórmula del volumen, V, de un prisma $V = Bh$, donde B representa el área de una base y h representa la altura del prisma.

Volume of a pyramid The volume of a pyramid is the number of unit cubes needed to fill the pyramid. The formula for the volume V of a pyramid is $V = \frac{1}{3}Bh$, where B represents the area of the base and h represents the height of the pyramid.

Volumen de una pirámide El volumen de una pirámide es el número de bloques de unidades, o unidades cúbicas, que se necesitan para llenar la pirámide. La fórmula del volumen, V, de una pirámide es $V = \frac{1}{3}Bh$, donde B representa el área de la base y h representa la altura de la pirámide.

English/Spanish Glossary

Volume of a sphere The volume of a sphere is the number of unit cubes, or cubic units, needed to fill the sphere. The formula for the volume of a sphere is $V = \frac{4}{3}\pi r^3$.

Volumen de una esfera El volumen de una esfera es el número de bloques de unidades, o unidades cúbicas, que se necesitan para llenar la esfera. La fórmula del volumen de una esfera es $V = \frac{4}{3}\pi r^3$.

W

Whole numbers The whole numbers consist of the number 0 and all of the natural numbers.

Números enteros no negativos Los números enteros no negativos son el número 0 y todos los números naturales.

Withdrawal A transaction that takes money out of a bank account is a withdrawal.

Retirada Una transacción que toma dinero fuera de una cuenta bancaria es una retirada.

Withholding allowance You can exclude a portion of your earned wages, called a withholding allowance, from federal income tax. You can claim one withholding allowance for yourself and one for each person dependent upon your income.

Retener concesión Puede excluir una porción de sus sueldos ganados, llamó una concesión que retiene, del impuesto de renta federal. Puede reclamar una concesión que retiene para usted mismo y para uno para cada dependiente de persona sobre sus ingresos.

Word form of a number The word form of a number is the number written in words.

Número en palabras Un número en palabras es un número escrito con palabras en lugar de dígitos.

Work-Study Work-study is a type of need-based aid that schools might offer to a student. A student must earn work-study money by working certain jobs.

Práctica estudiantil La práctica estudiantil es un tipo de ayuda necesidad-basado que escuelas quizás ofrezcan a un estudiante. Un estudiante debe ganar dinero de práctica estudiantil por ciertos trabajos de trabajo.

English/Spanish Glossary

····················· **X** ·····················

x-axis The x-axis is the horizontal number line that, together with the y-axis, forms the coordinate plane.

Eje de las x El eje de las x es la recta numérica horizontal que, junto con el eje de las y, forma el plano de coordenadas.

x-coordinate The x-coordinate is the first number in an ordered pair. It tells the number of horizontal units a point is from 0.

Coordenada x La coordenada x (abscisa) es el primer número de un par ordenado. Indica cuántas unidades horizontales hay entre un punto y 0.

····················· **Y** ·····················

y-axis The y-axis is the vertical number line that, together with the x-axis, forms the coordinate plane.

Eje de las y El eje de las y es la recta numérica vertical que, junto con el eje de las x, forma el plano de coordenadas.

y-coordinate The y-coordinate is the second number in an ordered pair. It tells the number of vertical units a point is from 0.

Coordenada y La coordenada y (ordenada) es el segundo número de un par ordenado. Indica cuántas unidades verticales hay entre un punto y 0.

y-intercept The y-intercept of a line is the y-coordinate of the point where the line crosses the y-axis.

Intercepto en y El intercepto en y de una recta es la coordenada y del punto por donde la recta cruza el eje de las y.

····················· **Z** ·····················

Zero exponent property For any nonzero number a, $a^0 = 1$.

Propiedad del exponente cero Para cualquier número distinto de cero a, $a^0 = 1$.

Zero Property of Multiplication The product of 0 and any number is 0. For any number n, $n \cdot 0 = 0$ and $0 \cdot n = 0$.

Propiedad del cero en la multiplicación El producto de 0 y cualquier número es 0. Para cualquier número n, $n \cdot 0 = 0$ and $0 \cdot n = 0$.

Formulas

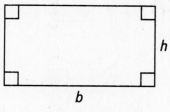

$$P = 2b + 2h$$
$$A = bh$$

Rectangle

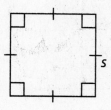

$$P = 4s$$
$$A = s^2$$

Square

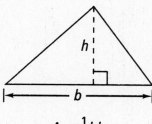

$$A = \frac{1}{2}bh$$

Triangle

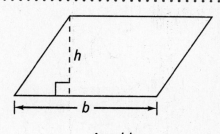

$$A = bh$$

Parallelogram

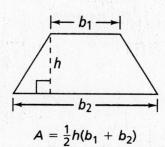

$$A = \frac{1}{2}h(b_1 + b_2)$$

Trapezoid

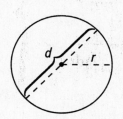

$$C = 2\pi r \text{ or } C = \pi d$$
$$A = \pi r^2$$

Circle

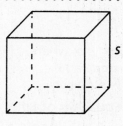

$$\text{S.A.} = 6s^2$$
$$V = s^3$$

Cube

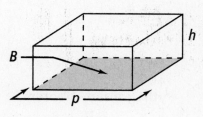

$$V = Bh$$
$$\text{L.A.} = ph$$
$$\text{S.A.} = \text{L.A.} + 2B$$

Rectangular Prism

Formulas

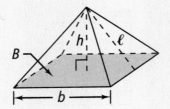

$V = \frac{1}{3}Bh$
L.A. $= 2b\ell$
S.A. $=$ L.A. $+ B$
Square Pyramid

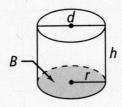

$V = Bh$
L.A. $= 2\pi rh$
S.A. $=$ L.A. $+ 2B$
Cylinder

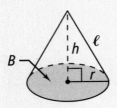

$V = \frac{1}{3}Bh$
L.A. $= \pi r\ell$
S.A. $=$ L.A. $+ B$
Cone

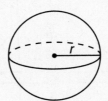

$V = \frac{4}{3}\pi r^3$
S.A. $= 4\pi r^2$
Sphere

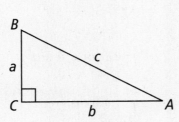

$a^2 + b^2 = c^2$

Pythagorean Theorem

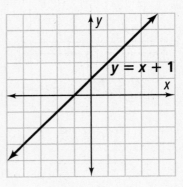

$y = mx + b$, where
$m =$ slope and
$b = y$-intercept
Equation of Line

Math Symbols

$+$	plus (addition)
$-$	minus (subtraction)
$\times$, $\cdot$	times (multiplication)
$\div$, $\overline{)}$, $\frac{a}{b}$	divide (division)
$=$	is equal to
$<$	is less than
$>$	is greater than
$\leq$	is less than or equal to
$\geq$	is greater than or equal to
$\neq$	is not equal to
$(\ )$	parentheses for grouping
$[\ ]$	brackets for grouping
$-a$	opposite of a
$\ldots$	and so on
$^\circ$	degrees
$\lvert a \rvert$	absolute value of a
$\stackrel{?}{=}, \stackrel{?}{<}, \stackrel{?}{>}$	Is the statement true?
$\approx$	is approximately equal to
$\frac{b}{a}$	reciprocal of $\frac{a}{b}$
A	area
ℓ	length
w	width
h	height
d	distance
r	rate
t	time
P	perimeter
b	base length
C	circumference
d	diameter

r	radius
S.A.	surface area
B	area of base
L.A.	lateral area
ℓ	slant height
V	volume
a^n	nth power of a
$\sqrt{x}$	nonnegative square root of x
π	pi, an irrational number approximately equal to 3.14
(a, b)	ordered pair with x-coordinate a and y-coordinate b
$\overline{AB}$	segment AB
A'	image of A, A prime
$\triangle ABC$	triangle with vertices A, B, and C
$\rightarrow$	arrow notation
$a : b$, $\frac{a}{b}$	ratio of a to b
$\cong$	is congruent to
$\sim$	is similar to
$\angle A$	angle with vertex A
AB	length of segment $\overline{AB}$
$\overrightarrow{AB}$	ray AB
$\angle ABC$	angle formed by $\overrightarrow{BA}$ and $\overrightarrow{BC}$
$m\angle ABC$	measure of angle ABC
$\perp$	is perpendicular to
$\overleftrightarrow{AB}$	line AB
$\parallel$	is parallel to
$\%$	percent
P (event)	probability of an event

Measures

Customary	Metric
Length	**Length**
1 foot (ft) = 12 inches (in.) 1 yard (yd) = 36 in. 1 yd = 3 ft 1 mile (mi) = 5,280 ft 1 mi = 1,760 yd	1 centimeter (cm) = 10 millimeters (mm) 1 meter (m) = 100 cm 1 kilometer (km) = 1,000 m 1 mm = 0.001 m
Area	**Area**
1 square foot (ft^2) = 144 square inches ($in.^2$) 1 square yard (yd^2) = 9 ft^2 1 square mile (mi^2) = 640 acres	1 square centimeter (cm^2) = 100 square millimeters (mm^2) 1 square meter (m^2) = 10,000 cm^2
Volume	**Volume**
1 cubic foot (ft^3) = 1,728 cubic inches ($in.^3$) 1 cubic yard (yd^3) = 27 ft^3	1 cubic centimeter (cm^3) = 1,000 cubic millimeters (mm^3) 1 cubic meter (m^3) = 1,000,000 cm^3
Mass	**Mass**
1 pound (lb) = 16 ounces (oz) 1 ton (t) = 2,000 lb	1 gram (g) = 1,000 milligrams (mg) 1 kilogram (kg) = 1,000 g
Capacity	**Capacity**
1 cup (c) = 8 fluid ounces (fl oz) 1 pint (pt) = 2 c 1 quart (qt) = 2 pt 1 gallon (gal) = 4 qt	1 liter (L) = 1,000 milliliters (mL) 1000 liters = 1 kiloliter (kL)

Customary Units and Metric Units	
Length	1 in. = 2.54 cm 1 mi ≈ 1.61 km 1 ft ≈ 0.3 m
Capacity	1 qt ≈ 0.94 L
Weight and Mass	1 oz ≈ 28.3 g 1 lb ≈ 0.45 kg

Properties

Unless otherwise stated, the variables a, b, c, m, and n used in these properties can be replaced with any number represented on a number line.

Identity Properties
Addition $n + 0 = n$ and $0 + n = n$
Multiplication $n \cdot 1 = n$ and $1 \cdot n = n$

Commutative Properties
Addition $a + b = b + a$
Multiplication $a \cdot b = b \cdot a$

Associative Properties
Addition $(a + b) + c = a + (b + c)$
Multiplication $(a \cdot b) \cdot c = a \cdot (b \cdot c)$

Inverse Properties
Addition
$a + (-a) = 0$ and $-a + a = 0$
Multiplication
$a \cdot \frac{1}{a} = 1$ and $\frac{1}{a} \cdot a = 1$, $(a \neq 0)$

Distributive Properties
$a(b + c) = ab + ac$ $(b + c)a = ba + ca$
$a(b - c) = ab - ac$ $(b - c)a = ba - ca$

Properties of Equality
Addition   If $a = b$,
             then $a + c = b + c$.
Subtraction   If $a = b$,
             then $a - c = b - c$.
Multiplication If $a = b$,
             then $a \cdot c = b \cdot c$.
Division   If $a = b$, and $c \neq 0$,
             then $\frac{a}{c} = \frac{b}{c}$.
Substitution   If $a = b$, then b can
             replace a in any
             expression.

Zero Property
$a \cdot 0 = 0$ and $0 \cdot a = 0$.

Properties of Inequality
Addition   If $a > b$,
             then $a + c > b + c$.
             If $a < b$,
             then $a + c < b + c$.
Subtraction   If $a > b$,
             then $a - c > b - c$.
             If $a < b$,
             then $a - c < b - c$.

Multiplication
If $a > b$ and $c > 0$, then $ac > bc$.
If $a < b$ and $c > 0$, then $ac < bc$.
If $a > b$ and $c < 0$, then $ac < bc$.
If $a < b$ and $c < 0$, then $ac > bc$.

Division
If $a > b$ and $c > 0$, then $\frac{a}{c} > \frac{b}{c}$.
If $a < b$ and $c > 0$, then $\frac{a}{c} < \frac{b}{c}$.
If $a > b$ and $c < 0$, then $\frac{a}{c} < \frac{b}{c}$.
If $a < b$ and $c < 0$, then $\frac{a}{c} > \frac{b}{c}$.

Properties of Exponents
For any nonzero number n and any integers m and n:

Zero Exponent $a^0 = 1$
Negative Exponent $a^{-n} = \frac{1}{a^n}$
Product of Powers $a^m \cdot a^n = a^{m+n}$
Power of a Product $(ab)^n = a^n b^n$
Quotient of Powers $\frac{a^m}{a^n} = a^{m-n}$
Power of a Quotient $\left(\frac{a}{b}\right)^n = \frac{a^n}{b^n}$
Power of a Power $(a^m)^n = a^{mn}$